THE KAMA SUTRA
OF VATSYAYANA

TRANSLATED BY SIR RICHARD BURTON
AND F. F. ARBUTHNOT

and

THE PHAEDRUS
OF PLATO

TRANSLATED BY BENJAMIN JOWETT

———

EDITED WITH AN INTRODUCTION BY
KENNETH WALKER
M.A., F.R.C.S.

KIMBER POCKET EDITIONS
46 WILTON PLACE, LONDON, S.W.1

This edition first published in 1963 by
WILLIAM KIMBER & CO. LIMITED
46 Wilton Place, London, S.W.1

Printed in England by
Hunt, Barnard & Co., Ltd.,
at the Sign of the Dolphin, Aylesbury, Bucks.

THE
KAMA SUTRA
AND
THE PHAEDRUS

CONTENTS

INTRODUCTION

by

KENNETH WALKER

M.A., F.R.C.S.

IN this volume are set side by side two of the earliest classical texts from East and West on the subject of love, which have powerfully influenced the course of thought on the place of sex in the two civilisations.

Plato, who was born in 428-7 B.C., devoted four of his dialogues mainly to this theme, the *Lysis*, the *Symposium*, the *Phaedrus* and the *Philebus*, of which the *Symposium* and the *Phaedrus* are by far the most important. The opening words of the *Philebus* state in the clearest possible form the opposing points of view of the popular pursuit of pleasure and the sterner Platonic attitude:

"Philebus was saying that enjoyment and pleasure and delight, and the class of feelings akin to them, are a good to every living being, whereas I contend, that not these, but wisdom and intelligence and memory, and their kindred, right opinion and true reasoning, are better and more desirable than pleasure for all who are able to partake of them, and that to all such who are or ever will be they are the most advantageous of all things. Have I not given, Philebus, a fair statement of the two sides of the argument?"

Although in the *Lysis* and the *Symposium* the treatment is poetical and romantic, in the latter dialogue the inferiority of physical love is considerably stressed. The seeker for truth is advised to proceed step by step, from the love of human forms to the virtually mystical contemplation of the abstract ideal of beauty itself. This is summarised at the conclusion of Socrates' famous speech:

"He who has been instructed thus far in the things of love, and who has learned to see the beautiful in due order and succession, when he comes toward the end will suddenly

7

perceive a nature of wondrous beauty—a nature which in the first place is everlasting, not growing and decaying, or waxing and waning; secondly, not fair in one point of view and foul in another, or at one time or in one relation or at one place fair, at another time or in another relation or at another place foul, as if fair to some and foul to others, or in the likeness of a face or hands or any other part of the bodily frame, or in any form of speech or knowledge, or existing in any other being, as for example, in an animal, or in heaven, or in earth, or in any other place; but beauty absolute separate simple and everlasting, which without diminution and without increase, or any change, is imparted to the ever-growing and perishing beauties of all other things. He who from these ascending under the influence of true love, begins to perceive that beauty, is not far from the end. And the true order of going, or being led by another, to the things of love, is to begin from the beauties of earth and mount upwards for the sake of that other beauty, using these as steps only, and from one going on to two, and from two to all fair forms, and from fair forms to fair practices, and from fair practices to fair notions, until from fair notions he arrives at the absolute beauty, and at last knows what the essence of beauty is . . . In that communion only, beholding beauty with the eye of the mind, he will be enabled to bring forth, not images of beauty, but realities (for he has hold not of an image but of a reality), and bringing forth and nourishing true virtue to become the friend of god and be immortal, if mortal man may."

The *Phaedrus* was written in Athens in the fourth century B.C. and probably in Plato's middle years. The opening theme of the work is the art of rhetoric and this leads to a discussion of love. There follows the memorable allegory of the charioteer, Reason, and his two horses, representing the moral and concupiscent elements in human nature. This formulation of the tripartite nature of the soul, has been fundamental to Western philosophy. Here is the distinction which is reflected in the warring of the flesh and the spirit, of which St. Paul and so many later Christian teachers speak. Plato, it is true, did not make an absolute separation of these two aspects of the soul, aware as he was of the ease with

8

which the higher passes into the lower or the lower can be "tamed and humbled, and follow the will of the charioteer". Such concepts are common in the strains of Christian mysticism. St. Francis would gladly have echoed the sentiment of the great final prayer of this work: "Beloved Pan, and all ye other gods who haunt this place, give me beauty in the inward soul: and may the outward and the inward man be at one". But it is undoubted that from the denigration of the senses, clearly laid down in Plato's last work, the *Laws*, and which is certainly implicit in the *Phaedrus*, stems the tenacious tradition in the West that the body and its desires should be treated with severe discipline, as unworthy of the higher nature of man and tending to deprive him of true happiness and harmony.

The end of the *Philebus* presents us with a discussion in which pleasure (which of course includes sexual pleasure) has been shown to be the lowest of the values in life:

"*Socrates:* And, according to the judgement which has now been given, pleasure will rank fifth.

"*Protarchus:* True.

"*Socrates:* But not first; no, not even if all the oxen and horses and animals in the world by their pursuit of enjoyment proclaim her to be so; although the many trusting in them as diviners trust in birds, determine that pleasures make up the good of life, and deem the lusts of animals to be better witnesses than the inspirations of divine philosophy."

In the *Lysis*, the *Symposium* and the *Phaedrus* Plato was concerned mainly with the homosexual romanticism of the society in which he lived but his later thought prohibited both homosexuality of any kind and any other form of sexual promiscuity. This is expressed with uncompromising severity in the *Laws*: "God willing, in the matter of love we may be able to enforce one of two things—either that no one shall venture to touch any person of the freeborn or noble class except his wedded wife, or sow the unconsecrated and bastard seed among harlots, or in barren and unnatural lusts; or at least we may abolish altogether the connexion of men with men; and as to women, if any man has to do with any but those who come into his house duly married by sacred rites, whether they be bought or acquired in any other way,

9

and he offends publicly in the face of all mankind, we shall be right in enacting that he be deprived of civic honours and privileges, that he be deemed to be, as he truly is, a stranger."

In 1883 Sir Richard Burton published his translation of the *Kama Sutra* anonymously in collaboration with his friend Arbuthnot, under the imprint of the fictitious "Kama Shastra Society of Benares" and circulated privately, and during the years 1885-7 appeared the sixteen volumes of Burton's unexpurgated translation of *The Arabian Nights*, which had appeared earlier in the century in a bowdlerised version. In 1880 he had published the first two volumes of his work on *The Lusiads* of Camoens, and in 1893 after his death his wife, as his literary executor permitted the publication of his translation of *The Pentameron* of Basile, the Neapolitan compiler of the first book of European fairy stories. All these translations have their place in the literary spirit of the time, for the Romantics saw themselves isolated from the materialistic civilisation of the nineteenth century, and looked to other times and other cultures for a permanent standard of values—and in particular they looked to the classical or mediaeval.

But a more striking way in which Burton followed the Romantic school was in his translations concerned in the main with sexual passion, *The Arabian Nights,* the *Kama Sutra,* and several other Asiatic works. The torch of the Marquis de Sade had been kept alight by the Romantics in France, Italy and in England; Baudelaire and Gautier with their morbid preoccupation with sexual ecstasy influenced Swinburne in whose work sensuousness and eroticism were exploited to their maximum, and who paved the way for the *fin de siècle* Decadent movement in which the ideal standards of the earlier Romantics coexisting for them with the macabre were absorbed into an aesthetic conception of life as an imitation of art, of passion for its own sake. "In no other period," considers Mario Praz, "has sex been so obviously the mainspring of works of imagination." All the elements essential to the Romantics, exemplified in Swinburne, could be drawn from these translations by Burton—fascination with the "savage Orient" unbound by social convention, the unknown, the bizarre, the erotic, the sensuous, and the sadistic—though perhaps more from the *Arabian Nights* than from a treatise such as the *Kama Sutra*, which is a systematic study of the relations between men and women in Hindu life.

Inevitably such translations would lay Burton open to the charge of pornography from the rigid Victorian public guardians of society. To this he supplied his own defence in a characteristically blunt manner: "I don't care a button about being prosecuted and if the matter comes to a fight, I will walk into court with my Bible and my Shakespeare and my Rabelais under my arm, and prove to them that before they condemn me they must cut half of them out and not allow them to be circulated to the public".

There is a mystical element in Plato but a much greater one in the philosophy of Plotinus (A.D. 204-270). This is not surprising. Plotinus did not obtain his philosophy from the official Greek lecturers to whom he listened in the University of Alexandria. He obtained it from Ammonius Saccas, an Oriental who made his living as a porter. Plotinus almost certainly had received it from an Indian *guru*. Hence the similarity between Neo-Platonism and Hinduism, and their mutual recognition of the two varieties of love, human and divine.

It is unlikely that everybody will agree with Burton's statement that the *Kama Sutra* "has placed Vatsyayana amongst the immortals". Some critics may go so far as to deny that a treatise on love-making could possibly be a medium for the expression of genius, however ably it were to be written. Yet another criticism could be brought forward against Vatsyayana's book. It might be objected that the two statements that Vatsyayana was a holy man and that he had written an authoritative work on the technique of love-making were in conflict with one another. They were incompatible statements, because a *Saddhu*, or holy man, practised *branachariya* or complete sexual continence. This being so he would not possess any personal experience of love-making.

The criticism that religion and love-making are incompatible is not a valid criticism. Religion and love have much in common, for both of them are emotional experiences, and both are the outcome of different forms of love. Ouspensky has drawn attention to the similarity between religious and erotic emotions in his book *A New Model of the Universe*. He writes: "Of all we know of life only in sexual love is there a taste of ecstasy. Nothing else in our life brings us so near to the limits of human possibilities, beyond which begins the unknown". Ouspensky is right. Religious ecstasy and sexual ecstasy have much in common. They are both associated with a raising of the level of consciousness and with a marked change in the sense of time. So also are both the result of the expenditure of a very fine quality of nervous energy and this explains why the Indian holy man and the Christian priest subject themselves to long periods of sexual abstinence. Because of this there is some basis for the criticism that a *Saddhu* usually has much less experience of sexual intercourse than has the ordinary married man.

But this does not mean that love-making and religious practices are by their very nature opposed to one another. Vatsyayana starts his treatise on love-making with the statement that there are three great goals to be attained in human life, namely the goals of *Dharma*, *Artha* and *Kama*. The Sanskrit word *Dharma* stands for the various disciplines to which the religious man subjects himself for the purpose of attaining his spiritual goal. But a well-balanced individual possesses earthly as well as celestial needs, and these worldly objectives may take the form of worldly fame and riches. *Artha*, or man's worldly aspirations should not be regarded as being of no account to him, even if they are of less importance to him than his spiritual welfare.

Kama is the Sanskrit word for all forms of sensual pleasures, amongst which are sexual pleasures. Vatsyayana reassures his readers that *Kama* is not necessarily opposed to the attainment of the higher goal of spiritual development. But he recommends *moderation* in all sensual pleasure. This being so he does not advise that his readers should indulge in *all* of the forms of love-making which are described in his book. He advises them to make use only of those which make a personal appeal to them. He writes: "A scientific work, which deals with a subject as a whole, must be exhaustive, but there is no reason why any particular practice should be used". Vatsyayana explains that he has described many alternative methods of making love because he is treating his subject in a scientific manner, and this means that he has to provide a very complete account. He even goes so far as to condemn some of the methods of love-making which have been described in his scientific treatise as being undesirable because he regards them as being of a *lustful* rather than of an *erotic* nature.

The year in which Vatsyayana wrote his scientific treatise on love is uncertain but, from his description of social life at that time, it was obviously a prosperous era in Indian history, an era in which the more successful town-dwelling merchants must have made a great deal of money. This permitted them to live in very great luxury. So also was it an era when men enjoyed many liberties and privileges in married life, liberties and privileges which were denied to their wives. For example, a wealthy man was allowed to marry as many wives as he wished. He was also permitted to take into his home a number of concubines.

Megasthenes, a Greek writer who visited India towards the end of the fourth century B.C., describes the manner in which upper-cast and well-educated men lived at that time. He writes: "After living in this manner (namely in the strict observance of religious disciplines and in the study of philosophy for seven and thirty years) a man usually retires to his own property, where he lives for the rest of his days in ease and security. Such men are accustomed to array themselves in fine muslin, and to wear a few trinkets of gold on their fingers and in their ears. They eat flesh and they marry as many wives as they please." In all probability Vatsyayana was engaged in writing his manual on love during what is now known as the Age of Imperial Guptas, that is to say between the years A.D. 300 and 400. This was an age of culture as well as of wealth, an age in which a successful citizen was expected to display a high degree of literary and aesthetic culture.

The society which Vatsyayana depicts in the *Kama Sutra* is very different from the society now to be found in India.

Dr. P. C. Bagchi, a Parisian historian and writer, gives the following description of this age of the Imperial Guptas: "To be a fashionable man it was not necessary to have more than one wife but it was impossible for a man to be fashionable without having many mistresses. The rightfully married wife had great responsibilities. She attended on her husband with all the love and the devotion that a devotee shows to the deity she worships. She ministers to her husband's personal needs, looks after his food and drinks, his toilet and his amusements. She tries to appreciate his likes and his dislikes and welcomes his friends with presents . . . When she finds that her husband is returning home she hastens to meet him and waits upon him herself . . . She may attend a festive assembly, but only with his permission, and in the company of her friends."

It is obvious, therefore, that the relationship existing between an Indian husband and wife was entirely different, in those far-off days, from the relationship which exists now in Western countries. This being so the *Kama Sutra* must be regarded as being an unsuitable guide to modern married life and alien to our contemporary outlook on sexual morality. But the physiology and the psychology of sexual intercourse remain much the same as they were in the years in which the *Kama Sutra* was written. So also do the errors made today in sexual technique remain the same. For example, Vatsyayana complains that many husbands approach sexual intimacies with their wives with the abruptness and the lack of art displayed by the animals in sexual congress. The same could be said of many husbands at the present day. This is particularly true of a husband's earlier efforts to consummate his marriage. Many men think that instinct will be sufficient to guide their actions on their marriage night and, as a result of their lack of knowledge, their wives have a very unfortunate introduction to the intimacies of married life. A woman does not trust her instinct to guide her in the care of her newly born baby, but supplements her maternal instinct by studying the art of mothercraft. Surely the man should do the same in the sphere of sexual intercourse.

I do not mean by this that husbands should obtain their

first knowledge of the art of sexual intercourse from the *Kama Sutra*. The relationship existing between modern Western men and women is so utterly different from that which existed in ancient India that the *Kama Sutra* cannot be regarded as a marriage handbook.

Yet another and final criticism may be brought against the *Kama Sutra* by certain people, namely the criticism that it is too outspoken on the subject of sexual intimacies. In answering this criticism I admit that I am only expressing a *personal* opinion on a subject concerning which other people may have entirely different views. The Hindu has always regarded sexuality and the procreation of children as essentials in man's natural endowments and responsibilities in life. They have a sacramental and religious significance and in fact the male and female sexual organs are represented in the symbols of religious worship. Sexuality has never been considered to be a weakness of the flesh, or a low form of animal activity as it has sometimes been regarded in European civilisation. As a result of this various forms of sexual neurosis and impotence are less common in India than they are in Europe.

The modern European attitude to sexuality, and to all that pertains to it, is now in the process of changing. The majority of modern people are coming to the conclusion that it was a mistake for children and young people to be brought up with regard to the subject of sex as the children of the Victorian age were brought up. I can here speak from my own personal experience, for it was in the Victorian manner that I, personally, was reared as a child. For me, and for all my companions, "sex" was either a shameful secret or a dirty joke. We learned also to regard the manifestations of sexuality in ourselves as being both degrading and sinful. Personally I welcome the change which is now taking place in our attitude to sex, for I have seen many adults who are still suffering from the wrong ideas they acquired during their childhood. The natural completeness with which statements are made in the *Kama Sutra* constitutes a virtue. I am even prepared to go so far as to accept the verdict of some of the literary critics that it is a work of genius.

THE
PHAEDRUS
OF
PLATO

TRANSLATED BY BENJAMIN JOWETT

PHAEDRUS

Socrates: My dear Phaedrus, whence come you, and whither are you going?

Phaedrus: I have come from Lysias the son of Cephalus, and I am going to take a walk outside the wall, for I have been sitting with him the whole morning; and our common friend Acumenus tells me that it is much more refreshing to walk in the open air than to be shut up in a cloister.

Soc.: There he is right. Lysias then, I suppose, was in the town?

Phaedr.: Yes, he was staying with Epicrates, here at the house of Morychus; that house which is near the temple of Olympian Zeus.

Soc.: And how did he entertain you? Can I be wrong in supposing that Lysias gave you a feast of discourse?

Phaedr.: You shall hear, if you can spare time to accompany me.

Soc.: And should I not deem the conversation of you and Lysias "a thing of higher import", as I may say in the words of Pindar, "than any business"?

Phaedr.: Will you go on?

Soc.: And will you go on with the narration?

Phaedr.: My tale, Socrates, is one of your sort, for love was the theme which occupied us—love after a fashion: Lysias has been writing about a fair youth who was being tempted, but not by a lover; and this was the point: he ingeniously proved that the non-lover should be accepted rather than the lover.

Soc.: O that is noble of him! I wish that he would say the poor man rather than the rich, and the old man rather than the young one; then he would meet the case of me and of many a man; his words would be quite refreshing, and he would be a public benefactor. For my part, I do so long to hear his speech, that if you walk all the way to Megara, and when you have reached the wall come back, as Herodicus recommends, without going in, I will keep you company.

Phaedr.: What do you mean, my good Socrates? How can you imagine that my unpractised memory can do justice to an elaborate work, which the greatest rhetorician of the age spent a long time in composing. Indeed, I cannot; I would give a great deal if I could.

Soc.: I believe that I know Phaedrus about as well as I know myself, and I am very sure that the speech of Lysias was repeated to him not once only, but again and again;— he insisted on hearing it many times over and Lysias was very willing to gratify him; at last, when nothing else would do, he got hold of the book, and looked at what he most wanted to see,—this occupied him during the whole morning;—and then when he was tired with sitting, he went out to take a walk, not until, by the dog, as I believe, he had simply learned by heart the entire discourse, unless it was un-usually long, and he went to a place outside the wall that he might practise his lesson. There he saw a certain lover of discourse who had a similar weakness; he saw and rejoiced; now thought he, "I shall have a partner in my revels". And he invited him to come and walk with him. But when the lover of discourse begged that he would repeat the tale, he gave himself airs and said, "No I cannot", as if he were indisposed; although, if the hearer had refused, he would sooner or later have been compelled by him to listen whether he would or no. Therefore, Phaedrus, bid him do at once what he will soon do whether bidden or not.

Phaedr.: I see that you will not let me off until I speak in some fashion or other; verily therefore my best plan is to speak as I best can.

Soc.: A very true remark, that of yours.

Phaedr.: I will do as I say; but believe me, Socrates, I did not learn the very words—O no; nevertheless I have a general notion of what he said, and will give you a summary of the points in which the lover differed from the non-lover. Let me begin at the beginning.

Soc.: Yes, my sweet one; but you must first of all show what you have in your left hand under your cloak, for that roll, as I suspect, is the actual discourse. Now, much as I love you, I would not have you suppose that I am going to have your memory exercised at my expense, if you have Lysias himself here.

Phaedr.: Enough; I see that I have no hope of practising my art upon you. But if I am to read, where would you please to sit?

Soc.: Let us turn aside and go by the Ilissus; we will sit down at some quiet spot.

Phaedr.: I am fortunate in not having my sandals, and as you never have any, I think that we may go along the brook and cool our feet in the water; this will be the easiest way, and at midday and in the summer is far from being unpleasant.

Soc.: Lead on, and look out for a place in which we can sit down.

Phaedr.: Do you see that tallest plane-tree in the distance?

Soc.: Yes.

Phaedr.: There are shade and gentle breezes, and grass on which we may either sit or lie down.

Soc.: Move forward.

Phaedr.: I should like to know, Socrates, whether the place is not somewhere here at which Boreas is said to have carried off Orithyia from the banks of the Ilissus?

Soc.: Such is the tradition.

Phaedr.: And is this the exact spot? The little stream is delightfully clear and bright; I can fancy that there might be maidens playing near.

Soc.: I believe that the spot is not exactly here, but about a quarter of a mile lower down, where you cross to the temple of Artemis, and there is, I think, some sort of an altar of Boreas at the place.

Phaedr.: I have never noticed it; but I beseech you to tell me, Socrates, do you believe this tale?

Soc.: The wise are doubtful, and I should not be singular if, like them, I too doubted. I might have a rational explanation that Orithyia was playing with Pharmacia, when a northern gust carried her over the neighbouring rocks; and this being the manner of her death, she was said to have been carried away by Boreas. There is a discrepancy, however, about the locality; according to another version of the story she was taken from the Areopagus, and not from this place. Now I quite acknowledge that these allegories are very nice, but he is not to be envied who has to invent them; much labour and ingenuity will be required of him; and when he has once begun, he must go on and rehabilitate Hippocentaurs and chimeras dire. Gorgons and winged steeds flow in apace, and numberless other inconceivable and portentous natures. And if he is sceptical about them, and would fain reduce them one after another to the rules of probability, this sort of crude philosophy will take up a great deal of time.

Now I have no leisure for such enquiries; shall I tell you why? I must first know myself, as the Delphian inscription says; to be curious about that which is not my concern, while I am still in ignorance of my own self, would be ridiculous. And therefore I bid farewell to all this; the common opinion is enough for me. For, as I was saying, I want to know not about this, but about myself: am I a monster more complicated and swollen with passion than the serpent Typho, or a creature of a gentler and simpler sort, to whom Nature has given a diviner and lowlier destiny? But let me ask you friend: have we not reached the plane-tree to which you were conducting us?

Phaedr.: Yes, this is the tree.

Soc.: By Herè, a fair resting-place, full of summer sounds and scents. Here is this lofty and spreading plane-tree, and the agnus castus high and clustering, in the fullest blossom and the greatest fragrance; and the stream which flows beneath the plane-tree is deliciously cold to the feet. Judging from the ornaments and images, this must be a spot sacred to Achelous and the Nymphs. How delightful is the breeze: so very sweet; and there is a sound in the air shrill and summerlike which makes answer to the chorus of the cicadae. But the greatest charm of all is the grass, like a pillow gently sloping to the head. My dear Phaedrus, you have been an admirable guide.

Phaedr.: What an incomprehensible being you are,

Socrates: when you are in the country, as you say, you really are like some stranger who is led about by a guide. Do you ever cross the border? I rather think that you never venture even outside the gates.

Soc.: Very true, my good friend; and I hope that you will excuse me when you hear the reason, which is, that I am a lover of knowledge, and the men who dwell in the city are my teachers, and not the trees or the country. Though I do indeed believe that you have found a spell with which to draw me out of the city into the country, like a hungry cow before whom a bough or a bunch of fruit is waved. For only hold up before me in like manner a book, and you may lead me all round Attica, and over the wide world. And now having arrived, I intend to lie down, and do you choose any posture in which you can read best. Begin.

Phaedr.: Listen. You know how matters stand with me; and how, as I conceive, this affair may be arranged for the advantage of both of us. And I maintain that I ought not to fail in my suit, because I am not your lover: for lovers repent of the kindnesses which they have shown when their passion ceases, but to the non-lovers who are free and not under any compulsion, no time of repentance ever comes; for they confer their benefits according to the measure of their ability, in the way which is most conducive to their own interest. Then again, lovers consider how by reason of their love they have neglected their own concerns and rendered service to others: and when to these benefits conferred they add on the troubles which they have endured, they think that they have long ago made to the beloved a very ample return.

But the non-lover has no such tormenting recollections; he has never neglected his affairs or quarrelled with his relations; he has no troubles to add up or excuses to invent; and being well rid of all these evils, why should he not freely do what will gratify the beloved? If you say that the lover is more to be esteemed, because his love is thought to be greater; for he is willing to say and do what is hateful to other men, in order to please his beloved;—that, if true, is only a proof that he will prefer any future love to his present, and will injure his old love at the pleasure of the

23

new. And how, in a matter of such infinite importance, can a man be right in trusting himself to one who is afflicted with a malady which no experienced person would attempt to cure, for the patient himself admits that he is not in his right mind, and acknowledges that he is wrong in his mind, but says that he is unable to control himself? And if he came to his right mind, would he ever imagine that the desires were good which he conceived when in his wrong mind?

Once more, there are many more non-lovers than lovers; and if you choose the best of the lovers, you will not have many to choose from; but if from the non-lovers, the choice will be larger, and you will be far more likely to find among them a person who is worthy of your friendship. If public opinion be your dread, and you would avoid reproach, in all probability the lover, who is always thinking that other men are as emulous of him as he is of them, will boast to some one of his successes, and make a show of them openly in the pride of his heart; he wants others to know that his labour has not been lost; but the non-lover is more his own master, and is desirous of solid good, and not of the opinion of mankind. Again, the lover may be generally noted or seen following the beloved (this is his regular occupation), and whenever they are observed to exchange two words they are supposed to meet about some affair of love either past or in contemplation; but when non-lovers meet, no one asks the reason why, because people know that talking to another is natural, whether friendship or mere pleasure be the motive.

Once more, if you fear the fickleness of friendship, consider that in any other case a quarrel might be a mutual calamity; but now, when you have given up what is most precious to you, you will be the greater loser, and therefore, you will have more reason in being afraid of the lover, for his vexations are many, and he is always fancying that every one is leagued against him. Wherefore also he debars his beloved from society; he will not have you intimate with the wealthy, lest they should exceed him in wealth, or with men of education, lest they should be his superiors in understanding; and he is equally afraid of anybody's influence who has any other advantage over himself. If he can persuade you to break with them, you are left without a friend in the world; or if, out of a regard to your own interest, you have more sense than to comply with his desire, you will have to quarrel with him. But those who are non-lovers, and whose success in love is the reward of their merit, will not be jealous of the companions of their beloved, and will rather hate those who refuse to be his associates, thinking that their favourite is slighted by the latter and benefited by the former; for more love than hatred may be expected to come to him out of his friendship with others.

Many lovers too have loved the person of a youth before they knew his character or his belongings; so that when their passion has passed away, there is no knowing whether they will continue to be his friends; whereas, in the case of non-lovers who were always friends, the friendship is not lessened by the favours granted; but the recollection of these remains with them, and is an earnest of good things to come. Further, I say that you are likely to be improved by me, whereas the lover will spoil you. For they praise your words and actions in a wrong way; partly, because they are afraid of offending you, and also, their judgment is weakened by passion. Such are the feats which love exhibits; he makes things painful to the disappointed which give no pain to others; he compels the successful lover to praise what ought not to give him pleasure, and therefore the beloved is to be pitied rather than envied.

But if you listen to me, in the first place, I, in my intercourse with you, shall not merely regard present enjoyment, but also future advantage, being not mastered by love, but my own master; nor for small causes taking violent dislikes, but even when the cause is great, slowly laying up little wrath—unintentional offences I shall forgive, and intentional ones I shall try to prevent; and these are the marks of a friendship which will last. Do you think that a lover only can be a firm friend? reflect: if this were true, we should set small value on sons, or fathers, or mothers; nor should we ever have loyal friends, for our love of them arises not from passion, but from other associations. Further, if we ought to shower favours on those who are the most eager suitors; on that principle, we ought always to do good, not to the most virtuous, but to the most needy; for they are the persons who will be most relieved, and will therefore be the most grateful; and when you make a feast you should invite not your friend, but the beggar and the empty soul; for they will love you, and attend you, and come about your doors, and will be the best pleased, and the most grateful, and will invoke many a blessing on your head. Yet surely you ought not to be granting favours to those who besiege you with prayer, but to those who are best able to reward you; nor to the lover only, but to those who are worthy of love; nor to those who will enjoy the bloom of your youth, but to those who will share their possessions with you in age; nor to those who, having succeeded, will glory in their success to others, but to those who will be modest and tell no tales; nor to those who care about you for a moment only, but to those who will continue your friends through life; nor to those who, when their passion is over, will pick a quarrel with you, but rather to those who, when the charm of youth has left you, will show their own virtue. Remember what I have said; and consider yet this further point: friends admonish the lover under the idea that his way of life is bad, but no one of his kindred ever yet censured the non-lover, or thought that he was ill-advised about his own interests.

Perhaps you will ask me whether I propose that you should indulge every non-lover. To which I reply that not even the lover would advise you to indulge all lovers, for the indiscriminate favour is less esteemed by the rational recipient, and less easily hidden by him who would escape the censure of the world. Now love ought to be for the advantage of both parties, and for the injury of neither.

I believe that I have said enough; but if there is anything more which you desire or which in your opinion needs to be supplied, ask and I will answer.

Now, Socrates, what do you think? Is not the discourse excellent, more especially in the matter of the language?

Soc.: Yes, quite admirable; the effect on me was ravishing. And this I owe to you, Phaedrus, for I observed you while reading to be in an ecstasy, and thinking that you are more

26

experienced in these matters than I am, I followed your example, and, like you, my divine darling, I became inspired with a frenzy.

Phaedr.: Indeed, you are pleased to be merry.

Soc.: Do you mean that I am not in earnest?

Phaedr.: Now don't talk in that way, Socrates, but let me have your real opinion; I adjure you, by Zeus, the god of friendship, to tell me whether you think that any Hellene could have said more or spoken better on the same subject.

Soc.: Well, but are you and I expected to praise the sentiments of the author, or only the clearness, and roundness, and finish, and tournure of the language? As to the first I willingly submit to your better judgment, for I am not worthy to form an opinion, having only attended to the rhetorical manner; and I was doubting whether this could have been defended even by Lysias himself; I thought, though I speak under correction, that he repeated himself two or three times, either from want of words or from want of pains; and also, he appeared to me ostentatiously to exult in showing how well he could say the same thing in two or three ways.

Phaedr.: Nonsense, Socrates; what you call repetition was the especial merit of the speech; for he omitted no topic of which the subject rightly allowed, and I do not think that any one could have spoken better or more exhaustively.

Soc.: There I cannot go along with you. Ancient sages, men and women, who have spoken and written of these things, would rise up in judgment against me, if out of complaisance I assented to you.

Phaedr.: Who are they, and where did you hear anything better than this?

Soc.: I am sure that I must have heard; but at this moment I do not remember from whom; perhaps from Sappho the fair, or Anacreon the wise; or, possibly, from a prose writer. Why do I say so? Why, because I perceive that my bosom is full, and that I could make another speech as good as that of Lysias, and different. Now I am certain that this is not an invention of my own, who am well aware that I know nothing, and therefore I can only infer that I have been filled through the ears, like a pitcher, from the waters of another, though I have actually forgotten in my stupidity who was my informant.

Phaedr.: That is grand: but never mind where you heard the discourse or from whom; let that be a mystery not to be divulged even at my earnest desire. Only, as you say, promise to make another and better oration, equal in length and entirely new, on the same subject; and I, like the nine Archons, will promise to set up a golden image at Delphi, not only of myself, but of you, and as large as life.

Soc.: You are a dear golden ass if you suppose me to mean that Lysias has altogether missed the mark, and that I can make a speech from which all his arguments are to be excluded. The worst of authors will say something which is to the point. Who, for example, could speak on this thesis of yours without praising the discretion of the non-lover and blaming the indiscretion of the lover? These are the commonplaces of the subject which must come in (for what else is there to be said?) and must be allowed and excused; the only merit is in the arrangement of them, for there can be none in the invention; but when you leave the common-places, then there may be some originality.

Phaedr.: I admit that there is reason in what you say, and I too will be reasonable, and will allow you to start with the premiss that the lover is more disordered in his wits than the non-lover; if in what remains you make a longer and better speech than Lysias, and use other arguments, then I say again, that a statue you shall have of beaten gold, and take your place by the colossal offerings of the Cypselids at Olympia.

Soc.: How profoundly in earnest is the lover, because to tease him I lay a finger upon his love! And so, Phaedrus, you really imagine that I am going to improve upon the ingenuity of Lysias?

Phaedr.: There I have you as you had me, and you must just speak "as you best can". Do not let us exchange "tu quoque" as in a farce, or compel me to say to you as you said to me, "I know Socrates as well as I know myself, and he was wanting to speak, but he gave himself airs". Rather I would have you consider that from this place we stir not until you have unbosomed yourself of the speech; for here are we all alone, and I am stronger, remember, and younger than you. Wherefore perpend, and do not compel me to use violence.

Soc.: But, my sweet Phaedrus, how ridiculous it would be of me to compete with Lysias in an extempore speech! He is a master in his art and I am an untaught man.

Phaedr.: You see how matters stand; and therefore let there be no more pretences; for, indeed, I know the word that is irresistible.

Soc.: Then don't say it.

Phaedr.: Yes, but I will; and my word shall be an oath. "I say, or rather swear"—but what god will be the witness of my oath?—"By this plane-tree I swear, that unless you repeat the discourse here in the face of this very plane-tree, I will never tell you another; never let you have word of another!"

Soc.: Villain! I am conquered; the poor lover of discourse has no more to say.

Phaedr.: Then why are you still at your tricks?

Soc.: I am not going to play tricks now that you have taken the oath, for I cannot allow myself to be starved.

Phaedr.: Proceed.

Soc.: Shall I tell you what I will do?

Phaedr.: What?

Soc.: I will veil my face and gallop through the discourse as fast as I can, for if I see you I shall feel ashamed and not know what to say.

Phaedr.: Only go on and you may do anything else which you please.

Soc.: Come, O ye Muses, melodious, as ye are called, whether you have received this name from the character of your strains, or because the Melians are a musical race, help, O help me in the tale which my good friend here desires me to rehearse, in order that his friend whom he always deemed wise may seem to him to be wiser now than ever.

Once upon a time there was a fair boy, or, more properly speaking, a youth; he was very fair and had a great many lovers; and there was one special cunning one, who had persuaded the youth that he did not love him, but he really loved him all the same; and one day when he was paying his addresses to him, he used this very argument—that he ought to accept the non-lover rather than the lover; his words were as follows:

"All good counsel begins in the same way; a man should know what he is advising about, or his counsel will all come to nought. But people imagine that they know about the nature of things, when they don't know about them, and, not having come to an understanding at first because they think that they know, they end, as might be expected, in contradicting one another and themselves. Now you and I must not be guilty of this fundamental error which we condemn in others; but as our question is whether the lover or non-lover is to be preferred, let us first of all agree in defining the nature and power of love, and then, keeping our eyes upon the definition and to this appealing, let us further enquire whether love brings advantage or dis-advantage.

"Every one sees that love is a desire, and we know also that non-lovers desire the beautiful and good. Now in what way is the lover to be distinguished from the non-lover? Let us note that in every one of us there are two guiding and ruling principles which lead us whither they will; one is the natural desire of pleasure, the other is an acquired opinion which aspires after the best; and these two are sometimes in harmony and then again at war, and some-times the one, sometimes the other conquers. When opinion by the help of reason leads us to the best, the conquering principle is called temperance; but when desire, which is devoid of reason, rules in us and drags us to pleasure, that power of misrule is called excess. Now excess has many names, and many members, and many forms, and any of these forms when very marked gives a name, neither honour-able nor creditable, to the bearer of the name. The desire of eating, for example, which gets the better of the higher reason and the other desires, is called gluttony, and he who is possessed by it is called a glutton; the tyrannical desire of drink, which inclines the possessor of the desire to drink, has a name which is only too obvious, and there can be as little doubt by what name any other appetite of the same family would be called; it will be the name of that which happens to be dominant. And now I think that you will perceive the drift of my discourse; but as every spoken word is in a manner plainer than the unspoken, I had better say further that the irrational desire which overcomes the tendency of opinion towards right, and is led away to the enjoyment of beauty, and especially of personal beauty, by the desires which are her own kindred—that supreme desire, I say, which by leading conquers and by the force of passion is reinforced, from this very force, receiving a name, is called love."

And now, dear Phaedrus, I shall pause for an instant to ask whether you do not think me, as I appear to myself, inspired?

Phaedr.: Yes, Socrates, you seem to have a very unusual flow of words.

Soc.: Listen to me, then, in silence; for surely the place is holy; so that you must not wonder, if, as I proceed, I appear to be in a divine fury, for already I am getting into dithyrambics.

Phaedr.: Nothing can be truer.

Soc.: The responsibility rests with you. But hear what follows, and perhaps the fit may be averted; all is in their hands above. I will go on talking to my youth. Listen:

Thus, my friend, we have declared and defined the nature of the subject. Keeping the definition in view, let us now enquire what advantage or disadvantage is likely to ensue from the lover or the non-lover to him who accepts their advances.

He who is the victim of his passions and the slave of pleasure will of course desire to make his beloved as agreeable to himself as possible. Now to him who has a mind diseased anything is agreeable which is not opposed to him, but that which is equal or superior is hateful to him, and therefore the lover will not brook any superiority or equality on the part of his beloved; he is always employed in reducing him to inferiority. And the ignorant is the inferior of the wise, the coward of the brave, the slow of speech of the speaker, the dull of the clever. These, and not these only, are the mental defects of the beloved; defects which, when implanted by nature, are necessarily a delight to the lover, and, when not implanted, he must contrive to implant them in him, if he would not be deprived of his fleeting joy. And therefore he cannot help being jealous, and will debar his beloved from the advantages of society which would make a man of him, and especially from that society which would have given him wisdom, and thereby he cannot fail to do him great harm. That is to say, in his excessive fear lest he should come to be despised in his eyes he will be compelled to banish from him divine philosophy; and there is no greater injury which he can inflict upon him than this. He will contrive that his beloved shall be wholly ignorant, and in everything shall look to him; he is to be the delight of the lover's heart, and a curse to himself. Verily, a lover is a profitable guardian and associate for him in all that relates to his mind.

Let us next see how his master, whose law of life is pleasure and not good, will keep and train the body of his servant. Will he not choose a beloved who is delicate rather than sturdy and strong? One brought up in shady bowers and not in the bright sun, a stranger to manly exercises and the sweat of toil, accustomed only to a soft and luxurious diet, instead of the hues of health having the colours of paint and ornament, and the rest of a piece?—such a life as any one can imagine and which I need not detail at length. But I may sum up all that I have to say in a word, and pass on. Such a person in war, or in any of the great crises of life, will be the anxiety of his friends and also of his lover, and certainly not the terror of his enemies; which nobody can deny.

And now let us tell what advantage or disadvantage the beloved will receive from the guardianship and society of his lover in the matter of his property; this is the next point to be considered. The lover will be the first to see what, indeed, will be sufficiently evident to all men, that he desires above all things to deprive his beloved of his dearest and best and holiest possessions, father, mother, kindred, friends, of all whom he thinks may be hinderers or reprovers of their most sweet converse; he will even cast a jealous eye upon his gold and silver or other property, because these make him a less easy prey, and when caught less manageable; hence he is of necessity displeased at his possession of them and rejoices at their loss; and he would like him to be wifeless, childless, homeless, as well; and the longer the better, for the longer he is all this, the longer he will enjoy him.

There are some sort of animals, such as flatterers, who are dangerous and mischievous enough, and yet nature has mingled a temporary pleasure and grace in their composition. You may say that a courtesan is hurtful, and disapprove of such creatures and their practices, and yet for the time they are very pleasant. But the lover is not only hurtful to his love; he is also an extremely disagreeable companion. The old proverb says that "birds of a feather flock together"; I suppose that equality of years inclines them to the same pleasures, and similarity begets friendship; yet you may have more than enough even of this; and verily constraint is always said to be grievous.

Now the lover is not only unlike his beloved, but he forces himself upon him. For he is old and his love is young, and neither day nor night will he leave him if he can help; necessity and the sting of desire drive him on, and allure him with the pleasure which he receives from seeing, hearing, touching, perceiving him in every way. And therefore he is delighted to fasten upon him and to minister to him. But what pleasure or consolation can the beloved be receiving all this time? Must he not feel the extremity of disgust when he looks at an old shrivelled face and the remainder to match, which even in a description is disagreeable, and quite detestable when he is forced into daily contact with his lover; moreover he is jealously watched and guarded against everything and everybody, and has to hear misplaced and exaggerated praises of himself, and censures equally inappropriate, which are intolerable when the man is sober, and, besides being intolerable, are published all over the place in all their indelicacy and wearisomeness when he is drunk.

And not only while his love continues is he mischievous and unpleasant, but when his love ceases he becomes a perfidious enemy of him on whom he showered his oaths and prayers and promises, and yet could hardly prevail upon him to tolerate the tedium of his company even from motives of interest. The hour of payment arrives, and now he is the servant of another master; instead of love and infatuation, wisdom and temperance are his bosom's lords; but the beloved has not discovered the change which has taken place in him, when he asks for a return and recalls to his recollection former sayings and doings; he believes himself to be speaking to the same person, and the other, not having the courage to confess the truth, and not knowing how to fulfil the oaths and promises which he made when under the dominion of folly, and having now grown wise and temperate, does not want to do as he did or to be as he was before.

And so he runs away and is constrained to be a defaulter; the oyster-shell has fallen with the other side uppermost—he changes pursuit into flight, while the other is compelled to follow him with passion and imprecation, not knowing that he ought never from the first to have accepted a demented lover instead of a sensible non-lover; and that in making such a choice he was giving himself up to a faithless, morose, envious, disagreeable being, hurtful to his estate, hurtful to his bodily health, and still more hurtful to the cultivation of his mind, than which there neither is nor ever will be anything more honoured in the eyes both of gods and men. Consider this, fair youth, and know that in the friendship of the lover there is no real kindness; he has an appetite and wants to feed upon you:

As wolves love lambs so lovers love their loves.

But I told you so, I am speaking in verse, and therefore I had better make an end; enough.

Phaedr.: I thought that you were only half-way and were going to make a similar speech about all the advantages of accepting the non-lover. Why do you not proceed?

Soc.: Does not your simplicity observe that I have got out of dithyrambics into heroics, when only uttering a censure on the lover? And if I am to add the praises of the non-lover what will become of me? Do you not perceive that I am already overtaken by the Nymphs to whom you have mischievously exposed me? And therefore I will only add that the non-lover has all the advantages in which the lover is accused of being deficient. And now I will say no more; there has been enough of both of them. Leaving the tale to its fate, I will cross the river and make the best of my way home, lest a worse thing be inflicted upon me by you.

Phaedr.: Not yet, Socrates; not until the heat of the day has passed; do you not see that the hour is almost noon? there is the midday sun standing still, as people say, in the meridian. Let us rather stay and talk over what has been said, and then return in the cool.

Soc.: Your love of discourse, Phaedrus, is superhuman, simply marvellous, and I do not believe that there is any one of your contemporaries who has either made or in one way or another has compelled others to make an equal number of speeches. I would except Simmias the Theban, but all the rest are far behind you. And now I do verily believe that you have been the cause of another.

Phaedr.: That is good news. But what do you mean?

Soc.: I mean to say that as I was about to cross the stream the usual sign was given to me,—that sign which always forbids, but never bids, me to do anything which I am going to do; and I thought that I heard a voice saying in my ear that I had been guilty of impiety, and that I must not go away until I had made an atonement. Now I am a diviner, though not a very good one, but I have enough religion for my own use, as you might say of a bad writer—his writing is good enough for him; and I am beginning to see that I was in error. O my friend, how prophetic is the human soul! At the time I had a sort of misgiving, and, like Ibycus, "I was troubled; I feared that I might be buying honour from men at the price of sinning against the gods". Now I recognize my error.

Phaedr.: What error?

Soc.: That was a dreadful speech which you brought with you, and you made me utter one as bad.

Phaedr.: How so?

Soc.: It was foolish, I say,—to a certain extent, impious; can anything be more dreadful?

Phaedr.: Nothing, if the speech was really such as you describe.

Soc.: Well, and is not Eros the son of Aphrodite, and a god?

Phaedr.: So men say.

Soc.: But that was not acknowledged by Lysias in his speech, not by you in that other speech which you by a charm drew from my lips. For if love be, as he surely is, a divinity, he cannot be evil. Yet this was the error of both the speeches. There was also a simplicity about them which was refreshing; having no truth or honesty in them, nevertheless they pretended to be something, hoping to succeed in deceiving the manikins of earth and gain celebrity among them. Wherefore I must have a purgation. And I bethink me of an ancient purgation of mythological error which was devised, not by Homer, for he never had the wit to discover why he was blind, but by Stesichorus, who was a philosopher and knew the reason why; and therefore, when he lost his eyes, for that was the penalty which was inflicted upon him for reviling the lovely Helen, he at once purged himself. And the purgation was a recantation, which began thus,—

False is that word of mine—the truth is that thou didst not embark in ships, nor ever go to the walls of Troy;

and when he had completed his poem, which is called "the recantation", immediately his sight returned to him. Now I will be wiser than either Stesichorus or Homer, in that I am going to make my recantation for reviling love before I suffer; and this I will attempt, not as before, veiled and ashamed, but with forehead bold and bare.

Phaedr.: Nothing could be more agreeable to me than to hear you say so.

Soc.: Only think, my good Phaedrus, what an utter want of delicacy was shown in the two discourses; I mean, in my own and in that which you recited out of the book. Would not any one who was himself of a noble and gentle nature, and who loved or ever had loved a nature like his own, when we tell of the petty causes of lovers' jealousies, and of their exceeding animosities, and of the injuries which they do to their beloved, have imagined that our ideas of love were taken from some haunt of sailors to which good manners

36

were unknown—he would certainly never have admitted the justice of our censure?

Phaedr.: I dare say not, Socrates.

Soc.: Therefore, because I blush at the thought of this person, and also because I am afraid of Love himself, I desire to wash the brine out of my ears with water from the spring; and I would counsel Lysias not to delay, but to write another discourse, which shall prove that "ceteris paribus" the lover ought to be accepted rather than the non-lover.

Phaedr.: Be assured that he shall. You shall speak the praises of the lover, and Lysias shall be compelled by me to write another discourse on the same theme.

Soc.: You will be true to your nature in that, and therefore I believe you.

Phaedr.: Speak, and fear not.

Soc.: But where is the fair youth whom I was addressing before, and who ought to listen now; lest, if he hear me not, he should accept a non-lover before he knows what he is doing?

Phaedr.: He is close at hand, and always at your service.

Soc.: Know then, fair youth, that the former discourse was the word of Phaedrus, the son of Vain Man, who dwells in the city of Myrrhina. And this which I am about to utter is the recantation of Stesichorus the son of Godly Man, who comes from the town of Desire, and is to the following effect: I told a lie when I said that the beloved ought to accept the non-lover when he might have the lover, because the one is sane, and the other mad. It might be so if madness were simply an evil; but there is also a madness which is a divine gift, and the source of the chiefest blessings granted to men. For prophecy is a madness, and the prophetess at Delphi and the priestesses at Dodona when out of their senses have conferred great benefits on Hellas, both in public and private life, but when in their senses few or none. And I might also tell you how the Sibyl and other inspired persons have given to many an one many an intimation of the future which has saved them from falling. But it would be tedious to speak of what every one knows.

There will be more reason in appealing to the ancient

inventors of names, who would never have connected prophecy, which foretells the future and is the noblest of arts,
with madness, or called them both by the same name, if
they had deemed madness to be a disgrace or dishonour;
they must have thought that there was an inspired madness
which was a noble thing. And this is confirmed by the name
which was given by them to the rational investigation of
futurity, whether made by the help of birds or of other
signs—and as prophecy is more perfect and august than
augury, both in name and fact, in the same proportion, as the
ancients testify, is madness superior to a sane mind, for
the one is only of human, but the other of divine origin.
Again, where plagues and mightiest woes have bred in
certain families, owing to some ancient blood-guiltiness,
there madness has entered with holy prayers and rites, and
by inspired utterances found a way of deliverance for those
who are in need; and he who has part in this gift, and is
truly possessed and duly out of his mind, is by the use of
purifications and mysteries made whole and exempt from
evil, future as well as present, and has a release from the
calamity which was afflicting him. The third kind is the
madness of those who are possessed by the Muses; which
taking hold of a delicate and virgin soul, and there inspiring
frenzy, awakens lyrical and all other numbers; with these
adorning the myriad actions of ancient heroes for the instruction of posterity. But he who, having no touch of the
Muses' madness in his soul, comes to the door and thinks
that he will get into the temple by the help of art—he, I
say, and his poetry are not admitted; the sane man dis-
appears and is nowhere when he enters into rivalry with the
madman.

  I might tell of many other noble deeds which have sprung
from inspired madness. And therefore, let no one frighten
or flutter us by saying that the temperate friend is to be
chosen rather than the inspired, but let him further show
that love is not sent by the gods for any good to lover or
beloved; if he can do so we will allow him to carry off the
palm. And we, on our part, will prove in answer to him that
the madness of love is the greatest of heaven's blessings, and
the proof shall be one which the wise will receive, and the

ignorant disbelieve. But first of all, let us view the affections and actions of the soul divine and human, and try to ascertain the truth about them. The beginning of our proof is as follows:

The soul through all her being is immortal, for that which is ever in motion is immortal; but that which moves another and is moved by another, in ceasing to move ceases also to live. Only the self-moving, never leaving self, never ceases to move, and is the fountain and beginning of motion to all that moves besides. Now, the beginning is unbegotten, for that which is begotten has a beginning; but the beginning is begotten of nothing, for if it were begotten of something, then the begotten would not come from a beginning. But if unbegotten, it must also be indestructible; for if beginning were destroyed, there could be no beginning out of anything, nor anything out of a beginning; and all things must have a beginning. And therefore the self-moving is the beginning of motion; and this can neither be destroyed nor begotten, else the whole heavens and all creation would collapse and stand still, and never again have motion or birth. But if the self-moving is proved to be immortal, he who affirms that self-motion is the very idea and essence of the soul will not be put to confusion. For the body which is moved from without is soulless; but that which is moved from within has a soul, for such is the nature of the soul. But if this be true, must not the soul be the self-moving, and therefore of necessity unbegotten and immortal? Enough of the soul's immortality.

Of the nature of the soul, though her true form be ever a theme of large and more than mortal discourse, let me speak briefly, and in a figure. And let the figure be composite—a pair of winged horses and a charioteer. Now the winged horses and the charioteers of the gods are all of them noble and of noble descent, but those of other races are mixed; the human charioteer drives his in a pair; and one of them is noble and of noble breed, and the other is ignoble and of ignoble breed; and the driving of them of necessity gives a great deal of trouble to him. I will endeavour to explain to you in what way the mortal differs from the immortal creature.

The soul in her totality has the care of inanimate being everywhere, and traverses the whole heaven in divers forms appearing;—when perfect and fully winged she soars upward, and orders the whole world; whereas the imperfect soul, losing her wings and drooping in her flight at last settles on the solid ground—there, finding a home, she receives an earthly frame which appears to be self-moved, but is really moved by her power; and this composition of soul and body is called a living and mortal creature. For immortal no such union can be reasonably believed to be; although fancy, not having seen nor surely known the nature of god, may imagine an immortal creature having both a body and also a soul which are united throughout all time. Let that, however, be as god wills, and be spoken of acceptably to him. And now let us ask the reason why the soul loses her wings!

The wing is the corporeal element which is most akin to the divine, and which by nature tends to soar aloft and carry that which gravitates downwards into the upper region, which is the habitation of the gods. The divine is beauty, wisdom, goodness, and the like; and by these the wing of the soul is nourished, and grows apace; but when fed upon evil and foulness and the opposite of good, wastes and falls away. Zeus, the mighty lord, holding the reins of a winged chariot, leads the way in heaven, ordering all and taking care of all; and there follows him the array of gods and demi-gods, marshalled in eleven bands; Hestia alone abides at home in the house of heaven; of the rest they who are reckoned among the princely twelve march in their appointed order. They see many blessed sights in the inner heaven, and there are many ways to and fro, along which the blessed gods are passing, every one doing his own work; he may follow who will and can, for jealousy has no place in the celestial choir. But when they go to banquet and festival, then they move up the steep to the top of the vault of heaven. The chariots of the gods in even poise, obeying the rein, glide rapidly; but the others labour, for the vicious steed goes heavily, weighing down the charioteer to the earth when his steed has not been thoroughly trained:—and this is the hour of agony and extremest conflict for the soul. For the immortals, when they are at the end of their course, go forth and stand upon the outside of heaven, and the revolution of the spheres carries them round, and they behold the things beyond. But of the heaven which is above the heavens, what earthly poet ever did or ever will sing worthily? It is such as I will describe; for I must dare to speak the truth, when truth is my theme.

There abides the very being with which true knowledge is concerned; the colourless, formless, intangible essence, visible only to mind, the pilot of the soul. The divine intelligence, being nurtured upon mind and pure knowledge, and the intelligence of every soul which is capable of receiving the food proper to it, rejoices at beholding reality, and once more gazing upon truth, is replenished and made glad, until the revolution of the worlds brings her round again to the same place. In the revolution she beholds justice, and temperance, and knowledge absolute, not in the form of generation or of relation, which men call existence, but knowledge absolute in existence absolute; and beholding the other true existences in like manner, and feasting upon them, she passes down into the interior of the heavens and returns home; and there the charioteer putting up his horses at the stall, gives them ambrosia to eat and nectar to drink.

Such is the life of the gods; but of other souls, that which follows god best and is likest to him lifts the head of the charioteer into the outer world, and is carried round in the revolution, troubled indeed by the steeds, and with difficulty beholding true being; while another only rises and falls, and sees, and again fails to see by reason of the unruliness of the steeds. The rest of the souls are also longing after the upper world and they all follow, but not being strong enough they are carried round below the surface, plunging, treading on one another, each striving to be first; and there is confusion and perspiration and the extremity of effort; and many of them are lamed or have their wings broken through the ill-driving of the charioteers; and all of them after a fruitless toil, not having attained to the mysteries of true being, go away, and feed upon opinion. The reason why the souls exhibit this exceeding eagerness to behold the plain of truth is that pasturage is found there, which is suited to the highest part of the soul; and the wing on which the soul soars is nourished with this.

And there is a law of Destiny, that the soul which attains any vision of truth in company with a god is preserved from harm until the next period, and if attaining always is always unharmed. But when she is unable to follow, and fails to behold the truth, and through some ill-hap sinks beneath the double load of forgetfulness and vice, and her wings fall from her and she drops to the ground, then the law ordains that this soul shall at her first birth pass, not into any other animal, but only into man; and the soul which has seen most of truth shall come to the birth as a philosopher, or artist, or some musical and loving nature; that which has seen truth in the second degree shall be some righteous king or warrior chief; the soul which is of the third class shall be a politician, or economist, or trader; the fourth shall be a lover of gymnastic toils, or a physician; the fifth shall lead the life of a prophet or hierophant; to the sixth the character of a poet or some other imitative artist will be assigned; to the seventh the life of an artisan or husbandman; to the eighth that of a sophist or demagogue; to the ninth that of a tyrant;—all these are states of probation, in which he who does righteously improves, and he who does unrighteously, deteriorates his lot.

Ten thousand years must elapse before the soul of each one can return to the place from whence she came, for she cannot grow her wings in less; only the soul of a philosopher, guileless and true, or the soul of a lover, who is not devoid of philosophy, may acquire wings in the third of the recurring periods of a thousand years; he is distinguished from the ordinary good man who gains wings in three thousand years: and they who choose this life three times in succession have wings given them, and go away at the end of three thousand years. But the others receive judgment when they have completed their first life, and after the judgment they go, some of them to the houses of correction which are under the earth, and are punished; others to some place in heaven whither they are lightly borne by justice, and there they live in a manner worthy of the life which they led here when in the form of men.

42

And at the end of the first thousand years the good souls and also the evil souls both come to draw lots and choose their second life, and they may take any which they please. The soul of a man may pass into the life of a beast, or from the beast return again into the man. But the soul which has never seen the truth will not pass into the human form. For a man must have intelligence of universals, and be able to proceed from the many particulars of sense to one conception of reason;—this is the recollection of those things which our soul once saw while following god—when regardless of that which we now call being she raised her head up towards the true being. And therefore the mind of the philosopher alone has wings; and this is just, for he is always, according to the measure of his abilities, clinging in recollection to those things in which god abides, and in beholding which he is what he is. And he who employs aright these memories is ever being initiated into perfect mysteries and alone becomes truly perfect. But, as he forgets earthly interests and is rapt in the divine, the vulgar deem him mad, and rebuke him; they do not see that he is inspired.

Thus far I have been speaking of the fourth and last kind of madness, which is imputed to him who, when he sees the beauty of earth, is transported with the recollection of the true beauty; he would like to fly away, but he cannot; he is like a bird fluttering and looking upward and careless of the world below; and he is therefore thought to be mad. And I have shown this of all inspirations to be the noblest and highest and the offspring of the highest to him who has or shares in it, and that he who loves the beautiful is called a lover because he partakes of it.

For, as has been already said, every soul of man has in the way of nature beheld true being; this was the condition of her passing into the form of man. But all souls do not easily recall the things of the other world; they may have seen them for a short time only, or they may have been unfortunate in their earthly lot, and, having had their hearts turned to unrighteousness through some corrupting influence, they may have lost the memory of the holy things which once they saw. Few only retain an adequate remembrance of them; and they, when they behold here any image

43

of that other world, are rapt in amazement; but they are
ignorant of what this rapture means, because they do not
clearly perceive. For there is no light of justice or temperance
or any of the higher ideas which are precious to souls in the
earthly copies of them: they are seen through a glass dimly;
and there are few who, going to the images, behold in them
the realities, and these only with difficulty. There was a
time when with the rest of the happy band they saw beauty
shining in brightness,—we philosophers following in the
train of Zeus, others in company with other gods; and then
we beheld the beatific vision and were initiated into a
mystery which may be truly called most blessed, celebrated
by us in our state of innocence, before we had any experience
of evils to come, when we were admitted to the sight of
apparitions innocent and simple and calm and happy, which
we beheld shining in pure light, pure ourselves and not yet
enshrined in that living tomb which we carry about, now
that we are imprisoned in the body, like an oyster in his shell.
Let me linger over the memory of scenes which have passed
away.

But of beauty, I repeat again that we saw her there shining
in company with the celestial forms; and coming to earth
we find her here too, shining in clearness through the clearest
aperture of sense. For sight is the most piercing of our
bodily senses; though not by that is wisdom seen; her
loveliness would have been transporting if there had been
a visible image of her, and the other ideas, if they had visible
counterparts, would be equally lovely. But this is the privi-
lege of beauty, that being the loveliest she is also the most
palpable to sight. Now he who is not newly initiated or
who has become corrupted, does not easily rise out of this
world to the sight of true beauty in the other; he looks only
at her earthly namesake, and instead of being awed at the
sight of her, he is given over to pleasure, and like a brutish
beast he rushes on to enjoy and beget; he consorts with
wantonness, and is not afraid or ashamed of pursuing
pleasure in violation of nature.

But he whose initiation is recent, and who has been the
spectator of many glories in the other world, is amazed
when he sees any one having a godlike face or form, which

44

is the expression of divine beauty; and at first a shudder runs through him, and again the old awe steals over him; then looking upon the face of his beloved as of a god he reverences him, and if he were not afraid of being thought a downright madman, he would sacrifice to his beloved as to the image of a god; then while he gazes on him there is a sort of reaction, and the shudder passes into an unusual heat and perspiration; for, as he receives the effluence of beauty through the eyes, the wing moistens and he warms. And as he warms, the parts out of which the wing grew, and which had been hitherto closed and rigid, and had prevented the wing from shooting forth, are melted, and as nourishment streams upon him, the lower end of the wing begins to swell and grow from the root upwards; and the growth extends under the whole soul—for once the whole was winged.

During this process the whole soul is all in a state of ebullition and effervescence,—which may be compared to the irritation and uneasiness in the gums at the time of cutting teeth,—bubbles up, and has a feeling of uneasiness and tickling; but when in like manner the soul is beginning to grow wings, the beauty of the beloved meets her eye and she receives the sensible warm motion of particles which flow towards her, therefore called emotion, and is refreshed and warmed by them, and then she ceases from her pain with joy. But when she is parted from her beloved and her moisture fails, then the orifices of the passage out of which the wing shoots dry up and close, and intercept the germ of the wing; which, being shut up with the emotion, throbbing as with the pulsations of an artery, pricks the aperture which is nearest, until at length the entire soul is pierced and maddened and pained, and at the recollection of beauty is again delighted. And from both of them together the soul is oppressed at the strangeness of her condition, and is in a great strait and excitement, and in her madness can neither sleep by night nor abide in her place by day. And wherever she thinks that she will behold the beautiful one, thither in her desire she runs.

And when she has seen him, and bathed herself in the waters of beauty, her constraint is loosened, and she is refreshed, and has no more pangs and pains; and this is the sweetest of all pleasures at the time, and is the reason why the soul of the lover will never forsake his beautiful one, whom he esteems above all; he has forgotten mother and brethren and companions, and he thinks nothing of the neglect and loss of his property; the rules and proprieties of life, on which he formerly prided himself, he now despises, and is ready to sleep like a servant, wherever he is allowed, as near as he can to his desired one, who is the object of his worship, and the physician who can alone assuage the greatness of his pain. And this state, my dear imaginary youth to whom I am talking, is by men called love, and among the gods has a name at which you, in your simplicity, may be inclined to mock; there are two lines in the apocryphal writings of Homer in which the name occurs. One of them is rather outrageous, and not altogether metrical. They are as follows:

> "Mortals call him fluttering love,
> But the immortals call him winged one,
> Because the growing of wings is a necessity to him."

You may believe this, but not unless you like. At any rate the loves of lovers and their causes are such as I have described.

Now the lover who is taken to be the attendant of Zeus is better able to bear the winged god, and can endure a heavier burden; but the attendants and companions of Ares, when under the influence of love, if they fancy that they have been at all wronged, are ready to kill and put an end to themselves and their beloved. And he who follows in the train of any other god, while he is unspoiled and the impression lasts, honours and imitates him, as far as he is able; and after the manner of his god he behaves in his intercourse with his beloved and with the rest of the world during the first period of his earthly existence. Every one chooses his love from the ranks of beauty according to his character, and this he makes his god, and fashions and adorns as a sort of image which he is to fall down and worship.

The followers of Zeus desire that their beloved should have a soul like him; and therefore they seek out some one of a philosophical and imperial nature, and when they have found him and loved him, they do all they can to confirm such a nature in him, and if they have no experience of such a disposition hitherto, they learn of any one who can teach them, and themselves follow in the same way. And they have the less difficulty in finding the nature of their own god in themselves, because they have been compelled to gaze intensely on him; their recollection clings to him, and they become possessed of him, and receive from him their character and disposition, so far as man can participate in god. The qualities of their god they attribute to the beloved, wherefore they love him all the more, and if, like the Bacchic Nymphs, they draw inspiration from Zeus, they pour out their own fountain upon him, wanting to make him as like as possible to their own god.

But those who are the followers of Herè seek a royal love, and when they have found him they do just the same with him; and in like manner the followers of Apollo, and of every other god walking in the ways of their god, seek a love who is to be made like him whom they serve, and when they have found him, they themselves imitate their god, and persuade their love to do the same, and educate him into the manner and nature of the god as far as they each can; for no feelings of envy or jealousy are entertained by them towards their beloved, but they do their utmost to create in him the greatest likeness of themselves and of the god whom they honour. Thus fair and blissful to the beloved is the desire of the inspired lover, and the initiation of which I speak into the mysteries of true love, if he be captured by the lover and their purpose is effected. Now the beloved is taken captive in the following manner:

As I said at the beginning of this tale, I divided each soul into three—two horses and a charioteer; and one of the horses was good and the other bad: the division may remain, but I have not yet explained in what the goodness or badness of either consists, and to that I will now proceed. The right-hand horse is upright and cleanly made; he has a lofty neck and an aquiline nose; his colour is white, and his eyes dark; he is a lover of honour and modesty and temperance, and the follower of true glory; he needs no touch of the whip, but is guided by word and admonition

47

only. The other is a crooked lumbering animal, put together anyhow; he has a short thick neck; he is flat-faced and of a dark colour, with grey eyes and blood-red complexion, the mate of insolence and pride, shag-eared and deaf, hardly yielding to whip and spur.

Now when the charioteer beholds the vision of love, and has his whole soul warmed through sense, and is full of the prickings and ticklings of desire, the obedient steed, then as always under the government of shame, refrains from leaping on the beloved; but the other, heedless of the pricks and of the blows of the whip, plunges and runs away, giving all manner of trouble to his companion and the charioteer, whom he forces to approach the beloved and to remember the joys of love. They at first indignantly oppose him and will not be urged on to do terrible and unlawful deeds; but at last, when he persists in plaguing them, they yield and agree to do as he bids them. And now they are at the spot and behold the flashing beauty of the beloved; which when the charioteer sees, his memory is carried to the true beauty, whom he beholds in company with Modesty like an image placed upon a holy pedestal. He sees her, but he is afraid and falls backwards in adoration, and by his fall is compelled to pull back the reins with such violence as to bring both the steeds on their haunches, the one willing and unresisting, the unruly one very unwilling; and when they have gone back a little, the one is overcome with shame and wonder, and his whole soul is bathed in perspiration; the other, when the pain is over which the bridle and the fall had given him, having with difficulty taken breath, is full of wrath and reproaches, which he heaps upon the charioteer and his fellow-steed, for want of courage and manhood, declaring that they have been false to their agreement and guilty of desertion. Again they refuse, and again he urges them on, and will scarce yield to their prayer that he would wait until another time.

When the appointed hour comes, they make as if they had forgotten, and he reminds them, fighting and neighing and dragging them on, until at length he on the same thoughts intent, forces them to draw near again. And when they are near he stoops his head and puts up his tail, and takes the bit in his teeth and pulls shamelessly. Then the charioteer is worse off than ever; he falls back like a racer at the barrier, and with a still more violent wrench drags the bit out of the teeth of the wild steed and covers his abusive tongue and jaws with blood, and forces his legs and haunches to the ground and punishes him sorely. And when this has happened several times and the villain has ceased from his wanton way, he is tamed and humbled, and follows the will of the charioteer, and when he sees the beautiful one he is ready to die of fear. And from that time forward the soul of the lover follows the beloved in modesty and holy fear.

And so the beloved who, like a god, has received every true and loyal service from his lover, not in pretence but in reality, being also himself of a nature friendly to his admirer, if in former days he has blushed to own his passion and turned away his lover, because his youthful companions or others slanderously told him that he would be disgraced, now as years advance, at the appointed age and time, is led to receive him into communion. For fate which has ordained that there shall be no friendship among the evil has also ordained that there shall ever be friendship among the good. And the beloved when he has received him into communion and intimacy, is quite amazed at the good-will of the lover; he recognises that the inspired friend is worth all other friends or kinsmen; they have nothing of friendship in them worthy to be compared with his.

And when this feeling continues and he is nearer to him and embraces him, in gymnastic exercises and at other times of meeting, then the fountain of that stream, which Zeus when he was in love with Ganymede named Desire, overflows upon the lover, and some enters into his soul, and some when he is filled flows out again; and as a breeze or an echo rebounds from the smooth rocks and returns whence it came, so does the stream of beauty, passing through the eyes which are the windows of the soul, come back to the beautiful one; there arriving and quickening the passages of the wings, watering them and inclining them to grow, and filling the soul of the beloved also with love. And thus he loves, but he knows not what; he does not understand and cannot explain his own state; he appears to have caught the infection of blindness from another; the lover is his mirror in whom he is beholding himself, but he is not aware of this.

When he is with the lover, both cease from their pain, but when he is away then he longs as he is longed for, and has love's image, love for love lodging in his breast, which he calls and believes to be not love but friendship only, and his desire is as the desire of the other, but weaker; he wants to see him, touch him, kiss, embrace him, and probably not long afterwards his desire is accomplished. When they meet, the wanton steed of the lover has a word to say to the charioteer; he would like to have a little pleasure in return for many pains, but the wanton steed of the beloved says not a word, for he is bursting with passion which he understands not;—he throws his arms round the lover and embraces him as his dearest friend; and, then they are side by side, he is not in a state in which he can refuse the lover anything, if he ask him; although his fellow-steed and the charioteer oppose him with the arguments of shame and reason. After this their happiness depends upon their self-control; if the better elements of the mind which lead to order and philosophy prevail, then they pass their life here in happiness and harmony—masters of themselves and orderly—enslaving the vicious and emancipating the virtuous elements of the soul; and when the end comes, they are light and winged for flight, having conquered in one of the three heavenly or truly Olympian victories; nor can human discipline or divine inspiration confer any greater blessing on man than this.

If, on the other hand, they leave philosophy and lead the lower life of ambition, then probably, after wine or in some other careless hour, the two wanton animals take the two souls when off their guard and bring them together, and they accomplish that desire of their hearts which to the many is bliss; and this having once enjoyed they continue to enjoy, yet rarely because they have not the approval of the whole soul. They too are dear, but not so dear to one another as the others, either at the time of their love or afterwards. They consider that they have given and taken from each other the most sacred pledges, and they may not break them and fall into enmity. At last they pass out of the body, unwinged, but eager to soar, and thus obtain no mean reward of love and madness. For those who have once begun the heavenward pilgrimage may not go down again to darkness and the journey beneath the earth, but they live in light always; happy companions in their pilgrimage, and when the time comes at which they receive their wings they have the same plumage because of their love.

Thus great are the heavenly blessings which the friendship of a lover will confer upon you, my youth. Whereas the attachment of the non-lover, which is alloyed with a worldly prudence and has worldly and niggardly ways of doling out benefits, will breed in your soul those vulgar qualities which the populace applaud, will send you bowling round the earth during a period of nine thousand years, and leave you a fool in the world below.

And thus, dear Eros, I have made and paid my recantation, as well and as fairly as I could; more especially in the matter of the poetical figures which I was compelled to use, because Phaedrus would have them. And now forgive the past and accept the present, and be gracious and merciful to me, and do not in thine anger deprive me of sight, or take from me the art of love which thou hast given me, but grant that I may be yet more esteemed in the eyes of the fair. And if Phaedrus or I myself said anything rude in our first speeches, blame Lysias, who is the father of the brat, and let us have no more of his progeny; bid him study philosophy, like his brother Polemarchus; and then his lover Phaedrus will no longer halt between two opinions, but will dedicate himself wholly to love and to philosophical discourses.

Phaedr.: I join in the prayer, Socrates, and say with you, if this be for my good, may your words come to pass. But why did you make your second oration so much finer than the first? I wonder why. And I begin to be afraid that I shall lose conceit of Lysias, and that he will appear tame in comparison, even if he be willing to put another as fine and as long as yours into the field, which I doubt. For quite lately one of your politicians was abusing him on this very account; and called him a "speech-writer" again and again. So that a feeling of pride may probably induce him to give up writing speeches.

Soc.: What a very amusing notion! But I think, my young man, that you are much mistaken in your friend if you imagine that he is frightened at a little noise; and, possibly, you think that his assailant was in earnest?

Phaedr.: I thought, Socrates, that he was. And you are aware that the greatest and most influential statesmen are ashamed of writing speeches and leaving them in a written form, lest they should be called Sophists by posterity.

Soc.: You seem to be unconscious, Phaedrus, that the "sweet elbow" of the proverb is really the long arm of the Nile. And you appear to be equally unaware of the fact that this sweet elbow of theirs is also a long arm. For there is nothing of which our great politicians are so fond as of writing speeches and bequeathing them to posterity. And they add their admirers' names at the top of the writing, out of gratitude to them.

Phaedr.: What do you mean? I do not understand.

Soc.: Why, do you not know that when a politician writes, he begins with the names of his approvers?

Phaedr.: How so?

Soc.: Why, he begins in this manner: "Be it enacted by the senate, the people, or both, on the motion of a certain person", who is our author; and so putting on a serious face, he proceeds to display his own wisdom to his admirers in what is often a long and tedious composition. Now what is that sort of thing but a regular piece of authorship?

Phaedr.: True.

Soc.: And if the law is finally approved, then the author leaves the theatre in high delight; but if the law is rejected and he is done out of his speech-making, and not thought good enough to write, then he and his party are in mourning.

Phaedr.: Very true.

Soc.: So far are they from despising, or rather so highly do they value the practice of writing.

Phaedr.: No doubt.

Soc.: And when the king or orator has the power, as Lycurgus or Solon or Darius had, of attaining an immortality of authorship in a state, is he not thought by posterity, when they see his compositions, and does he not think himself, while he is yet alive, to be a god?

Phaedr.: Very true.

Soc.: Then do you think that any one of this class, however ill-disposed, would reproach Lysias with being an author?

Phaedr.: Not upon your view; for according to you he would be casting a slur upon his own favourite pursuit.

Soc.: Any one may see that there is no disgrace in the mere fact of writing.

Phaedr.: Certainly not.

Soc.: The disgrace begins when a man writes not well, but badly.

Phaedr.: Clearly.

Soc.: And what is well and what is badly—need we ask Lysias, or any other poet or orator, who ever wrote or will write either a political or any other work, in metre or out of metre, poet or prose writer, to teach us this?

Phaedr.: Need we? For what should a man live if not for the pleasures of discourse? Surely not for the sake of bodily pleasures, which almost always have previous pain as a condition of them, and therefore are rightly called slavish.

Soc.: There is time enough. And I believe that the grasshoppers chirruping after their manner in the heat of the sun over our heads are talking to one another and looking down at us. What would they say if they saw that we, like the many, are not conversing, but slumbering at mid-day, lulled by their voices, too indolent to think? Would they not have a right to laugh at us? They might imagine that we were slaves, who, coming to rest at a place of resort of theirs, like sheep lie asleep at noon around the well. But if they see us discoursing, and like Odysseus sailing past them, deaf to their siren voices, they may perhaps, out of respect, give us of the gifts which they receive from the gods that they may impart them to men.

Phaedr.: What gifts do you mean? I never heard of any.

Soc.: A lover of music like yourself ought surely to have heard the story of the grasshoppers, who are said to have been human beings in an age before the Muses. And when the Muses came and song appeared they were ravished with delight; and singing always, never thought of eating and drinking, until at last in their forgetfulness they died. And now they live again in the grasshoppers; and this is the return which the Muses make to them—they neither hunger, nor thirst, but from the hour of their birth are always singing, and never eating or drinking; and when they die they go and inform the Muses in heaven who honours them on earth. They win the love of Terpsichore for the dancers by their report of them; or Erato for the lovers, and of the other Muses for those who do them honour, according to the several ways of honouring them; of Calliope the eldest Muse and of Urania who is next to her, for the philosophers, of whose music the grasshoppers make report to them; for these are the Muses who are chiefly concerned with heaven and thought, divine as well as human, and they have the sweetest utterance. For many reasons, then, we ought always to talk and not to sleep at mid-day.

Phaedr.: Let us talk.

Soc.: Shall we discuss the rules of writing and speech as we were proposing?

Phaedr.: Very good.

Soc.: In good speaking should not the mind of the speaker know the truth of the matter about which he is going to speak?

Phaedr.: And yet, Socrates, I have heard that he who would be an orator has nothing to do with true justice, but only with that which is likely to be approved by the many who sit in judgment; nor with the truly good or honourable, but only with opinion about them, and that from opinion comes persuasion, and not from the truth.

Soc.: The words of the wise are not to be set aside; for there is probably something in them; and therefore the meaning of this saying is not hastily to be dismissed.

Phaedr.: Very true.

Soc.: Let us put the matter thus: Suppose that I persuaded you to buy a horse and go to the wars. Neither of us knew what a horse was like, but I knew that you believed a horse to be of tame animals the one which has the longest ears.

Phaedr.: That would be ridiculous.

Soc.: There is something more ridiculous coming: Suppose, further, that in sober earnest I, having persuaded you of this, went and composed a speech in honour of an ass, whom I entitled a horse, beginning: "A noble animal and a most useful possession, especially in war, and you may get on his back and fight, and he will carry baggage or anything".

Phaedr.: How ridiculous!

Soc.: Ridiculous! Yes; but is not even a ridiculous friend better than a cunning enemy?

Phaedr.: Certainly.

Soc.: And when the orator instead of putting an ass in the place of a horse, puts good for evil, being himself as ignorant of their true nature as the city on which he imposes is ignorant; and having studied the notions of the multitude, falsely persuades them not about "the shadow of an ass", which he confounds with a horse, but about good which he confounds with evil,—what will be the harvest which rhetoric will be likely to gather after the sowing of that seed?

Phaedr.: The reverse of good.

Soc.: But perhaps rhetoric has been getting too roughly handled by us, and she might answer: What amazing nonsense you are talking! As if I force any man to learn to speak in ignorance of the truth! Whatever my advice may be worth, I should have told him to arrive at the truth first, and then come to me. At the same time I boldly assert that mere knowledge of the truth will not give you the art of persuasion.

Phaedr.: There is reason in the lady's defence of herself.

Soc.: Quite true; if only the other arguments which remain to be brought up bear her witness that she is an art at all. But I seem to hear them arraying themselves on the opposite side, declaring that she speaks falsely, and that rhetoric is a mere routine and trick, not an art. Lo! a Spartan appears, and says that there never is nor ever will be a real art of speaking which is divorced from the truth.

Phaedr.: And what are these arguments, Socrates? Bring them out that we may examine them.

Soc.: Come out, fair children, and convince Phaedrus, who is the father of similar beauties, but he will never be able to speak about anything as he ought to speak unless he have a knowledge of philosophy. And let Phaedrus answer you.

Phaedr.: Put the question.

Soc.: Is not rhetoric, taken generally, a universal art of enchanting the mind by arguments; which is practised not only in courts and public assemblies, but in private houses also, having to do with all matters, great as well as small, good and bad alike, and is in all equally right, and equally to be esteemed—that is what you have heard?

Phaedr.: Nay, not exactly that; I should say rather that I have heard the art confined to speaking and writing in law-suits, and to speaking in public assemblies—not extended farther.

Soc.: Then I suppose that you have only heard of the rhetoric of Nestor and Odysseus, which they composed in their leisure hours when at Troy, and never of the rhetoric of Palamedes?

Phaedr.: No more than of Nestor and Odysseus, unless Gorgias is your Nestor, and Thrasymachus or Theodorus your Odysseus.

Soc.: Perhaps that is my meaning. But let us leave them. And do you tell me, instead, what are plaintiff and defendant doing in a law-court—are they not contending?

Phaedr.: Exactly so.

Soc.: About the just and unjust—that is the matter in dispute?

Phaedr.: Yes.

Soc.: And a professor of the art will make the same thing appear to the same persons to be at one time just, at another time, if he is so inclined, to be unjust?

Phaedr.: Exactly.

Soc.: And when he speaks in the assembly, he will make the same things seem good to the city at one time, and at another time the reverse of good?

Phaedr.: That is true.

Soc.: Have we not heard of the Eleatic Palamedes (Zeno), who has an art of speaking by which he makes the same things appear to his hearers like and unlike, one and many, at rest and in motion?

Phaedr.: Very true.

Soc.: The art of disputation, then, is not confined to the courts and the assembly, but is one and the same in every use of language; this is the art, if there be such an art, which is able to find a likeness of everything to which a likeness can be found, and draws into the light of day the likenesses and disguises which are used by others?

Phaedr.: How do you mean?

Soc.: Let me put the matter thus: When will there be more chance of deception—when the difference is large or small?

Phaedr.: When the difference is small.

Soc.: And you will be less likely to be discovered in passing by degrees into the other extreme than when you go all at once?

Phaedr.: Of course.

Soc.: He, then, who would deceive others, and not be deceived, must exactly know the real likenesses and differences of things?

Phaedr.: He must.

Soc.: And if he is ignorant of the true nature of any subject, how can he detect the greater or less degree of likeness in other things to that of which by the hypothesis he is ignorant?

Phaedr.: He cannot.

Soc.: And when men are deceived and their notions are at variance with realities, it is clear that the error slips in through resemblances?

Phaedr.: Yes, that is the way.

Soc.: Then he who would be a master of the art must understand the real nature of everything; or he will never know either how to make the gradual departure from truth into the opposite of truth which is effected by the help of resemblances, or how to avoid it?

Phaedr.: He will not.

Soc.: He then, who being ignorant of the truth aims at appearances, will only attain an art of rhetoric which is ridiculous and is not an art at all?

Phaedr.: That may be expected.

Soc.: Shall I propose that we look for examples of art and want of art, according to our notion of them, in the speech of Lysias which you have in your hand, and in my own speech?

Phaedr.: Nothing could be better; and indeed I think that our previous argument has been too abstract and wanting in illustrations.

Soc.: Yes; and the two speeches happen to afford a very good example of the way in which the speaker who knows the truth may, without any serious purpose, steal away the hearts of his hearers. This piece of good-fortune I attribute to the local deities; and, perhaps, the prophets of the Muses who are singing over our heads may have imparted their inspiration to me. For I do not imagine that I have any rhetorical art of my own.

Phaedr.: Granted; if you will only please to get on.

Soc.: Suppose that you read me the first words of Lysias' speech.

Phaedr.: "You know how matters stand with me, and how, as I conceive, they might be arranged for our common interest; and I maintain that I ought not to fail in my suit, because I am not your lover. For lovers repent——"

Soc.: Enough:—Now, shall I point out the rhetorical error of those words?

Phaedr.: Yes.

Soc.: Every one is aware that about some things we are agreed, whereas about other things we differ.

Phaedr.: I think that I understand you; but will you explain yourself?

Soc.: When any one speaks of iron and silver, is not the same thing present in the minds of all?

Phaedr.: Certainly.

Soc.: But when any one speaks of justice and goodness we part company and are at odds with one another and with ourselves?

Phaedr.: Precisely.

Soc.: Then in some things we agree, but not in others?

Phaedr.: That is true.

Soc.: In which are we more likely to be deceived, and in which has rhetoric the greater power?

Phaedr.: Clearly, in the uncertain class.

Soc.: Then the rhetorician ought to make a regular division, and acquire a distinct notion of both classes, as well of that in which the many err, as of that in which they do not err?

Phaedr.: He who made such a distinction would have an excellent principle.

Soc.: Yes; and in the next place he must have a keen eye for the observation of particulars in speaking, and not make a mistake about the class to which they are to be referred.

Phaedr.: Certainly.

Soc.: Now to which class does love belong—to the debatable or to the undisputed class?

Phaedr.: To the debatable, clearly; for if not, do you think that love would have allowed you to say as you did, that he is an evil both to the lover and the beloved, and also the greatest possible good?

Soc.: Capital. But will you tell me whether I defined love at the beginning of my speech? for, having been in an ecstasy, I cannot well remember.

Phaedr.: Yes, indeed; that you did, and no mistake.

Soc.: Then I perceive that the Nymphs of Achelous and Pan the son of Hermes, who inspired me, were far better rhetoricians than Lysias the son of Cephalus. Alas! how inferior to them he is! But perhaps I am mistaken; and Lysias at the commencement of his lover's speech did insist on our supposing love to be something or other which he fancied him to be, and according to this model he fashioned and framed the remainder of his discourse. Suppose we read his beginning over again:

Phaedr.: If you please; but you will not find what you want.

Soc.: Read, that I may have his exact words.

Phaedr.: "You know how matters stand with me, and how, as I conceive, they might be arranged for our common interest; and I maintain I ought not to fail in my suit because I am not your lover, for lovers repent of the kindnesses which they have shown, when their love is over."

Soc.: Here he appears to have done just the reverse of what he ought; for he has begun at the end, and is swimming on his back through the flood to the place of starting. His address to the fair youth begins where the lover would have ended. Am I not right, sweet Phaedrus?

Phaedr.: Yes, indeed, Socrates; he does begin at the end.

Soc.: Then as to the other topics—are they not thrown down anyhow? Is there any principle in them? Why should the next topic follow next in order, or any other topic? I cannot help fancying in my ignorance that he wrote off boldly just what came into his head, but I dare say that you would recognize a rhetorical necessity in the succession of the several parts of the composition?

Phaedr.: You have too good an opinion of me if you think that I have any such insight into his principles of composition.

Soc.: At any rate, you will allow that every discourse ought to be a living creature, having a body of its own and a head and feet; there should be a middle, beginning, and end, adapted to one another and to the whole?

Phaedr.: Certainly.

Soc.: Can this be said of the discourse of Lysias? See whether you can find any more connexion in his words than in the epitaph which is said by some to have been inscribed on the grave of Midas the Phrygian.

Phaedr.: What is there remarkable in the epitaph?

Soc.: It is as follows:

> I am a maiden of bronze and lie on the tomb of Midas;
> So long as water flows and tall trees grow,
> So long here on this spot by his sad tomb abiding,
> I shall declare to passers-by that Midas sleeps below.

Now in this rhyme whether a line comes first or comes last, as you will perceive, makes no difference.

Phaedr.: You are making fun of that oration of ours.

Soc.: Well, I will say no more about your friend's speech lest I should give offence to you; although I think that it might furnish many other examples of what a man ought rather to avoid. But I will proceed to the other speech, which, as I think, is also suggestive to students of rhetoric.

Phaedr.: In what way?

Soc.: The two speeches, as you may remember, were unlike; the one argued that the lover and the other that the non-lover ought to be accepted.

Phaedr.: And right manfully.

Soc.: You should rather say "madly"; and madness was

the argument of them, for, as I said, "love is a madness".

Phaedr.: Yes.

Soc.: And of madness there were two kinds; one produced by human infirmity, the other was a divine release of the soul from the yoke of custom and convention.

Phaedr.: True.

Soc.: The divine madness was subdivided into four kinds, prophetic, initiatory, poetic, erotic, having four gods presiding over them; the first was the inspiration of Apollo, the second that of Dionysus, the third that of the Muses, the fourth that of Aphrodite and Eros. In the description of the last kind of madness, which was also said to be the best, we spoke of the affection of love in a figure, into which we introduced a tolerably credible and possibly true though partly erring myth, which was also a hymn in honour of Love, who is your lord and also mine, Phaedrus, and the guardian of fair children, and to him we sung the hymn in measures and solemn strain.

Phaedr.: I know that I had great pleasure in listening to you.

Soc.: Let us take this instance and note how the transition was made from blame to praise.

Phaedr.: What do you mean?

Soc.: I mean to say that the composition was mostly playful. Yet in these chance fancies of the hour were involved two principles of which we should be too glad to have a clearer description if art could give us one.

Phaedr.: What are they?

Soc.: First, the comprehension of scattered particulars in one idea; as in our definition of love, which whether true or false certainly gave clearness and consistency to the discourse, the speaker should define his several notions and so make his meaning clear.

Phaedr.: What is the other principle, Socrates?

Soc.: The second principle is that of division into species according to the natural formation, where the joint is, not breaking any part as a bad carver might. Just as our two discourses, alike assumed, first of all, a single form of unreason; and then, as the body which from being one becomes double and may be divided into a left side and right side, each having parts right and left of the same name—after this manner the speaker proceeded to divide the parts of the left side and did not desist until he found in them an evil or left-handed love which he justly reviled; and the other discourse leading us to the madness which lay on the right side found, another love, also having the same name, but divine, which the speaker held up before us and applauded and affirmed to be the author of the greatest benefits.

Phaedr.: Most true.

Soc.: I am myself a great lover of these processes of division and generalization; they help me to speak and to think. And if I find any man who is able to see "a One and Many" in nature, him I follow, and "walk in his footsteps as if he were a god". And those who have this art, I have hitherto been in the habit of calling dialecticians; but god knows whether the name is right or not. And I should like to know what name you would give to your or to Lysias' disciples, and whether this may not be that famous art of rhetoric which Thrasymachus and others teach and practise? Skilful speakers they are, and impart their skill to any who is willing to make kings of them and to bring gifts to them.

Phaedr.: Yes, they are royal men; but their art is not the same with the art of those whom you call, and rightly, in my opinion, dialecticians. Still we are in the dark about rhetoric.

Soc.: What do you mean? The remains of it, if there be anything remaining which can be brought under rules of art, must be a fine thing; and, at any rate, is not to be despised by you and me. But how much is left?

Phaedr.: There is a great deal surely to be found in books of rhetoric?

Soc.: Yes; thank you for reminding me. There is the exordium, showing how the speech should begin, if I remember rightly; that is what you mean—the niceties of the art?

Phaedr.: Yes.

Soc.: Then follows the statement of facts, and upon that witnesses; thirdly, proofs; fourthly, probabilities are to come; the great Byzantian word-maker also speaks, if I am not mistaken, of confirmation and further confirmation.

Phaedr.: You mean the excellent Theodorus.

Soc.: Yes; and he tells how refutation of further refutation is to be managed, whether in accusation or defence. I ought also to mention the illustrious Parian, Evenus, who first invented insinuations and indirect praises; and also indirect censures, which according to some he put into verse to help the memory. But shall I "to dumb forgetfulness consign" Tisias and Gorgias, who are not ignorant that probability is superior to truth, and who by force of argument make the little appear great and the great little, disguise the new in old fashions and the old in new fashions, and have discovered forms for everything, either short or going on to infinity. I remember Prodicus laughing when I told him of this; he said that he had himself discovered the true rule of art, which was to be neither long nor short, but of a convenient length.

Phaedr.: Well done, Prodicus!

Soc.: Then there is Hippias the Elean stranger, who probably agrees with him.

Phaedr.: Yes.

Soc.: And there is also Polus, who has treasuries of diplasiology, and gnomology, and eikonology, and who teaches in them the names of which Licymnius made him a present; they were to give a polish.

Phaedr.: Had not Protagoras something of the same sort?

Soc.: Yes, rules of correct diction and many other fine precepts; for the "sorrows of a poor old man", or any other pathetic case, no one is better than the Chalcedonian giant; he can put a whole company of people into a passion and out of one again by his mighty magic, and is first-rate at inventing or disposing of any sort of columny on any grounds or none. All of them agree in asserting that a speech should end in a recapitulation, though they do not all agree to use the same word.

Phaedr.: You mean that there should be a summing up of the arguments in order to remind the hearers of them.

Soc.: I have now said all that I have to say of the art of rhetoric: have you anything to add?

Phaedr.: Not much; nothing very important.

Soc.: Leave the unimportant and let us bring the really

important question into the light of day, which is: What power has this art of rhetoric, and when?

Phaedr.: A very great power in public meetings.

Soc.: It has. But I should like to know whether you have the same feeling as I have about the rhetoricians? To me there seem to be a great many holes in their web.

Phaedr.: Give an example.

Soc.: I will. Suppose a person to come to your friend Eryximachus, or to his father Acumenus, and to say to him: "I know how to apply drugs which shall have either a heating or a cooling effect, and I can give a vomit and also a purge, and all that sort of thing; and knowing all this, as I do, I claim to be a physician and to make physicians by imparting this knowledge to others", what do you suppose that they would say?

Phaedr.: They would be sure to ask him whether he knew "to whom" he would give his medicines, and "when", and "how much".

Soc.: And suppose that he were to reply: "No; I know nothing of all that; I expect the patient who consults me to be able to do these things for himself"?

Phaedr.: They would say in reply that he is a madman or a pedant who fancies that he is a physician because he has read something in a book, or has stumbled on a prescription or two, although he has no real understanding of the art of medicine.

Soc.: And suppose a person were to come to Sophocles or Euripides and say that he knows how to make a very long speech about a small matter, and a short speech about a great matter, and also a sorrowful speech, or a terrible, or threatening speech, or any other kind of speech, and in teaching this fancies that he is teaching the art of tragedy—?

Phaedr.: They too would surely laugh at him if he fancies that tragedy is anything but the arranging of these elements in a manner which will be suitable to one another and to the whole.

Soc.: But I do not suppose that they would be rude or abusive to him: Would they not treat him as a musician would a man who thinks that he is a harmonist because he knows how to pitch the highest and lowest note; happening to meet such an one he would not say to him savagely, "Fool, you are mad!" But like a musician, in a gentle and harmonious tone of voice, he would answer: "My good friend, he who would be a harmonist must certainly know this, and yet he may understand nothing of harmony if he has not got beyond your stage of knowledge, for you only know the preliminaries of harmony and not harmony itself".

Phaedr.: Very true.

Soc.: And will not Sophocles say to the display of the would-be tragedian, that this is not tragedy but the preliminaries of tragedy? and will not Acumenus say the same of medicine to the would-be physician?

Phaedr.: Quite true.

Soc.: And if Adrastus the mellifluous or Pericles heard of these wonderful arts, brachylogies and eikonologies and all the hard names which we have been endeavouring to draw into the light of day, what would they say? Instead of losing temper and applying uncomplimentary epithets, as you and I have been doing, to the authors of such an imaginary art, their superior wisdom would rather censure us, as well as them. "Have a little patience, Phaedrus and Socrates, they would say; you should not be in such a passion with those who from some want of dialectical skill are unable to define the nature of rhetoric, and consequently suppose that they have found the art in the preliminary conditions of it, and when these have been taught by them to others, fancy that the whole art of rhetoric has been taught by them; but as to using the several instruments of the art effectively, or making the composition a whole,—an application of it such as this is they regard as an easy thing which their disciples may make for themselves."

Phaedr.: I quite admit, Socrates, that the art of rhetoric which these men teach and of which they write is such as you describe—there I agree with you. But I still want to know where and how the true art of rhetoric and persuasion is to be acquired.

Soc.: The perfection which is required of the finished orator is, or rather must be, like the perfection of anything else, partly given by nature, but may also be assisted by art. If you have the natural power and add to it knowledge and practice, you will be a distinguished speaker; if you fall short in either of these, you will be to that extent defective. But the art, as far as there is an art, of rhetoric does not lie in the direction of Lysias or Thrasymachus.

Phaedr.: In what direction then?

Soc.: I conceive Pericles to have been the most accomplished of rhetoricians.

Phaedr.: What of that?

Soc.: All the great arts require discussion and high speculation about the truths of nature; hence come loftiness of thought and completeness of execution. And this, as I conceive, was the quality which, in addition to his natural gifts, Pericles acquired from his intercourse with Anaxagoras whom he happened to know. He was thus imbued with the higher philosophy, and attained the knowledge of Mind and the negative of Mind, which were favourite themes of Anaxagoras, and applied what suited his purpose to the art of speaking.

Phaedr.: Explain.

Soc.: Rhetoric is like medicine.

Phaedr.: How so?

Soc.: Why, because medicine has to define the nature of the body and rhetoric of the soul—if we would proceed, not empirically but scientifically, in the one case to impart health and strength by giving medicine and food, in the other to implant the conviction or virtue which you desire, by the right application of words and training.

Phaedr.: There, Socrates, I suspect that you are right.

Soc.: And do you think that you can know the nature of the soul intelligently without knowing the nature of the whole?

Phaedr.: Hippocrates the Asclepiad says that the nature even of the body can only be understood as a whole.

Soc.: Yes, friend, and he was right:—still, we ought not to be content with the name of Hippocrates, but to examine and see whether his argument agrees with his conception of nature.

Phaedr.: I agree.

Soc.: Then consider what truth as well as Hippocrates says about this or about any other nature. Ought we not consider first whether that which we wish to learn and to teach is a simple or multiform thing, and if simple, then to enquire what power it has of acting or being acted upon in relation to other things, and if multiform, then to number the forms; and see first in the case of one of them, and then in the case of all of them, what is that power of acting or being acted upon which makes each and all of them to be what they are?

Phaedr.: You may very likely be right, Socrates.

Soc.: The method which proceeds without analysis is like the groping of a blind man. Yet, surely, he who is an artist ought not to admit of a comparison with the blind, or deaf. The rhetorician, who teaches his pupil to speak scientifically, will particularly set forth the nature of that being to which he addresses his speeches; and this, I conceive, to be the soul.

Phaedr.: Certainly.

Soc.: His whole effort is directed to the soul; for in that he seeks to produce conviction.

Phaedr.: Yes.

Soc.: Then clearly, Thrasymachus or any one else who teaches rhetoric in earnest will give an exact description of the nature of the soul; which will enable us to see whether she be single and same, or, like the body, multiform. That is what we should call showing the nature of the soul.

Phaedr.: Exactly.

Soc.: He will explain, secondly, the mode in which she acts or is acted upon.

Phaedr.: True.

Soc.: Thirdly, having classified men and speeches, and their kinds and affections, and adapted them to one another, he will tell the reasons of his arrangement, and show why one soul is persuaded by a particular form of argument, and another not.

Phaedr.: You have hit upon a very good way.

Soc.: Yes, that is the true and only way in which any subject can be set forth or treated by rules of art, whether in speaking or writing. But the writers of the present day, at whose feet you have sat, craftily conceal the nature of the soul which they know quite well. Nor, until they adopt our method of reading and writing, can we admit that they write by rules of art?

Phaedr.: What is our method?

Soc.: I cannot give you the exact details; but I should like to tell you generally, as far as is in my power, how a man ought to proceed according to rules of art.

Phaedr.: Let me hear.

Soc.: Oratory is the art of enchanting the soul, and therefore he who would be an orator has to learn the differences of human souls—they are so many and of such a nature, and from them come the differences between man and man. Having proceeded thus far in his analysis, he will next divide speeches into their different classes:—"Such and such persons," he will say, "are affected by this or that kind of speech in this or that way", and he will tell you why. The pupil must have a good theoretical notion of them first, and then he must have experience of them in actual life, and be able to follow them with all his senses about him, or he will never get beyond the precepts of his masters. But when he understands what persons are persuaded by what arguments, and sees the person about whom he was speaking in the abstract actually before him, and knows that it is he, and can say to himself, "This is the man or this is the character who ought to have a certain argument applied to him in order to convince him of a certain opinion";—he who knows all this, and knows also when he should speak and when he should refrain, and when he should use pithy sayings, pathetic appeals, sensational effects, and all the other modes of speech which he has learned;—when, I say, he knows the times and seasons of all these things, then, and not till then, he is a perfect master of his art; but if he fail in any of these points, whether in speaking or teaching or writing them, and yet declares that he speaks by rules of art, he who says "I don't believe you" has the better of him. Well, the teacher will say, is this, Phaedrus and Socrates, your account of the so-called art of rhetoric, or am I to look for another?

Phaedr.: He must take this, Socrates, for there is no possibility of another, and yet the creation of such an art is not easy.

Soc.: Very true; and therefore let us consider this matter in every light, and see whether we cannot find a shorter and easier road; there is no use in taking a long rough roundabout way if there be a shorter and easier one. And I wish that you would try and remember whether you have heard from Lysias or any one else anything which might be of service to us.

Phaedr.: If trying would avail, then I might; but at the moment I can think of nothing.

Soc.: Suppose I tell you something which somebody who knows told me.

Phaedr.: Certainly.

Soc.: May not "the wolf", as the proverb says, "claim a hearing"?

Phaedr.: Do say what can be said for him.

Soc.: He will argue that there is no use in putting a solemn face on these matters, or in going round and round, until you arrive at first principles; for, as I said at first, when the question is of justice and good, or is a question in which men are concerned who are just and good, either by nature or habit, he who would be a skilful rhetorician has no need of truth— for that in courts of law men literally care nothing about truth, but only about conviction: and this is based on probability, to which he who would be a skilful orator should therefore give his whole attention. And they say also that there are cases in which the actual facts, if they are improbable, ought to be withheld, and only the probabilities should be told either in accusation or defence, and that always in speaking, the orator should keep probability in view, and say good-bye to the truth. And the observance of this principle throughout a speech furnishes the whole art.

Phaedr.: That is what the professors of rhetoric do actually say, Socrates. I have not forgotten that we have quite briefly touched upon this matter already; with them the point is all-important.

Soc.: I dare say that you are familiar with Tisias. Does he not define probability to be that which the many think?

Phaedr.: Certainly, he does.

Soc.: I believe that he has a clever and ingenious case of this sort:—He supposes a feeble and valiant man to have assaulted a strong and cowardly one, and to have robbed him of his coat or of something or other; he is brought into court, and then Tisias says that both parties should tell lies:

the coward should say that he was assaulted by more men than one; the other should prove that they were alone, and should argue thus: "How could a weak man like me have assaulted a strong man like him?" The complainant will not like to confess his own cowardice, and will therefore invent some other lie which his adversary will thus gain an opportunity of refuting. And there are other devices of the same kind which have a place in the system. Am I not right, Phaedrus?

Phaedr.: Certainly.

Soc.: Bless me, what a wonderfully mysterious art is this which Tisias or some other gentleman, in whatever name or country he rejoices, has discovered. Shall we say a word to him or not?

Phaedr.: What shall we say to him?

Soc.: Let us tell him that, before he appeared, you and I were saying that the probability of which he speaks was engendered in the minds of the many by the likeness of the truth, and we had just been affirming that he who knew the truth would always know best how to discover the resemblances of the truth. If he has anything else to say about the art of speaking we should like to hear him; but if not, we are satisfied with our own view, that unless a man estimates the various characters of his hearers and is able to divide all things into classes and to comprehend them under single ideas, he will never be a skilful rhetorician even within the limits of human power. And this skill he will not attain without a great deal of trouble, which a good man ought to undergo, not for the sake of speaking and acting before men, but in order that he may be able to say what is acceptable to god and always to act acceptably to him as far as in him lies; for there is a saying of wiser men than ourselves, that a man of sense should not try to please his fellow-servants (at least this should not be his first object) but his good and noble master; and therefore if the way is long and circuitous, marvel not at this, for, where the end is great, there we may take the longer road, but not for lesser ends such as yours. Truly, the argument may say, Tisias, that if you do not mind going so far, rhetoric has a fair beginning here.

Phaedr.: I think, Socrates, that this is admirable, if only practicable.

Soc.: But even to fail in an honourable object is honourable.

Phaedr.: True.

Soc.: Enough appears to have been said by us of a true and false art of speaking.

Phaedr.: Certainly.

Soc.: But there is something yet to be said of propriety and impropriety of writing.

Phaedr.: Yes.

Soc.: Do you know how you can speak or act about rhetoric in a manner which will be acceptable to god?

Phaedr.: No, indeed. Do you?

Soc.: I have heard a tradition of the ancients, whether true or not they only know; although if we had found the truth ourselves, do you think that we should care much about the opinions of men?

Phaedr.: Your question needs no answer; but I wish that you would tell me what you say that you have heard.

Soc.: At the Egyptian city of Naucratis, there was a famous old god, whose name was Theuth; the bird which is called the Ibis is sacred to him, and he was the inventor of many arts, such as arithmetic and calculation and geometry and astronomy and draughts and dice, but his great discovery was the use of letters. Now in those days the god Thamus was the king of the whole country of Egypt; and he dwelt in that great city of Upper Egypt which the Hellenes call Egyptian Thebes, and the god himself is called by them Ammon. To him came Theuth and showed his inventions, desiring that the other Egyptians might be allowed to have the benefit of them; he enumerated them, and Thamus enquired about their several uses, and praised some of them and censured others, as he approved or disapproved of them. It would take a long time to repeat all that Thamus said to Theuth in praise or blame of the various arts. But when they came to letters, This, said Theuth, will make the Egyptians wiser and give them better memories; it is a specific both for the memory and for the wit. Thamus replied: O most ingenious Theuth, the parent or inventor of an art is not always the best judge of the utility or inutility of his own inventions to the users of them. And in this instance, you who are the father of letters, from a paternal love of your own children have been led to attribute to them a quality which they cannot have; for this discovery of yours will create forgetfulness in the learners' souls, because they will not use their memories; they will trust to the external written characters and not remember of themselves. The specific which you have discovered is an aid not to memory, but to reminiscence, and you give your disciples not truth, but only the semblance of truth; they will be hearers of many things and will have learned nothing; they will appear to be omniscient and will generally know nothing; they will be tiresome company, having the show of wisdom without the reality.

Phaedr.: Yes, Socrates, you can easily invent tales of Egypt, or of any other country.

Soc.: There was a tradition in the temple of Dodona that oaks first gave prophetic utterances. The men of old, unlike in their simplicity to young philosophy, deemed that if they heard the truth even from "oak or rock", it was enough for them; whereas you seem to consider not whether a thing is or is not true, but who the speaker is and from what country the tale comes.

Phaedr.: I acknowledge the justice of your rebuke; and I think that the Theban is right in his view about letters.

Soc.: He would be a very simple person, and quite a stranger to the oracles of Thamus or Ammon, who should leave in writing or receive in writing any art under the idea that the written word would be intelligible or certain; or who deemed that writing was at all better than knowledge and recollection of the same matters?

Phaedr.: That is most true.

Soc.: I cannot help feeling, Phaedrus, that writing is unfortunately like painting; for the creations of the painter have the attitude of life, and yet if you ask them a question they preserve a solemn silence. And the same may be said of speeches. You would imagine that they had intelligence, but if you want to know anything and put a question to one of them, the speaker always gives one unvarying answer. And when they have been once written down they are tumbled about anywhere among those who may or may not understand them, and know not to whom they should reply, to whom not: and, if they are maltreated or abused, they have no parent to protect them; and they cannot protect or defend themselves.

Phaedr.: That again is most true.

Soc.: Is there not another kind of word or speech far better than this, and having far greater power—a son of the same family, but lawfully begotten?

Phaedr.: Whom do you mean, and what is his origin?

Soc.: I mean an intelligent word graven in the soul of the learner, which can defend itself, and knows when to speak and when to be silent.

Phaedr.: You mean the living word of knowledge which has a soul, and of which the written word is properly no more than an image?

Soc.: Yes, of course that is what I mean. And now may I be allowed to ask you a question: Would a husbandman, who is a man of sense, take the seeds, which he values and which he wishes to bear fruit, and in sober seriousness plant them during the heat of summer, in some garden of Adonis, that he may rejoice when he sees them in eight days appearing in beauty? at least he would do so, if at all, only for the sake of amusement and pastime. But when he is in earnest he sows in fitting soil, and practises husbandry, and is satisfied if in eight months the seeds which he has sown arrive at perfection?

Phaedr.: Yes, Socrates, that will be his way when he is in earnest; he will do the other, as you say, only in play.

Soc.: And can we suppose that he who knows the just and good and honourable has less understanding, than the husbandman, about his own seeds?

Phaedr.: Certainly not.

Soc.: Then he will not seriously incline to "write" his thoughts "in water" with pen and ink, sowing words which can neither speak for themselves nor teach the truth adequately to others?

Phaedr.: No, that is not likely.

Soc.: No, that is not likely—in the garden of letters he will sow and plant, but only for the sake of recreation and amusement; he will write them down as memorials to be treasured against the forgetfulness of old age, by himself, or by any other old man who is treading the same path. He will rejoice in beholding their tender growth; and while others are refreshing their souls with banqueting and the like, this will be the pastime in which his days are spent.

Phaedr.: A pastime, Socrates, as noble as the other is ignoble, the pastime of a man who can be amused by serious talk, and can discourse merrily about justice and the like.

Soc.: True, Phaedrus. But nobler far is the serious pursuit of the dialectician, who, finding a congenial soul, by the help of science sows and plants therein words which are able to help themselves and him who planted them, and are not unfruitful, but have in them a seed which others brought up in different soils render immortal, making the possessors of it happy to the utmost extent of human happiness.

Phaedr.: Far nobler, certainly.

Soc.: And now, Phaedrus, having agreed upon the premises we may decide about the conclusion.

Phaedr.: About what conclusion?

Soc.: About Lysias, whom we censured, and his art of writing, and his discourses, and the rhetorical skill or want of skill which was shown in them—these are the questions which we sought to determine, and they brought us to this point. And I think that we are now pretty well informed about the nature of art and its opposite.

Phaedr.: Yes, I think with you; but I wish that you would repeat what was said.

Soc.: Until a man knows the truth of the several particulars of which he is writing or speaking, and is able to define them as they are, and having defined them again to divide them until they can be no longer divided, and until in like manner he is able to discern the nature of the soul, and discover the different modes of discourse which are adapted to different natures, and to arrange and dispose them in such a way that the simple form of speech may be addressed to the simpler nature, and the complex and composite to the more complex nature—until he has accomplished all this, he will be unable

74

to handle arguments according to rules of art, as far as their nature allows them to be subjected to art, either for the purpose of teaching of persuading;—such is the view which is implied in the whole preceding argument.

Phaedr.: Yes, that was our view, certainly.

Soc.: Secondly, as to the censure which was passed on the speaking or writing of discourses, and how they might be rightly or wrongly censured—did not our previous argument show—?

Phardr.: Show what?

Soc.: That whether Lysias or any other writer that ever was or will be, whether private man or statesman, proposes laws and so becomes the author of a political treatise, fancying that there is any great certainty and clearness in his performance, the fact of his so writing is only a disgrace to him, whatever men may say. For not to know the nature of justice and injustice, and good and evil, and not to be able to distinguish the dream from the reality, cannot in truth be otherwise than disgraceful to him, even though he have the applause of the whole world.

Phaedr.: Certainly.

Soc.: But he who thinks that in the written word there is necessarily much which is not serious, and that neither poetry nor prose, spoken or written, is of any great value, if, like the compositions of the rhapsodes, they are only recited in order to be believed, and not with any view to criticism or instruction; and who thinks that even the best of writings are but a reminiscence of what we know, and that only in principles of justice and goodness and nobility taught and communicated orally for the sake of instruction and graven in the soul, which is the true way of writing, is there clearness and perfection and seriousness, and that such principles are a man's own and his legitimate offspring;—being, in the first place, the word which he finds in his own bosom; secondly, the brethren and descendants and relations of his idea which have been duly implanted by him in the souls of others;—and who cares for them and no others—this is the right sort of man; and you and I, Phaedrus, would pray that we may become like him.

Phaedr.: That is most assuredly my desire and prayer.

Soc.: And now the play is played out; and of rhetoric enough. Go and tell Lysias that to the fountain and school of the Nymphs we went down, and were bidden by them to convey a message to him and to other composers of speeches —to Homer and other writers of poems, whether set to music or not; and to Solon and others who have composed writings in the form of political discourses which they would term laws—to all of them we are to say that if their compositions are based on knowledge of the truth, and they can defend or prove them, when they are put to the test, by spoken arguments, which leave their writings poor in comparison of them, then they are to be called, not only poets, orators, legislators, but are worthy of a higher name, befitting the serious pursuit of their life.

Phaedr.: What name would you assign to them?

Soc.: Wise, I may not call them; for that is a great name which belongs to god alone,—lovers of wisdom or philosophers is their modest and befitting title.

Phaedr.: Very suitable.

Soc.: And he who cannot rise above his own compilations and compositions, which he has been long patching and piecing, adding some and taking away some, may be justly called poet or speech-maker or law-maker.

Phaedr.: Certainly.

Soc.: Now go and tell this to your companion.

Phaedr.: But there is also a friend of yours who ought not to be forgotten.

Soc.: Who is he?

Phaedr.: Isocrates the fair:—What message will you send to him, and how shall we describe him?

Soc.: Isocrates is still young, Phaedrus; but I am willing to hazard a prophecy concerning him.

Phaedr.: What would you prophesy?

Soc.: I think that he has a genius which soars above the orations of Lysias, and that his character is cast in a finer mould. My impression of him is that he will marvellously improve as he grows older, and that all former rhetoricians will be as children in comparison of him. And I believe that he will not be satisfied with rhetoric, but that there is in him a divine inspiration which will lead him to things higher still.

For he has an element of philosophy in his nature. This is the message of the gods dwelling in this place, and which I will myself deliver to Isocrates, who is my delight; and do you give the other to Lysias, who is yours.

Phaedr.: I will; and now as the heat is abated let us depart.

Soc.: Should we not offer up a prayer first of all to the local deities?

Phaedr.: By all means.

Soc.: Beloved Pan, and all ye other gods who haunt this place, give me beauty in the inward soul; and may the outward and inward man be at one. May I reckon the wise to be the wealthy, and may I have such a quantity of gold as a temperate man and he only can bear and carry. Anything more? The prayer, I think, is enough for me.

Phaedr.: Ask the same for me, for friends should have all things in common.

Soc.: Let us go.

THE

KAMA SUTRA

OF

VATSYAYANA

TRANSLATED FROM THE SANSCRIT

IN SEVEN PARTS,

WITH

PREFACE, INTRODUCTION,

AND

CONCLUDING REMARKS

by SIR RICHARD BURTON

and F. F. ARBUTHNOT

PREFACE
TO THE ORIGINAL EDITION

In the literature of all countries there will be found a certain number of works treating especially of love. Everywhere the subject is dealt with differently, and from various points of view. In the present publication it is proposed to give a complete translation of what is considered the standard work on love in Sanscrit literature, and which is called the *Vatsyayana Kama Sutra*, or Aphorisms on Love, by Vatsyayana.

While the introduction will deal with the evidence concerning the date of the writing, and the commentaries written upon it, the chapters following the introduction will give a translation of the work itself. It is, however, advisable to furnish here a brief analysis of works of the same nature, prepared by authors who lived and wrote years after Vatsya had passed away, but who still considered him as the great authority, and always quoted him as the chief guide to Hindoo erotic literature.

Besides the treatise of Vatsyayana the following works on the same subject are procurable in India:

1. The Ratirahasya, or secrets of love.
2. The Panchasakya, or the five arrows.
3. The Smara Pradipa, or the light of love.
4. The Ratimanjari, or the garland of love.
5. The Rasmanjari, or the sprout of love.
6. The Anunga Runga, or the stage of love; also called Kamaledhiplava, or a boat in the ocean of love.

The author of the *Secrets of Love* (No. 1) was a poet named Kukkoka. He composed his work to please one Venudutta, who was perhaps a king. When writing his own name at the end of each chapter he calls himself "Siddha patiya pandita", i.e., an ingenious man among learned men. The work was translated into Hindi years ago, and in this the author's name was written as Koka. And as the same name crept into all the translations into other languages in India, the book became generally known, and the subject was popularly called Koka Shastra, or doctrines of Koka, which is identical with the Kama Shastra, or doctrines of love, and the words Koka Shastra and Kama Shastra are used indiscriminately.

The work contains nearly eight hundred verses, and is divided into ten chapters, which are called Pachivedas. Some of the things treated of in this work are not to be found in the Vatsyayana, such as the four classes of women, viz., the Padmini, Chitrini, Shankini and Hastini, as also the enumeration of the days and hours on which the women of the different classes become subject to love. The author adds that he wrote these things from the opinions of Gonikaputra and Nandikeshwara, both of whom are mentioned by Vatsyayana, but their works are not now extant. It is difficult to give any approximate idea as to the year in which the work was composed. It is only to be presumed that it was written after that of Vatsyayana, and previous to the other works on this subject that are still extant. Vatsyayana gives the names of ten authors on the subject, all of whose works he had consulted, but none of which are extant, and does not mention this one. This would tend to show that Kukkoka wrote after Vatsya, otherwise Vatsya would assuredly have mentioned him as an author in this branch of literature along with the others.

The author of the *Five Arrows* (No. 2 in the list) was one Jyotirisha. He is called the chief ornament of poets, the treasure of the sixty-four arts, and the best teacher of the rules of music. He says that he composed the work after reflecting on the aphorisms of love as revealed by the gods, and studying the opinions of Gonikaputra, Muladeva, Babhravya, Ramtideva, Nundikeshwara and Kshemandra. It is impossible to say whether he had perused all the works of these authors, or had only heard about them; anyhow, none of them appear to be in existence now. This work contains nearly six hundred verses, and is divided into five chapters, called Sayakas or Arrows.

The author of the *Light of Love* (No. 3) was the poet Gunakara, the son of Vechapati. The work contains four hundred verses, and gives only a short account of the doctrines of love, dealing more with other matters.

The Garland of Love (No. 4) is the work of the famous poet Jayadeva, who said about himself that he is a writer on all subjects. This treatise is, however, very short, containing only one hundred and twenty-five verses.

The author of the *Sprout of Love* (No. 5) was a poet called Bhanudatta. It appears from the last verse of the manuscript that he was a resident of the province of Tirhoot, and son of a Brahman named Ganeshwar, who was also a poet. The work, written in Sanscrit, gives the descriptions of different classes of men and women, their classes being made out from their age, description, conduct, etc. It contains three chapters, and its date is not known, and cannot be ascertained.

The Stage of Love (No. 6) was composed by the poet Kullianmull, for the amusement of Ladkhan, the son of Ahmed Lodi, the same Ladkhan being in some places spoken of as Ladana Mull, and in others as Ladanaballa. He is supposed to have been a relation or connection of the house of Lodi, which reigned in Hindostan from A.D. 1450-1526. The work would, therefore, have been written in the fifteenth or sixteenth century. It contains ten chapters, and has been translated into English but only six copies were printed for private circulation. This is supposed to be the latest of the Sanscrit works on the subject, and the ideas in it were evidently taken from previous writings of the same nature.

The contents of these works are in themselves a literary curiosity. There are to be found both in Sanscrit poetry and in the Sanscrit drama a certain amount of poetical sentiment and romance, which have, in every country and in every language, thrown an immortal halo round the subject. But here it is treated in a plain, simple, matter of fact sort of way. Men and women are divided into classes and divisions in the same way that Buffon and other writers on natural history have classified and divided the animal world. As Venus was represented by the Greeks to stand forth as the type of the beauty of woman, so the Hindoos describe the Padmini or Lotus woman as the type of most perfect feminine excellence, as follows:

She in whom the following signs and symptoms appear is

called a Padmini. Her face is pleasing as the full moon; her body, well clothed with flesh, is soft as the Shiras or mustard flower, her skin is fine, tender and fair as the yellow lotus, never dark coloured. Her eyes are bright and beautiful as the orbs of the fawn, well cut, and with reddish corners. Her bosom is hard, full and high; she has a good neck; her nose is straight and lovely, and three folds or wrinkles cross her middle—about the umbilical region. Her yoni resembles the opening lotus bud, and her love seed (Kama salila) is perfumed like the lily that has newly burst. She walks with swan-like gait, and her voice is low and musical as the note of the Kokila bird, she delights in white raiments, in fine jewels, and in rich dresses. She eats little, sleeps lightly, and being as respectful and religious as she is clever and courteous, she is ever anxious to worship the gods, and to enjoy the conversation of Brahmans. Such, then, is the Padmini or Lotus woman.

Detailed descriptions then follow the Chitrini or Art woman; the Shankhini or Conch woman, and the Hastini or Elephant woman, their days of enjoyment, their various seats of passion, the manner in which they should be manipulated and treated in sexual intercourse, along with the characteristics of the men and women of the various countries in Hindostan. The details are so numerous, and the subjects so seriously dealt with, and at such length, that neither time nor space will permit of their being given here.

One work in the English language is somewhat similar to these works of the Hindoos. It is called *Kalogynomia: or the Laws of Female Beauty*, being the elementary principles of that science, by T. Bell, M.D., with twenty-four plates, and printed in London in 1821. It treats of Beauty, of Love, of Sexual Intercourse, of the Laws regulating that Intercourse, of Monogamy and Polygamy, of Prostitution, of Infidelity, ending with a *catalogue raisonnée* of the defects of female beauty.

Other works in English also enter into great details of private and domestic life. *The Elements of Social Science, or Physical, Sexual and Natural Religion, by a Doctor of Medicine,* London, 1880, and *Every Woman's Book*, by Dr. Waters, 1826. To persons interested in the above subjects these works will be found to contain such details as have been seldom before published, and which ought to be thoroughly understood by all philanthropists and benefactors of society.

After a perusal of the Hindoo work, and of the English books above mentioned, the reader will understand the subject, at all events from a materialistic, realistic and practical point of view. If all science is founded more or less on a stratum, of facts, there can be no harm in making known to mankind generally certain matters intimately connected with their private, domestic and social life.

Alas! complete ignorance of them has unfortunately wrecked many a man and many a woman, while a little knowledge of a subject generally ignored by the masses would have enabled numbers of people to have understood many things which they believed to be quite incomprehensible, or which were not thought worthy of their consideration.

INTRODUCTION
TO THE ORIGINAL EDITION

It may be interesting to some persons to learn how it came about that Vatsyayana was first brought to light and translated into the English language. It happened thus. While translating with the pundits the "Anunga runga, or the stage of love", reference was frequently found to be made to one Vatsya. The sage Vatsya was of this opinion, or of that opinion. The sage Vatsya said this, and so on. Naturally questions were asked who the sage was, and the pundits replied that Vatsya was the author of the standard work on love in Sanscrit literature, that no Sanscrit library was complete without his work, and that it was most difficult now to obtain in its entire state. The copy of the manuscript obtained in Bombay was defective, and so the pundits wrote to Benares, Calcutta and Jeypoor for copies of the manuscript from Sanscrit libraries in those places. Copies having been obtained, they were then compared with each other, and with the aid of a Commentary called *Jayamangla* a revised copy of the entire manuscript was prepared, and from this copy the English translation was made. The following is the certificate of the chief pundit:

"The accompanying manuscript is corrected by me after comparing four different copies of the work. I had the assistance of a Commentary called *Jayamangla* for correcting the portion in the first five parts, but found great difficulty in correcting the remaining portion, because, with the exception of one copy thereof which was tolerably correct, all the other copies I had were far too incorrect. However, I took that portion as correct in which the majority of the copies agreed with each other."

The *Aphorisms on Love* by Vatsyayana contain about one thousand two hundred and fifty slokas or verses, and are divided into parts, parts into chapters, and chapters into paragraphs. The whole consists of seven parts, thirty-six chapters, and sixty-four paragraphs. Hardly anything is known about the author. His real name is supposed to be Mallinaga or Mrillana, Vatsyayana being his family name. At the close of the work this is what he writes about himself:

"After reading and considering the works of Babhravya and other ancient authors, and thinking over the meaning of the rules given by them, this treatise was composed, according to the precepts of the Holy Writ, for the benefit of the world, by Vatsyayana, while leading the life of a religious student at Benares, and wholly engaged in the contemplation of the Deity. This work is not to be used merely as an instrument for satisfying our desires. A person acquainted with the true principles of this science, who preserves his Dharma (virtue or religious merit), his Artha (worldly wealth) and his Kama (pleasure or sensual gratification), and who has regard to the customs of the people, is sure to obtain the mastery over his senses. In short, an intelligent and knowing person, attending to Dharma and Artha and also to Kama, without becoming the slave of his passions, will obtain success in everything that he may do."

It is impossible to fix the exact date either of the life of Vatsyayana or of his work. It is supposed that he must have lived between the first and sixth century of the Christian era, on the following grounds:—He mentions that Satkarni Satvahan, a king of Kuntal, killed Malayevati his wife with an instrument called kartari by striking her in the passion of love, and Vatsya quotes this case to warn people of the danger arising from some old customs of striking women when under the influence of this passion. Now this king of Kuntal is believed to have lived and reigned during the first century B.C., and consequently Vatsya must have lived after him. On the other hand, Virahamihira, in the eighteenth chapter of his *Brihatsanhita*, treats of the science of love, and appears to have borrowed largely from Vatsyayana on the subject. Now Virahamihira is said to have lived during the sixth century A.D., and as Vatsya must have written his works previously, therefore not earlier than the first century B.C., and not later than the sixth century A.D., must be considered as the approximate date of his existence.

On the text of the *Aphorisms on Love*, by Vatsyayana, only

two commentaries have been found. One called *Jayamangla* or *Sutrabashya*, and the other *Sutra vritti*. The date of the *Jayamangla* is fixed between the tenth and thirteenth century A.D., because while treating of the sixty-four arts an example is taken from the *Kávyaprakásha*, which was written about the tenth century A.D. Again, the copy of the commentary procured was evidently a transcript of a manuscript which once had a place in the library of a Chaulukyan king named Vishaladeva, a fact elicited from the following sentence at the end of it:

"Here ends the part relating to the art of love in the commentary on the *Vatsyayana Kama Sutra*, a copy from the library of the king of kings, Vishaladeva, who was a powerful hero, as it were a second Arjuna, and head jewel of the Chaulukya family."

Now it is well known that this king ruled in Guzerat from A.D. 1244 to 1262, and founded a city called Visalnagur. The date, therefore, of the commentary is taken to be not earlier than the tenth and not later than the thirteenth century. The author of it is supposed to be one Yashodhara, the name given him by his preceptor being Indrapada. He seems to have written it during the time of affliction caused by his separation from a clever and shrewd woman, at least that is what he himself says at the end of each chapter. It is presumed that he called his work after the name of his absent mistress, or the word may have some connection with the meaning of her name.

This commentary was most useful in explaining the true meaning of Vatsyayana, for the commentator appears to have had a considerable knowledge of the times of the older author, and gives in some places very minute information. This cannot be said of the other commentary, called *Sutra vritti*, which was written about A.D. 1789, by Narsing Shastri, a pupil of a Sarveshwar Shastri; the latter was a descendant of Bhaskur, and so also was our author, for at the conclusion of every part he calls himself Bhaskur Narsing Shastri. He was induced to write the work by order of the learned Raja Vrijalala, while he was residing in Benares, but as to the merits of this commentary it does not deserve much commendation. In many cases the writer does not appear to have understood the meaning of the original author, and has changed the text in many places to fit in with his own explanations.

A complete translation of the original work now follows. It has been prepared in complete accordance with the text of the manuscript, and is given, without further comments, as made from it.

PART I

THE VATSYAYANA SUTRA

Salutation to Dharma, Artha and Kama

IN the beginning, the Lord of Beings created men and women, and in the form of commandments in one hundred thousand chapters laid down rules for regulating their existence with regard to Dharma,* Artha,† and Kama.‡ Some of these commandments, namely those which treated of Dharma, were separately written by Swayambhu Manu; those that related to Artha were compiled by Brihaspati; and those that referred to Kama were expounded by Nandi, the follower of Mahadeva, in one thousand chapters.

Now these "Kama Sutra" (Aphorisms on Love), written by Nundi in one thousand chapters, were reproduced by Shvetaketu, the son of Uddvalaka, in an abbreviated form in five hundred chapters, and this work was again similarly reproduced in an abridged form, in one hundred and fifty chapters, by Babhravya, an inheritant of the Punchala (South of Delhi) country. These one hundred and fifty chapters were then put together under seven heads or parts named severally—

1st. Sadharana (general topics).

2nd. Samprayogika (embraces, etc.).

3rd. Kanya Samprayuktaka (union of males and females).

4th. Bharyadhikarika (on one's own wife).

---

* Dharma is acquisition of religious merit, and is fully described in Chapter 5, Volume III., of Talboys Wheeler's *History of India,* and in the edicts of Asoka.

† Artha is acquisition of wealth and property, etc.

‡ Kama is love, pleasure and sensual gratification.

These three words are retained throughout in their original, as technical terms. They may also be defined as virtue, wealth and pleasure, the three things repeatedly spoken of in the Laws of Manu.

5th. Pardika (on the wives of other people).

6th. Vaisika (on courtesans).

7th. Aupamishadika (on the arts of seduction, tonic medicines, etc.).

The sixth part of this last work was separately expounded by Dattaka at the request of the public women of Pataliputra (Patna), and in the same way Charayana explained the first part of it. The remaining parts, viz., the second, third, fourth, fifth, and seventh were each separately expounded by—

Suvarnanabha (second part).

Ghotakamukha (third part).

Gonardiya (fourth part).

Gonikaputra (fifth part).

Kuchumara (seventh part), respectively.

Thus the work being written in parts by different authors was almost unobtainable, and as the parts which were expounded by Dattaka and the others treated only of the particular branches of the subject to which each part related, and moreover as the original work of Babhravya was difficult to be mastered on account of its length, Vatsyayana, therefore, composed his work in a small volume as an abstract of the whole of the works of the above-named authors.

PART I

CHAPTER I

Being the Index to or Contents of the Work

PART II

On Sexual Union

PART III

About the Acquisition of a Wife

PART IV

About a Wife

PART V

About the Wives of Other People

PART VI

About Courtesans

PART VII

On the Means of Attracting Others to One's Self

PART I

CHAPTER II

On the Acquisition of Dharma, Artha and Kama

MAN, the period of whose life is one hundred years, should practise Dharma, Artha and Kama at different times and in such a manner that they may harmonize together and not clash in any way. He should acquire learning in his childhood, in his youth and middle age he should attend to Artha and Kama, and in his old age he should perform Dharma, and thus seek to gain Moksha, i.e., release from further transmigration. Or, on account of the uncertainty of life, he may practise them at times when they are enjoined to be practised. But one thing is to be noted, he should lead the life of a religious student until he finishes his education.

Dharma is obedience to the command of the Shastra or Holy Writ of the Hindoos to do certain things, such as the performance of sacrifices, which are not generally done, because they do not belong to this world, and produce no visible effect; and not to do other things, such as eating meat, which is often done because it belongs to this world, and has visible effects.

Dharma should be learnt from the Shruti (Holy Writ), and from those conversant with it.

Artha is the acquisition of arts, land, gold, cattle, wealth, equipages and friends. It is, further, the protection of what is acquired, and the increase of what is protected.

Artha should be learnt from the king's officers, and from merchants who may be versed in the ways of commerce.

Kama is the enjoyment of appropriate objects by the five senses of hearing, feeling, seeing, tasting and smelling, assisted by the mind together with the soul. The ingredient in this is a peculiar contact between the organ of sense and its object, and the consciousness of pleasure which arises from that contact is called Kama.

Kama is to be learnt from the Kama Sutra (aphorisms on love) and from the practice of citizens.

When all the three, viz., Dharma, Artha and Kama come together, the former is better than the one which follows it, i.e., Dharma is better than Artha, and Artha is better than Kama. But Artha should always be first practised by the king, for the livelihood of men is to be obtained from it only. Again, Kama being the occupation of public women, they should prefer it to the other two, and these are exceptions to the general rule.

Objection 1

Some learned men say that as Dharma is connected with things not belonging to this world, it is appropriately treated of in a book; and so also is Artha, because it is practised only by the application of proper means, and a knowledge of those means can only be obtained by study and from books. But Kama being a thing which is practised even by the brute creation, and which is to be found everywhere, does not want any work on the subject.

Answer

This is not so. Sexual intercourse being a thing dependent on man and woman requires the application of proper means by them, and those means are to be learnt from the Kama Shastra. The non-application of proper means, which we see in the brute creation, is caused by their being unrestrained, and by the females among them only being fit for sexual intercourse at certain seasons and no more, and by their intercourse not being preceded by thought of any kind.

Objection 2

The Lokayatikas* say:—Religious ordinances should not be observed, for they bear a future fruit, and at the same time it is also doubtful whether they will bear any fruit at all. What foolish person will give away that which is in his own hands into the hands of another? Moreover, it is better to have a pigeon today than a peacock tomorrow; and a copper coin which we have the certainty of obtaining, is better than a gold coin, the possession of which is doubtful.

Answer

It is not so. 1st Holy Writ, which ordains the practice of Dharma, does not admit of a doubt.

2nd. Sacrifices such as those made for the destruction of enemies, or for the fall of rain, are seen to bear fruit.

3rd. The sun, moon, stars, planets and other heavenly bodies appear to work intentionally for the good of the world.

4th. The existence of this world is effected by the observance of the rules respecting the four classes† of men and their four stages of life.

5th. We see that seed is thrown into the ground with the hope of future crops.

Vatsyayana is therefore of opinion that the ordinances of religion must be obeyed.

Objection 3

Those who believe that destiny is the prime mover of all things say:—We should not exert ourselves to acquire wealth, for sometimes it is not acquired although we strive to get it, while at other times it comes to us of itself without

* These were certainly materialists who seemed to think that a bird in the hand was worth two in the bush.

† Among the Hindoos the four classes of men are the Brahmans or priestly class, the Kshutrya or warlike class, the Vaishya or agricultural and mercantile class, and the Shoodra or menial class. The four stages of life are, the life of a religious student, the life of a householder, the life of a hermit, and the life of a Sunyasi or devotee.

any exertion on our part. Everything is therefore in the power of destiny, who is the lord of gain and loss, of success and defeat, of pleasure and pain. Thus we see that Bali* was raised to the throne of Indra by destiny, and was also put down by the same power, and it is destiny only that can reinstate him.

Answer

It is not right to say so. As the acquisition of every object presupposes at all events some exertion on the part of man, the application of proper means may be said to be the cause of gaining all our ends, and this application of proper means being thus necessary (even where a thing is destined to happen), it follows that a person who does nothing will enjoy no happiness.

Objection 4

Those who are inclined to think that Artha is the chief object to be obtained argue thus. Pleasures should not be sought for, because they are obstacles to the practice of Dharma and Artha, which are both superior to them, and are also disliked by meritorious persons. Pleasures also bring a man into distress, and into contact with low persons; they cause him to commit unrighteous deeds, and produce impurity in him; they make him regardless of the future, and encourage carelessness and levity. And lastly, they cause him to be disbelieved by all, received by none, and despised by everybody, including himself. It is notorious, moreover, that many men who have given themselves up to pleasure alone, have been ruined along with their families and relations. Thus, King Dandakya,† of the Bhoja dynasty, carried off a Brahman's daughter with evil intent, and was eventually ruined and lost his kingdom. Indra, too, having violated the

* Bali was a demon who had conquered Indra and gained his throne, but was afterwards overcome by Vishnu at the time of his fifth incarnation.

† Dandakya is said to have abducted from the forest the daughter of a Brahman, named Bhargava, and being cursed by the Brahman, was buried with his kingdom under a shower of dust. The place was called after his name the Dandaka forest, celebrated in the Ramayana, but now unknown.

chastity of Ahalya,* was made to suffer for it. In a like, manner the mighty Kichaka,† who tried to seduce Draupadi and Ravana,‡ who attempted to gain over Sita, were punished for their crimes. These and many others fell by reason of their pleasures.

Answer

This objection cannot be sustained, for pleasures, being as necessary for the existence and well-being of the body as food, are consequently equally required. They are, moreover, the results of Dharma and Artha. Pleasures are, therefore, to be followed with moderation and caution. No one refrains from cooking food because there are beggars to ask for it, or from sowing seed because there are deer to destroy the corn when it is grown up.

Thus a man practising Dharma, Artha and Kama enjoys happiness both in this world and in the world to come. The good perform those actions in which there is no fear as to what is to result from them in the next world, and in which there is no danger to their welfare. Any action which conduces to the practice of Dharma, Artha and Kama together, or of any two, or even one of them, should be performed, but an action which conduces to the practice of one of them at the expense of the remaining two should not be performed.

* Ahalya was the wife of the sage Gautama. Indra caused her to believe that he was Gautama, and thus enjoyed her. He was cursed by Gautama and subsequently afflicted with a thousand ulcers on his body.

† Kichaka was the brother-in-law of King Virata, with whom the Pandavas had taken refuge for one year. Kichaka was killed by Bhima, who assumed the disguise of Draupadi. For this story the Mahabarata should be referred to.

‡ The story of Ravana is told in the Ramayana, which with the Mahabarata form the two great epic poems of the Hindoos; the latter was written by Vyasa, and the former by Valmiki.

CHAPTER III

On the Arts and Sciences to be Studied

MAN should study the Kama Sutra and the arts and sciences
subordinate thereto, in addition to the study of the arts and
sciences contained in Dharma and Artha. Even young maids
should study this Kama Sutra along with its arts and sciences
before marriage, and after it they should continue to do so
with the consent of their husbands.

Here some learned men object, and say that females, not
being allowed to study any science, should not study the
Kama Sutra.

But Vatsyayana is of opinion that this objection does not
hold good, for women already know the practice of Kama
Sutra, and that practice is derived from the Kama Shastra, or
the science of Kama itself. Moreover, it is not only in this
but in many other cases that though the practice of a science
is known to all, only a few persons are acquainted with the
rules and laws on which the science is based. Thus the
Yadnikas or sacrificers, though ignorant of grammar, make
use of appropriate words when addressing the different
Deities, and do not know how these words are framed.
Again, persons do the duties required of them on auspicious
days, which are fixed by astrology, though they are not
acquainted with the science of astrology. In a like manner
riders of horses and elephants train these animals without
knowing the science of training animals, but from practice
only. And similarly the people of the most distant provinces
obey the laws of the kingdom from practice, and because
there is a king over them, and without further reason.*
And from experience we find that some women, such as
daughters of princes and their ministers, and public women,
are actually versed in the Kama Shastra.

A female, therefore, should learn the Kama Shastra, or at

* The author wishes to prove that a great many things are done by people
from practice and custom, without their being acquainted with the reason
of things, or the laws on which they are based, and this is perfectly true.

least a part of it, by studying its practice from some confidential friend. She should study alone in private the sixty-four practices that form a part of the Kama Shastra. Her teacher should be one of the following persons, viz., the daughter of a nurse brought up with her and already married,* or a female friend who can be trusted in everything, or the sister of her mother (i.e., her aunt), or an old female servant, or a female beggar who may have formerly lived in the family, or her own sister, who can always be trusted.

The following are the arts to be studied, together with the Kama Sutra:

1. Singing.

2. Playing on musical instruments.

3. Dancing.

4. Union of dancing, singing, and playing instrumental music.

5. Writing and drawing.

6. Tattooing.

7. Arraying and adorning an idol with rice and flowers.

8. Spreading and arranging beds or couches of flowers, or flowers upon the ground.

9. Colouring the teeth, garments, hair, nails and bodies, i.e., staining, dyeing, colouring and painting the same.

10. Fixing stained glass into a floor.

11. The art of making beds, and spreading out carpets and cushions for reclining.

12. Playing on musical glasses filled with water.

13. Storing and accumulating water in aqueducts, cisterns and reservoirs.

14. Picture making, trimming and decorating.

15. Stringing of rosaries, necklaces, garlands and wreaths.

16. Binding of turbans and chaplets, and making crests and top-knots of flowers.

17. Scenic representations. Stage playing.

18. Art of making ear ornaments.

19. Art of preparing perfumes and odours.

20. Proper disposition of jewels and decorations, and adornment in dress.

21. Magic or sorcery.

* The proviso of being married applies to all the teachers.

22. Quickness of hand or manual skill.

23. Culinary art, i.e., cooking and cookery.

24. Making lemonades, sherbets, acidulated drinks, and spirituous extracts with proper flavour and colour.

25. Tailor's work and sewing.

26. Making parrots, flowers, tufts, tassels, bunches, bosses, knobs, etc., out of yarn or thread.

27. Solution of riddles, enigmas, covert speeches, verbal puzzles and enigmatical questions.

28. A game, which consisted in repeating verses, and as one person finished, another person had to commence at once, repeating another verse, beginning with the same letter with which the last speaker's verse ended, whoever failed to repeat was considered to have lost, and to be subject to pay a forfeit or stake of some kind.

29. The art of mimicry or imitation.

30. Reading, including chanting and intoning.

31. Study of sentences difficult to pronounce. It is played as a game chiefly by women and children, and consists of a difficult sentence being given, and when repeated quickly, the words are often transposed or badly pronounced.

32. Practice with sword, single stick, quarter staff and bow and arrow.

33. Drawing inferences, reasoning or inferring.

34. Carpentry, or the work of a carpenter.

35. Architecture, or the art of building.

36. Knowledge about gold and silver coins, and jewels and gems.

37. Chemistry and mineralogy.

38. Colouring jewels, gems and beads.

39. Knowledge of mines and quarries.

40. Gardening; knowledge of treating the diseases of trees and plants, of nourishing them, and determining their ages.

41. Art of cock fighting, quail fighting and ram fighting.

42. Art of teaching parrots and starlings to speak.

43. Art of applying perfumed ointments to the body, and of dressing the hair with unguents and perfumes and braiding it.

44. The art of understanding writing in cypher, and the writing of words in a peculiar way.

45. The art of speaking by changing the forms of words. It is of various kinds. Some speak by changing the beginning and end of words, others by adding unnecessary letters between every syllable of a word, and so on.

46. Knowledge of language and of the vernacular dialects.

47. Art of making flower carriages.

48. Art of framing mystical diagrams, of addressing spells and charms, and binding armlets.

49. Mental exercises, such as completing stanzas or verses on receiving a part of them; or supplying one, two or three lines when the remaining lines are given indiscriminately from different verses, so as to make the whole an entire verse with regard to its meaning; or arranging the words of a verse written irregularly by separating the vowels from the consonants, or leaving them out altogether; or putting into verse or prose sentences represented by signs or symbols. There are many other such exercises.

50. Composing poems.

51. Knowledge of dictionaries and vocabularies.

52. Knowledge of ways of changing and disguising the appearance of persons.

53. Knowledge of the art of changing the appearance of things, such as making cotton to appear as silk, coarse and common things to appear as fine and good.

54. Various ways of gambling.

55. Art of obtaining possession of the property of others by means of muntras or incantations.

56. Skill in youthful sports.

57. Knowledge of the rules of society, and of how to pay respects and compliments to others.

58. Knowledge of the art of war, of arms, of armies, etc.

59. Knowledge of gymnastics.

60. Art of knowing the character of a man from his features.

61. Knowledge of scanning or constructing verses.

62. Arithmetical recreations.

63. Making artificial flowers.

64. Making figures and images in clay.

A public woman, endowed with a good disposition, beauty and other winning qualities, and also versed in the above arts, obtains the name of a Ganika, or public woman of high quality, and receives a seat of honour in an assemblage of men. She is, moreover, always respected by the king, and praised by learned men, and her favour being sought for by all, she becomes an object of universal regard. The daughter of a king too, as well as the daughter of a minister, being learned in the above arts, can make their husbands favourable to them, even though these may have thousands of other wives besides themselves. And in the same manner, if a wife becomes separated from her husband, and falls into distress, she can support herself easily, even in a foreign country, by means of her knowledge of these arts. Even the bare knowledge of them gives attractiveness to a woman, though the practice of them may be only possible or otherwise according to the circumstances of each case. A man who is versed in these arts, who is loquacious and acquainted with the arts of gallantry, gains very soon the hearts of women, even though he is only acquainted with them for a short time.

CHAPTER IV

The Life of a Citizen*

HAVING thus acquired learning, a man, with the wealth that he may have gained by gift, conquest, purchase, deposit,† or inheritance from his ancestors, should become a householder, and pass the life of a citizen. He should take a house in a city, or large village, or in the vicinity of good men, or in a place which is the resort of many persons. This abode should be situated near some water, and divided into different compartments for different purposes. It should be surrounded by a garden, and also contain two rooms, an outer and an inner one. The inner room should be occupied

* This term would appear to apply generally to an inhabitant of Hindoostan. It is not meant only for a dweller in a city, like the Latin Urbanus as opposed to Rusticus.

† Gift is peculiar to a Brahman, conquest to a Kshatrya, while purchase, deposit, and other means of acquiring wealth belongs to the Vaishya.

by the females, while the outer room, balmy with rich perfumes, should contain a bed, soft, agreeable to the sight, covered with a clean white cloth, low in the middle part, having garlands and bunches of flowers* upon it, and a canopy above it, and two pillows, one at the top, another at the bottom. There should be also a sort of couch besides, and at the head of this a sort of stool, on which should be placed the fragrant ointments for the night, as well as flowers, pots containing collyrium and other fragrant substances, things used for perfuming the mouth, and the bark of the common citron tree. Near the couch, on the ground, there should be a pot for spitting, a box containing ornaments, and also a lute hanging from a peg made of the tooth of an elephant, a board for drawing, a pot containing perfume, some books, and some garlands of the yellow amaranth flowers. Not far from the couch, and on the ground, there should be a round seat, a toy cart, and a board for playing with dice; outside the outer room there should be cages of birds,† and a separate place for spinning, carving and such like diversions. In the garden there should be a whirling swing and a common swing, as also a bower of creepers covered with flowers, in which a raised parterre should be made for sitting.

Now the householder having got up in the morning and performed his necessary duties,‡ should wash his teeth, apply a limited quantity of ointments and perfumes to his body, put some ornaments on his person and collyrium on his eyelids and below his eyes, colour his lips with alacktaka,§ and look at himself in the glass. Having then eaten betel leaves, with other things that give fragrance to the mouth, he should perform his usual business. He should bathe daily, anoint his body with oil every other day, apply a lathering‖ substance to his body every three days, get his head (including face) shaved every four days, and the other

* Natural garden flowers.
† Such as quails, partridges, parrots, starlings, etc.
‡ The calls of nature always performed by the Hindoos the first thing in the morning.
§ A colour made from lac.
‖ This would act instead of soap, which was not introduced until the rule of the Mahomedans.

106

parts of his body every five or ten days.* All these things should be done without fail, and the sweat of the armpits should also be removed. Meals should be taken in the forenoon, in the afternoon, and again at night, according to Charayana. After breakfast, parrots and other birds should be taught to speak, and the fighting of cocks, quails, and rams should follow. A limited time should be devoted to diversions with Pithamardas, Vitas, and Vidushakas,† and then should be taken the midday sleep.‡ After this the householder, having put on his clothes and ornaments, should, during the afternoon, converse with his friends. In the evening there should be singing, and after that the householder, along with his friend, should await in his room, previously decorated and perfumed, the arrival of the woman that may be attached to him, or he may send a female messenger for her, or go for her himself. After her arrival at his house, he and his friend should welcome her, and entertain her with a loving and agreeable conversation. Thus end the duties of the day.

The following are the things to be done occasionally as diversions or amusements.

1. Holding festivals§ in honour of different Deities.
2. Social gatherings of both sexes.
3. Drinking parties.
4. Picnics.
5. Other social diversions.

Festivals

On some particular auspicious day, an assembly of citizens should be convened in the temple of Saraswati.‖ There the

---

* Ten days are allowed when the hair is taken out with a pair of pincers.
† These are characters generally introduced in the Hindoo drama; their characteristics will be explained further on.
‡ Noonday sleep is only allowed in summer, when the nights are short.
§ These are very common in all parts of India.
‖ In the *Asiatic Miscellany*, and in Sir W. Jones's works, will be found a spirited hymn addressed to this goddess, who is adored as the patroness of the fine arts, especially of music and rhetoric, as the inventress of the Sanscrit language, etc. She is the goddess of harmony, eloquence and language, and is somewhat analogous to Minerva. For further information about her, see Edward Moor's *Hindoo Pantheon*.

skill of singers, and of others who may have come recently to the town, should be tested, and on the following day they should always be given some rewards. After that they may either be retained or dismissed, according as their performances are liked or not by the assembly. The members of the assembly should act in concert, both in times of distress as well as in times of prosperity, and it is also the duty of these citizens to show hospitality to strangers who may have come to the assembly. What is said above should be understood to apply to all the other festivals which may be held in honour of the different Deities, according to the present rules.

Social Gatherings

When men of the same age, disposition and talents, fond of the same diversions and with the same degree of education, sit together in company with public women,* or in an assembly of citizens, or at the abode of one among themselves, and engage in agreeable discourse with each other, such is called a sitting in company or a social gathering. The subjects of discourse are to be the completion of verses half composed by others, and the testing the knowledge of one another in the various arts. The women who may be the most beautiful, who may like the same things that the men like, and who may have power to attract the minds of others, are here done homage to.

Drinking Parties

Men and women should drink in one another's houses. And here the men should cause the public women to drink,

* The public women, or courtesans (Vesya), of the early Hindoos have often been compared with the Hetera of the Greeks. The subject is dealt with at some length in H. H. Wilson's *Select Specimens of the Theatre of the Hindoos,* in two volumes, Trubner & Co., 1871. It may be fairly considered that the courtesan was one of the elements, and an important element, too, of early Hindoo society, and that her education and intellect were both superior to that of the women of the household. Wilson says: "By the Vesya or courtesan, however, we are not to understand a female who has disregarded the obligation of law or the precepts of virtue, but a character reared by a state of manners unfriendly to the admission of wedded females into society, and opening it only at the expense of reputation to women who were trained for association with men by personal and mental acquirements to which the matron was a stranger."

and should then drink themselves, liquors such as the Madhu, Aireya, Sara, and Asawa, which are of bitter and sour taste; also drinks concocted from the barks of various trees, wild fruits and leaves.

Going to Gardens or Picnics

In the forenoon, men, having dressed themselves should go to gardens on horseback, accompanied by public women and followed by servants. And having done there all the duties of the day, and passed the time in various agreeable diversions, such as the fighting of quails, cocks and rams, and other spectacles, they should return home in the afternoon in the same manner, bringing with them bunches of flowers, etc.

The same also applies to bathing in summer in water from which wicked or dangerous animals have previously been taken out, and which has been built in on all sides.

Other Social Diversions

Spending nights playing with dice. Going out on moonlight nights. Keeping the festive day in honour of spring. Plucking the sprouts and fruits of the mangoe trees. Eating the fibres of lotuses. Eating the tender ears of corn. Picnicing in the forests when the trees get their new foliage. The Udakakashvedika or sporting in the water. Decorating each other with the flowers of some trees. Pelting each other with the flowers of the Kadamba tree, and many other sports which may either be known to the whole country, or may be peculiar to particular parts of it. These and similar other amusements should always be carried on by citizens.

The above amusements should be followed by a person who diverts himself alone in company with a courtesan, as well as by a courtesan who can do the same in company with her maid servants or with citizens.

A Pithamarda* is a man without wealth, alone in the

* According to this description a Pithamarda would be a sort of professor of all the arts, and as such received as the friend and confidant of the citizens.

world, whose only property consists of his Mallika,* some lathering substance and a red cloth, who comes from a good country, and who is skilled in all the arts; and by teaching these arts is received in the company of citizens, and in the abode of public women.

A Vita† is a man who has enjoyed the pleasures of fortune, who is a compatriot of the citizens with whom he associates, who is possessed of the qualities of a householder, who has his wife with him, and who is honoured in the assembly of citizens and in the abodes of public women, and lives on their means and on them.

A Vidushaka‡ (also called a Vaihasaka, i.e., one who provokes laughter) is a person only acquainted with some of the arts, who is a jester, and who is trusted by all.

These persons are employed in matters of quarrels and reconciliations between citizens and public women.

This remark applies also to female beggars, to women with their heads shaved, to adulterous women, and to old public women skilled in all the various arts.

Thus a citizen living in his town or village, respected by all, should call on the persons of his own caste who may be worth knowing. He should converse in company and gratify his friends by his society, and obliging others by his assistance in various matters, he should cause them to assist one another in the same way.

There are some verses on this subject as follows:

A citizen discoursing, not entirely in the Sanscrit

* A seat in the form of the letter T.

† The Vita is supposed to represent somewhat the character of the Parasite of the Greek comedy. It is possible that he was retained about the person of the wealthy and dissipated as a kind of private instructor, as well as an entertaining companion.

‡ Vidushaka is evidently the buffoon and jester. Wilson says of him that he is the humble companion, not the servant, of a prince or man of rank, and it is a curious peculiarity that he is always a Brahman. He bears more affinity to Sancho Panza, perhaps, than any other character in western fiction, imitating him in his combination of shrewdness and simplicity, his fondness of good living and his love of ease. In the dramas of intrigue he exhibits some of the talents of Mercury, but with less activity and ingenuity, and occasionally suffers by his interference. According to the technical definition of his attributes he is to excite mirth by being ridiculous in person, age, and attire.

language,* nor wholly in the dialects of the country, on various topics in society, obtains great respect. The wise should not resort to a society disliked by the public, governed by no rules, and intent on the destruction of others. But a learned man living in a society which acts according to the wishes of the people, and which has pleasure for its only object is highly respected in this world.

CHAPTER V

About the Kinds of Women Resorted to by the Citizens, and of Friends and Messengers

WHEN Kama is practised by men of the four castes according to the rules of the Holy Writ (i.e., by lawful marriage) with virgins of their own caste, it then becomes a means of acquiring lawful progeny and good fame, and it is not also opposed to the customs of the world. On the contrary the practice of Kama with women of the higher castes, and with those previously enjoyed by others, even though they be of the same caste, is prohibited. But the practice of Kama with women of the lower castes, with women excommunicated from their own caste, with public women, and with women twice married,† is neither enjoined nor prohibited. The object of practising Kama with such women is pleasure only.

Nayikas,‡ therefore, are of three kinds, viz., maids,

* This means, it is presumed, that the citizen should be acquainted with several languages. The middle part of this paragraph might apply to the Nihilists and Fenians of the day, or to secret societies. It was perhaps a reference to the Thugs.

† This term does not apply to a widow, but to a woman who has probably left her husband, and is living with some other person as a married woman, maritalement, as they say in France.

‡ Any woman fit to be enjoyed without sin. The object of the enjoyment of women is twofold, viz., pleasure and progeny. Any woman who can be enjoyed without sin for the purpose of accomplishing either the one or the other of these two objects is a Nayika. The fourth kind of Nayika which Batsya admits further on is neither enjoyed for pleasure or for progeny, but merely for accomplishing some special purpose in hand. The word Nayika is retained as a technical term throughout.

women twice married, and public women. Gonikaputra has expressed an opinion that there is a fourth kind of Nayika, viz., a woman who is resorted to on some special occasion even though she be previously married to another. These special occasions are when a man thinks thus:

(a) This woman is self-willed, and has been previously enjoyed by many others besides myself. I may, therefore, safely resort to her as to a public woman though she belongs to a higher caste than mine, and, in so doing I shall not be violating the ordinances of Dharma.

Or thus:

(b) This is a twice-married woman and has been enjoyed by others before me, there is, therefore, no objection to my resorting to her.

Or thus:

(c) This woman has gained the heart of her great and powerful husband, and exercises a mastery over him, who is a friend of my enemy; if, therefore, she becomes united with me she will cause her husband to abandon my enemy.

Or thus:

(d) This woman will turn the mind of her husband, who is very powerful, in my favour, he being at present disaffected towards me, and intent on doing me some harm.

Or thus:

(e) By making this woman my friend I shall gain the object of some friend of mine, or shall be able to effect the ruin of some enemy, or shall accomplish some other difficult purpose.

Or thus:

(f) By being united with this woman, I shall kill her husband, and so obtain his vast riches which I covet.

Or thus:

(g) The union of this woman with me is not attended with any danger, and will bring me wealth, of which, on account of my poverty and inability to support myself, I am very much in need. I shall, therefore obtain her vast riches in this way without any difficulty.

Or thus:

(h) This woman loves me ardently, and knows all my weak points, if therefore, I am unwilling to be united with her, she will make my faults public, and thus tarnish my character and reputation. Or she will bring some gross accusation against me, of which it may be hard to clear myself, and I shall be ruined. Or perhaps she will detach from me her husband who is powerful, and yet under her control, and will unite him to my enemy, or will herself join the latter.

Or thus:

(i) The husband of this woman has violated the chastity of my wives, I shall therefore return that injury by seducing his wives.

Or thus:

(j) By the help of this woman I shall kill an enemy of the king, who has taken shelter with her, and whom I am ordered by the king to destroy.

Or thus:

(k) The woman whom I love is under the control of this woman. I shall, through the influence of the latter, be able to get at the former.

Or thus:

(l) This woman will bring to me a maid, who possesses wealth and beauty, but who is hard to get at, and under the control of another.

Or lastly thus:

(m) My enemy is a friend of this woman's husband, I shall therefore cause her to join him, and will thus create an enmity between her husband and him.

For these and similar other reasons the wives of other men may be resorted to, but it must be distinctly understood that is only allowed for special reasons, and not for mere carnal desire.

Charayana thinks that under these circumstances there is also a fifth kind of Nayika, viz., a woman who is kept by a minister, or who repairs to him occasionally; or a widow who accomplishes the purpose of a man with the person to whom she resorts.

Suvarnanabha adds that a woman who passes the life of an ascetic and in the condition of a widow may be considered as a sixth kind of Nayika.

Ghotakamukha says that the daughter of a public woman, and a female servant, who are still virgins, form a seventh kind of Nayika.

Gonardiya puts forth his doctrine that any woman born of good family, after she has come of age, is an eighth kind of Nayika.

But these four latter kinds of Nayikas do not differ much from the first four kinds of them, as there is no separate object in resorting to them. Therefore, Vatsyayana is of opinion that there are only four kinds of Nayikas, i.e., the maid, the twice-married woman, the public woman, and the woman resorted to for a special purpose.

The following women are not to be enjoyed:

A leper.

A lunatic.

A woman turned out of caste.

A woman who reveals secrets.

A woman who publicly expresses desire for sexual intercourse.

A woman who is extremely white.

A woman who is extremely black.

A bad-smelling woman.

A woman who is a near relation.

A woman who is a female friend.

A woman who leads the life of an ascetic.

And, lastly the wife of a relation, of a friend, of a learned Brahman, and of the king.

The followers of Babhravya say that any woman who has been enjoyed by five men is a fit and proper person to be enjoyed. But Gonikaputra is of opinion that even when this is the case, the wives of a relation, of a learned Brahman and of a king should be excepted.

The following are of the kind of friends:

One who has played with you in the dust, i.e., in childhood.

One who is bound by an obligation.

One who is of the same disposition and fond of the same things.

One who is a fellow student.

One who is acquainted with your secrets and faults, and whose faults and secrets are also known to you.

One who is a child of your nurse.

One who is brought up with you.

One who is an hereditary friend.

These friends should possess the following qualities:

They should tell the truth.

They should not be changed by time.

They should be favourable to your designs.

They should be firm.

They should be free from covetousness.

They should not be capable of being gained over by others.

They should not reveal your secrets.

Charayana says that citizens form friendship with washermen, barbers, cowherds, florists, druggists, betel-leaf sellers, tavern keepers, beggars, Pithamardas, Vitas and Vidushekas, as also with the wives of all these people.

A messenger should possess the following qualities:

Skilfulness.

Boldness.

Knowledge of the intention of men by their outward signs.

Absence of confusion, i.e., no shyness.

Knowledge of the exact meaning of what others do or say.

Good manners.

Knowledge of appropriate times and places for doing different things.

Ingenuity in business.

Quick comprehension.

Quick application of remedies, i.e., quick and ready resources.

And this part ends with a verse:

The man who is ingenious and wise, who is accompanied by a friend, and who knows the intentions of others, as also the proper time and place for doing everything, can gain over, very easily, even a woman who is very hard to be obtained.

PART II

of Sexual Union

CHAPTER I

Kinds of Sexual Union According to
    (a) Dimensions.
    (b) Force of Desire or Passion.
    (c) Time.

Kinds of Union

MAN is divided into three classes, viz., the hare man, the bull man, and the horse man, according to the size of his lingam. Woman also, according to the depth of her yoni, is either a female deer, a mare, or a female elephant.

There are thus three equal unions between persons of corresponding dimensions, and there are six unequal unions, when the dimensions do not correspond, or nine in all, as the following table shows:

EQUAL		UNEQUAL	
Men	*Women*	*Men*	*Women*
Hare	Deer	Hare	Mare
Bull	Mare	Hare	Elephant
Horse	Elephant	Bull	Deer
		Bull	Elephant
		Horse	Deer
		Horse	Mare

In these unequal unions, when the male exceeds the female in point of size, his union with a woman who is immediately next to him in size is called high union, and is of two kinds; while his union with the woman most remote from him in size is called the highest union, and is of one kind only.

On the other hand, when the female exceeds the male in point of size, her union with a man immediately next to her in size is called low union, and is of two kinds; while her union with a man most remote from her in size is called the lowest union, and is of one kind only.

In other words, the horse and mare, the bull and deer, form the high union, while the horse and deer form the highest union. On the female side, the elephant and bull, the mare and hare, form low unions, while the elephant and the hare make the lowest unions.

There are then, nine kinds of union according to dimensions. Amongst all these, equal unions are the best, those of a superlative degree, i.e., the highest and the lowest, are the worst, and the rest are middling, and with them the high* are better than the low.

There are also nine kinds of union according to the force of passion or carnal desire, as follows:

Men	Women	Men	Women
Small	Small	Small	Middling
Middling	Middling	Small	Intense
Intense	Intense	Middling	Small
		Middling	Intense
		Intense	Small
		Intense	Middling

A man is called a man of small passion whose desire at the time of sexual union is not great, whose semen is scanty, and who cannot bear the warm embraces of the female.

Those who differ from this temperament are called men of middling passion, while those of intense passion are full of desire.

In the same way, women are supposed to have the three degrees of feeling as specified above.

Lastly, according to time there are three kinds of men and women, viz., the short-timed, the moderate-timed, and the

* High unions are said to be better than low ones, for in the former it is possible for the male to satisfy his own passion without injuring the female, while in the latter it is difficult for the female to be satisfied by any means.

long-timed, and of these as in the previous statements, there are nine kinds of union.

But on this last head there is a difference of opinion about the female, which should be stated.

Auddalika says, "Females do not emit as males do. The males simply remove their desire, while the females, from their consciousness of desire, feel a certain kind of pleasure, which gives them satisfaction, but it is impossible for them to tell you what kind of pleasure they feel. The fact from which this becomes evident is, that males, when engaged in coition, cease of themselves after emission, and are satisfied, but it is not so with females."

This opinion is however objected to on the grounds, that if a male be a long-timed, the female loves him the more, but if he be short-timed, she is dissatisfied with him. And this circumstance, some say, would prove that the female emits also.

But this opinion does not hold good, for if it takes a long time to allay a woman's desire, and during this time she is enjoying great pleasure, it is quite natural then that she should wish for its continuation. And on this subject there is a verse as follows:

"By union with men the lust, desire, or passion of women is satisfied, and the pleasure derived from the consciousness of it is called their satisfaction."

The followers of Babhravya, however, say that the semen of women continues to fall from the beginning of the sexual union to its end, and it is right that it should be so, for if they had no semen there would be no embryo.

To this there is an objection. In the beginning of coition the passion of the woman is middling, and she cannot bear the vigorous thrusts of her lover, but by degrees her passion increases until she ceases to think about her body, and then finally she wishes to stop from further coition.

This objection, however, does not hold good, for even in ordinary things that revolve with great force, such as a potter's wheel, or a top, we find that the motion at first is slow, but by degrees it becomes very rapid. In the same way the passion of the woman having gradually increased, she has a desire to discontinue coition, when all the semen has fallen away. And there is a verse with regard to this as follows:

"The fall of the semen of the man takes place only at the end of coition, while the semen of the woman falls continually, and after the semen of both has all fallen away then they wish for the discontinuance of coition."*

Lastly, Vatsyayana is of opinion that the semen of the female falls in the same way as that of the male.

Now some may ask here: If men and women are beings of the same kind, and are engaged in bringing about the same result, why should they have different works to do.

Vatsya says that this is so, because the ways of working as well as the consciousness of pleasure in men and women are different. The difference in the ways of working, by which men are the actors, and women are the persons acted upon, is owing to the nature of the male and the female, otherwise the actor would be sometimes the person acted upon, and vice versa. And from this difference in the ways of working follows the difference in the consciousness of pleasure, for a man thinks, "this woman is united with me", and a woman thinks, "I am united with this man".

It may be said that if the ways of working in men and women are different, why should not there be a difference, even in the pleasure they feel, and which is the result of those ways.

But this objection is groundless, for the person acting and the person acted upon being of different kinds, there is a reason for the difference in their ways of working; but there is no reason for any difference in the pleasure they feel, because they both naturally derive pleasure from the act they perform.†

* The strength of passion with women varies a great deal, some being easily satisfied, and others eager and willing to go on for a long time. To satisfy these last thoroughly a man must have recourse to art. It is certain that a fluid flows from the woman in larger or smaller quantities, but her satisfaction is not complete until she has experienced the "spasme génêsique", as described in a French work recently published and called *Breviare de l' Amour Experimental par le Dr. Jules Guyot.*

† This is a long dissertation very common among Sanscrit authors, both when writing and talking socially. They start certain propositions, and then argue for and against them. What it is presumed the author means, is that, though both men and women derive pleasure from the act of coition, the

120

On this again some may say that when different persons are engaged in doing the same work, we find that they accomplish the same end or purpose; while, on the contrary, in the case of men and women we find that each of them accomplishes his or her own end separately, and this is inconsistent. But this is a mistake, for we find that sometimes two things are done at the same time, as for instance in the fighting of rams, both the rams receive the shock at the same time on their heads. Again, in throwing one wood apple against another, and also in a fight or struggle of wrestlers.

If it be said that in these cases the things employed are of the same kind, it is answered that even in the case of men and women, the nature of the two persons is the same. And as the difference in their ways of working arises from the difference of their conformation only, it follows that men experience the same kind of pleasure as women do.

There is also a verse on this subject as follows: "Men and women being of the same nature, feel the same kind of pleasure, and therefore a man should marry such a woman as will love him ever afterwards".

The pleasure of men and women being thus proved to be of the same kind, it follows that in regard to time, there are nine kinds of sexual intercourse, in the same way as there are nine kinds, according to the force of passion.

There being thus nine kinds of union with regard to dimensions, force of passion, and time, respectively, by making combinations of them, innumerable kinds of union would be produced. Therefore in each particular kind of sexual union, men should use such means as they may think suitable for the occasion.*

way it is produced is brought about by different means, each individual performing his own work in the matter, irrespective of the other, and each deriving individually their own consciousness of pleasure from the act they perform. There is a difference in the work that each does, and a difference in the consciousness of pleasure that each has, but no difference in the pleasure they feel, for each feel that pleasure to a greater or lesser degree.

* This paragraph should be particularly noted, for it specially applies to married men and their wives. So many men utterly ignore the feelings of the women, and never pay the slightest attention to the passion of the latter. To understand the subject thoroughly, it is absolutely necessary to study it, and then a person will know that, as dough is prepared for baking, so must a woman be prepared for sexual intercourse, if she is to derive satisfaction from it.

At the first time of sexual union the passion of the male is intense, and his time is short, but in subsequent unions on the same day the reverse of this is the case. With the female, however, it is the contrary, for at the first time her passion is weak, and then her time long, but on subsequent occasions on the same day, her passion is intense and her time short, until her passion is satisfied.

On the Different Kinds of Love

Men learned in the humanities are of opinion that love is of four kinds, viz.:

1. Love acquired by continual habit.
2. Love resulting from the imagination.
3. Love resulting from belief.
4. Love resulting from the perception of external objects.

(1) Love resulting from the constant and continual performance of some act, is called love acquired by constant practice and habit, as for instance the love of sexual intercourse, the love of hunting, the love of drinking, the love of gambling, etc.

(2) Love which is felt for things to which we are not habituated, and which proceeds entirely from ideas, is called love resulting from imagination, as for instance, that love which some men and women and eunuchs feel for the Auparishtaka or mouth congress, and that which is felt by all for such things as embracing, kissing, etc.

(3) The love which is mutual on both sides, and proved to be true, when each looks upon the other as his or her very own, such is called love resulting from belief by the learned.

(4) The love resulting from the perception of external objects is quite evident and well known to the world, because the pleasure which it affords is superior to the pleasure of the other kinds of love, which exists only for its sake.

What has been said in this chapter upon the subject of sexual union is sufficient for the learned; but for the edification of the ignorant, the same will now be treated of at length and in detail.

CHAPTER II

Of the Embrace

THIS part of the Kama Shastra, which treats of sexual union, is also called "Sixty-four" (Chatushshashti). Some old authors say that it is called so, because it contains sixty-four chapters. Other are of opinion that the author of this part being a person named Panchala, and the person who recited the part of the Rig Veda called Dashatapa, which contains sixty-four verses, being also called Panchala, the name "sixty-four" has been given to the part of the work in honour of the Rig Vedas. The followers of Brabhravya say on the other hand that this part contains eight subjects, viz., the embrace, kissing, scratching with the nails or fingers, biting, lying down, making various sounds, playing the part of a man, and the Auparishtaka, or mouth congress. Each of these subjects being of eight kinds, and eight multiplied by eight being sixty-four, this part is therefore named "sixty-four". But Vatsyayana affirms that as this part contains also the following subjects, viz., striking, crying, the acts of a man during congress, the various kinds of congress, and other subjects, the name "sixty-four" is given to it only accidentally. As, for instance, we say this tree is "Saptaparna", or seven-leaved, this offering of rice is "Panchavarna", or five-coloured, but the tree has not seven leaves, neither has the rice seven colours.

However the part sixty-four is now treated of, and the embrace, being the first subject, will now be considered.

Now the embrace which indicates the mutual love of a man and women who have come together is of four kinds, viz.:

Touching
Piercing
Rubbing
Pressing

The action in each case is denoted by the meaning of the word which stands for it.

(1) When a man under some pretext or other goes in front or alongside of a woman and touches her body with his own, it is called the "touching embrace".

(2) When a woman in a lonely place bends down, as if to pick up something, and pierces, as it were, a man sitting or standing, with her breasts, and the man in return takes hold of them, if is called a "piercing embrace".

The above two kinds of embrace takes place only between persons who do not, as yet, speak freely with each other.

(3) When two lovers are walking slowly together, either in the dark, or in a place of public resort, or in a lonely place, and rub their bodies against each other, it is called a "rubbing embrace".

(4) When on the above occasion one of them presses the other's body forcibly against a wall or pillar, it is called a "pressing embrace".

These two last embraces are peculiar to those who know the intentions of each other.

At the time of the meeting the four following kinds of embrace are used, viz.:

Jataveshtitaka, or the twining of a creeper.

Vrikshadhirudhaka, or climbing a tree.

Tila-Tandulaka, or the mixture of sesamum seed with rice.

Kshiraniraka, or milk and water embrace.

(1) When a woman, clinging to a man as a creeper twines round a tree, bends his head down to hers with the desire of kissing him and slightly makes the sound of sut sut, embraces him, and looks lovingly towards him, it is called an embrace like the "twining of a creeper".

(2) When a woman, having placed one of her feet on the foot of her lover, and the other on one of his thighs, passes one of her arms round his back, and the other on his shoulders, makes slightly the sounds of singing and cooing, and wishes, as it were, to climb up him in order to have a kiss, it is called an embrace like the "climbing of a tree".

These two kinds of embrace take place when the lover is standing.

(3) When lovers lie on a bed, and embrace each other so closely that the arms and thighs of the one are encircled by the arms and thighs of the other, and are, as it were, rubbing up against them, this is called an embrace like "the mixture of sesamum seed with rice".

(4) When a man and a woman are very much in love with each other, and, not thinking of any pain or hurt, embrace each other as if they were entering into each other's bodies either while the woman is sitting on the lap of the man, or in front of him, or on a bed, then it is called an embrace like a "mixture of milk and water".

These two kinds of embrace take place at the time of sexual union.

Babhravya has thus related to us the above eight kinds of embraces.

Suvarnanabha moreover gives us four ways of embracing simple members of the body, which are:

The embrace of the thighs.

The embrace of the jaghana, i.e., the part of the body from the navel downwards to the thighs.

The embrace of the breasts.

The embrace of the forehead.

(1) When one of two lovers presses forcibly one or both of the thighs of the other between his or her own, it is called the "embrace of thighs".

(2) When a man presses the jaghana or middle part of the woman's body against his own, and mounts upon her to practise, either scratching with the nail or finger, or biting, or striking, or kissing, the hair of the woman being loose and flowing, it is called the "embrace of the jaghana".

(3) When a man places his breast between the breasts of a woman and presses her with it, it is called the "embrace of the breasts".

(4) When either of the lovers touches the mouth, the eyes and the forehead of the other with his or her own, it is called the "embrace of the forehead".

Some say that even shampooing is a kind of embrace, because there is a touching of bodies in it. But Vatsyayana thinks that shampooing is performed at a different time, and for a different purpose, and it is also of a different character, it cannot be said to be included in the embrace.

There are also some verses on the subject as follows: "The whole subject of embracing is of such a nature that men who ask questions about it, or who hear about it, or who talk about it, acquire thereby a desire for enjoyment. Even those embraces that are not mentioned in the Kama Shastra should be practised at the time of sexual enjoyment, if they are in any way conducive to the increase of love or passion. The rules of the Shastra apply so long as the passion of man is middling, but when the wheel of love is once set in motion, there is then no Shastra and no order."

CHAPTER III

On Kissing

IT is said by some that there is no fixed time or order between the embrace, the kiss, and the pressing or scratching with the nails or fingers, but that all these things should be done generally before sexual union takes place, while striking and making the various sounds generally takes place at the time of the union. Vatsyayana however, thinks that anything may take place at any time, for love does not care for time or order.

On the occasion of the first congress, kissing and the other things mentioned above should be done moderately, they should not be continued for a long time, and should be done alternately. On subsequent occasions however the reverse of all this may take place, and moderation will not be necessary, they may continue for a long time, and for the purpose of kindling love, they may be all done at the same time.

The following are the places for kissing, viz., the forehead, the eyes, the cheeks, the throat, the bosom, the breasts, the lips, and the interior of the mouth. Moreover the people of the Lat country kiss also on the following places, viz., the joints of the thighs, the arms and the navel. But Vatsyayana thinks that though kissing is practised by these people in the above places on account of the intensity of their love, and the customs of their country, it is not fit to be practised by all.

Now in a case of a young girl there are three sorts of kisses, viz.:

The nominal kiss
The throbbing kiss
The touching kiss

(1) When a girl only touches the mouth of her lover with her own, but does not herself do anything, it is called the "nominal kiss".

(2) When a girl, setting aside her bashfulness a little, wishes to touch the lip that is pressed into her mouth, and with that object moves her lower lip, but not the upper one, it is called the "throbbing kiss".

(3) When a girl touches her lover's lip with her tongue, and having shut her eyes, places her hands on those of her lover, it is called the "touching kiss".

Other authors describe four other kinds of kisses, viz.:

The straight kiss
The bent kiss
The turned kiss
The pressed kiss

(1) When the lips of two lovers are brought into direct contact with each other, it is called a "straight kiss".

(2) When the heads of two lovers are bent towards each other, and when so bent, kissing takes place, it is called a "bent kiss".

(3) When one of them turns up the face of the other by holding the head and chin, and then kissing, it is called a "turned kiss".

(4) Lastly when the lower lip is pressed with much force, it is called a "pressed kiss".

There is also a fifth kind of kiss called the "greatly pressed kiss", which is effected by taking hold of the lower lip between two fingers, and then after touching it with the tongue, pressing it with great force with the lip.

As regards kissing, a wager may be laid as to which will

get hold of the lips of the other first. If the woman loses, she should pretend to cry, should keep her lover off by shaking her hands, and turn away from him and dispute with him saying, "let another wager be laid". If she loses this a second time, she should appear doubly distressed, and when her lover is off his guard or asleep, she should get hold of his lower lip, and hold it in her teeth, so that it should not slip away, and then she should laugh, make a loud noise, deride him, dance about, and say whatever she likes in a joking way, moving her eyebrows, and rolling her eyes. Such are the wagers and quarrels as far as kissing is concerned, but the same may be applied with regard to the pressing or scratching with the nails and fingers, biting and striking. All these however are only peculiar to men and women of intense passion.

When a man kisses the upper lip of a woman, while she in return kisses his lower lip, it is called the "kiss of the upper lip".

When one of them takes both the lips of the other between his or her own, it is called "a clasping kiss". A woman, however, only takes this kind of kiss from a man who has no moustache. And on the occasion of this kiss, if one of them touches the teeth, the tongue, and the palate of the other, with his or her tongue, it is called the "fighting of the tongue". In the same way, the pressing of the teeth of the one against the mouth of the other is to be practised.

Kissing is of four kinds, viz., moderate, contracted, pressed, and soft, according to the different parts of the body which are kissed, for different kinds of kisses are appropriate for different parts of the body.

When a woman looks at the face of her lover while he is asleep, and kisses it to show her intention or desire, it is called a "kiss that kindles love".

When a woman kisses her lover while he is engaged in business, or while he is quarrelling with her, or while he is looking at something else, so that his mind may be turned away, it is called a "kiss that turns away".

When a lover coming home late at night kisses his beloved, who is asleep on her bed, in order to show her his desire, it is called a "kiss that awakens". On such an occasion the woman may pretend to be asleep at the time of her lover's arrival, so that she may know his intention and obtain respect from him.

When a person kisses the reflection of the person he loves in a mirror, in water, or on a wall, it is called a "kiss showing the intention".

When a person kisses a child sitting on his lap, or a picture, or an image, or figure, in the presence of the person beloved by him, it is called a "transferred kiss".

When at night at a theatre, or in an assembly of caste men, a man coming up to a woman kisses a finger of her hand if she be standing, or a toe of her foot if she be sitting, or when a woman is shampooing her lover's body, places her face on his thigh (as if she was sleepy) so as to inflame his passion, and kisses his thigh or great toe, it is called a "demonstrative kiss".

There is also a verse on this subject as follows:

"Whatever things may be done by one of the lovers to the other, the same should be returned by the other, i.e., if the woman kisses him he should kiss her in return, if she strikes him he should also strike her in return.

CHAPTER IV

On Pressing, or Marking, or Scratching with the Nails

WHEN love becomes intense, pressing with the nails or scratching the body with them is practised, and it is done on the following occasions: on the first visit; at the time of setting out on a journey; on the return from a journey; at the time when an angry lover is reconciled; and lastly when the woman is intoxicated.

But pressing with the nails is not an usual thing except with those who are intensely passionate, i.e., full of passion. It is employed together with biting, by those to whom the practice is agreeable.

Pressing with the nails is of the eight following kinds, according to the forms of the marks which are produced, viz.:

1. Sounding.
2. Half moon.
3. A circle.
4. A line.
5. A tiger's nail or claw.
6. A peacock's foot.
7. The jump of a hare.
8. The leaf of a blue lotus.

The places that are to be pressed with the nails are as follows: the arm pit, the throat, the breasts, the lips, the jaghana, or middle parts of the body, and the thighs. But Suvarnanabha is of opinion that when the impetuosity of passion is excessive, then the places need not be considered.

The qualities of good nails are that they should be bright, well set, clean, entire, convex, soft, and glossy in appearance. Nails are of three kinds according to their size, viz.:

Small

Middling

Large

Large nails, which give grace to the hands, and attract the hearts of women from their appearance, are possessed by the Bengalees.

Small nails, which can be used in various ways, and are to be applied only with the object of giving pleasure, are possessed by the people of the southern districts.

Middling nails, which contain the properties of both the above kinds, belong to the people of the Maharashtra.

(1) When a person presses the chin, the breasts, the lower lip, or the jaghana or another so softly that no scratch or mark is left, but only the hair on the body becomes erect from the touch of the nails, and the nails themselves make a sound, it is called a "sounding or pressing with the nails".

This pressing is used in the case of a young girl when her lover shampoos her, scratches her head, and wants to trouble or frighten her.

(2) The curved mark with the nails, which is impressed on the neck and the breasts, is called the "half moon".

(3) When the half moons are impressed opposite to each other, it is called a "circle". This mark with the nails is generally made on the navel, the small cavities about the buttocks, and on the joints of the thigh.

(4) A mark in the form of a small line, and which can be made on any part of the body, is called a "line".

(5) This same line, when it is curved, and made on the breast, is called a "tiger's nail".

(6) When a curved mark is made on the breast by means of the five nails, it is called a "peacock's foot". This mark is made with the object of being praised, for it requires a great deal of skill to make it properly.

(7) When five marks with the nails are made close to one another near the nipple of the breast, it is called "the jump of a hare".

(8) A mark made on the breast or on the hips in the form of a leaf of the blue lotus, is called the "leaf of a blue lotus".

When a person is going on a journey, and makes a mark on the thighs, or on the breast, it is called a "token of remembrance". On such an occasion three or four lines are impressed close to one another with the nails.

Here ends the marking with the nails. Marks of other kinds than the above may also be made with the nails, for the ancient authors say, that as there are innumerable degrees of skill among men (the practice of this art being known to all), so there are innumerable ways of making these marks. And as pressing or marking with the nails is independent on love, no one can say with certainty how many different kinds of marks with the nails do actually exist. The reason of this is, Vatsyayana says, that as variety is necessary in love, so love is to be produced by means of variety. It is on this account that courtesans, who are well acquainted with various ways and means, become so desirable, for if variety is sought in all the arts and amusements, such as archery and others, how much more should it be sought after in the present case.

The marks of the nails should not be made on married women, but particular kinds of marks may be made on their private parts for the remembrance and increase of love.

There are also some verses on the subject, as follows:
"The love of a woman who sees the marks of nails on the

131

private parts of her body, even though they are old and almost worn out, becomes again fresh and new. If there be no marks of nails to remind a person of the passages of love, then love is lessened in the same way as when no union takes place for a long time".

Even when a stranger sees at a distance a young woman with the marks of nails on her breast,* he is filled with love and respect for her.

A man, also, who carried the marks of nails and teeth on some parts of his body, influences the mind of a woman, even though it be ever so firm. In short, nothing tends to increase love so much as the effects of marking with the nails, and biting.

CHAPTER V

On Biting, and the Means to be Employed with Regard to Women of Different Countries

ALL the places that can be kissed, are also the places that can be bitten, except the upper lip, the interior of the mouth, and the eyes.

The qualities of good teeth are as follows: They should be equal, possessed of a pleasing brightness, capable of being coloured, of proper proportions, unbroken, and with sharp ends.

The defects of teeth on the other hand are, that they are blunt, protruding from the gums, rough, soft, large, and loosely set.

The following are the different kinds of biting, viz.:

> The hidden bite
> The swollen bite
> The point
> The line of points

* From this it would appear that in ancient times the breasts of women were not covered, and this is seen in the paintings of the Ajunta and other caves, where we find that the breasts of even royal ladies and others are exposed.

The coral and the jewel
The line of jewels
The broken cloud
The biting of the boar

(1) The biting which is shown only by the excessive redness of the skin that is bitten, is called the "hidden bite".

(2) When the skin is pressed down on both sides, it is called the "swollen bite".

(3) When a small portion of the skin is bitten with two teeth only, it is called the "point".

(4) When such small portions of the skin are bitten with all the teeth, it is called the "line of points".

(5) The biting which is done by bringing together the teeth and the lips, is called the "coral and the jewel". The lip is the coral, and the teeth the jewel.

(6) When biting is done with all the teeth, it is called the "line of jewels".

(7) The biting which consists of unequal risings in a circle, and which comes from the space between the teeth, is called the "broken cloud". This is impressed on the breasts.

(8) The biting which consists of many broad rows of marks near to one another, and with red intervals, is called the "biting of a boar". This is impressed on the breasts and the shoulders; and these two last modes of biting are peculiar to persons of intense passion.

The lower lip is the place on which the "hidden bite", the "swollen bite", and the "point" are made; again the "swollen bite", and the "coral and the jewel" bite are done on the cheek. Kissing, pressing with the nails, and biting are the ornaments of the left cheek, and when the word cheek is used it is to be understood as the left cheek.

Both the "line of points" and the "line of jewels" are to be impressed on the throat, the arm pit, and the joints of the thighs; but the "line of points" alone is to be impressed on the forehead and the thighs.

The marking with the nails, and the biting of the following things, viz., an ornament of the forehead, an ear ornament, a bunch of flowers, a betel leaf, or a tamala leaf, which are worn by, or belong to the woman that is beloved, are signs of the desire of enjoyment.

Here end the different kinds of biting.

In the affairs of love a man should do such things as are agreeable to the women of different countries.

The women of the central countries (i.e., between the Ganges and the Jumna) are noble in their character, not accustomed to disgraceful practices, and dislike pressing the nails and biting.

The women of the Balhika country are gained over by striking.

The women of Avantika are fond of foul pleasures, and have not good manners.

The women of the Maharashtra are fond of practising the sixty-four arts, they utter low and harsh words, and like to be spoken to in the same way, and have an impetuous desire of enjoyment.

The women of Pataliputra (i.e., the modern Patna) are of the same nature as the women of the Maharashtra, but show their likings only in secret.

The women of the Dravida country, though they are rubbed and pressed about at the time of sexual enjoyment, have a slow fall of semen, that is they are very slow in the act of coition.

The women of Vanavasi are moderately passionate, they go through every kind of enjoyment, cover their bodies, and abuse those who utter low, mean and harsh words.

The women of Avanti hate kissing, marking with the nails, and biting, but they have a fondness for various kinds of sexual union.

The women of Malwa like embracing and kissing, but not wounding, and they are gained over by striking.

The women of Abhira, and those of the country about the Indus and five rivers (i.e., the Punjab), are gained over by the Auparishtaka or mouth congress.

The women of Aparatika are full of passion, and make slowly the sound "Sit".

The women of the Lat country have even more impetuous desire, and also make the sound "Sit".

The women of the Stri Rajya, and of Koshola (Oude), are

full of impetuous desire, their semen falls in large quantities, and they are fond of taking medicine to make it do so.

The women of the Audhra country have tender bodies, they are fond of enjoyment, and have a liking for voluptuous pleasures.

The women of Ganda have tender bodies, and speak sweetly.

Now Suvarnanabha is of opinion that that which is agreeable to the nature of a particular person, is of more consequence than that which is agreeable to a whole nation, and that therefore the peculiarities of the country should not be observed in such cases. The various pleasures, the dress, and the sports of one country are in time borrowed by another, and in such a case these things must be considered as belonging originally to that country.

Among the things mentioned above, viz., embracing, kissing, etc., those which increase passion should be done first, and those which are only for amusement or variety should be done afterwards.

There are also some verses on this subject as follows:

"When a man bites a woman forcibly, she should angrily do the same to him with double force. Thus a 'point' should be returned with a 'line of points', and a 'line of points' with a 'broken cloud', and if she be excessively chafed, she should at once begin a love quarrel with him. At such a time she should take hold of her lover by the hair, and bend his head down, and kiss his lower lip, and then, being intoxicated with love, she should shut her eyes and bite him in various places. Even by day, and in a place of public resort, when her lover shows her any mark that she may have inflicted on his body, she should smile at the sight of it, and turning her face as if she were going to chide him, she should show him with an angry look the marks on her own body that have been made by him. Thus if men and women act according to each other's liking, their love for each other will not be lessened even in one hundred years."

Of the Different Ways of Lying Down, and Various Kinds of Congress

ON the occasion of a "high congress" the Mrigi (Deer) woman should lie down in such a way as to widen her yoni, while in a "low congress" the Hastini (Elephant) woman should lie down so as to contract hers. But in an "equal congress" they should lie down in the natural position. What is said above concerning the Mrigi and the Hastini applies also to the Vadawa (Mare) woman. In a "low congress" the women should particularly make use of medicine, to cause her desires to be satisfied quickly.

The Deer-woman has the following three ways of lying down.

> The widely opened position
> The yawning position
> The position of the wife of Indra

(1) When she lowers her head and raises her middle parts, it is called the "widely opened position". At such a time the man should apply some unguent, so as to make the entrance easy.

(2) When she raises her thighs and keeps them wide apart and engages in congress, it is called the "yawning position".

(3) When she places her thighs with her legs doubled on them upon her sides, and thus engages in congress, it is called the position of Indrani, and this is learnt only by practice. The position is also useful in the case of the "highest congress".

The "clasping position" is used in "low congress", and in the "lowest congress", together with the "pressing position", the "twining position", and the "mare's position".

When the legs of both the male and the female are stretched straight out over each other, it is called the "clasping position". It is of two kinds, the side position and the supine position, according to the way in which they lie down. In the side position the male should invariably lie on his left side, and cause the women to lie on her right side, and this rule is to be observed in lying down with all kinds of women.

When, after congress has begun in the clasping position, the woman presses her lover with her thighs, it is called the "pressing position".

When the woman places one of her thighs across the thigh of her lover, it is called the "twining position".

When a woman forcibly holds in her yoni the lingam after it is in, it is called the "mare's position". This is learnt by practice only, and is chiefly found among the women of the Andra country.

The above are the different ways of lying down, mentioned by Babhravya; Suvarnanabha, however, gives the following in addition.

When the female raises both of her thighs straight up, it is called the "rising position".

When she raises both of her legs, and places them on her lover's shoulders, it is called the "yawning position".

When the legs are contracted, and thus held by the lover before his bosom, it is called the "pressed position".

When only one of her legs is stretched out, it is called the "half pressed position".

When the woman places one of her legs on her lover's shoulder, and stretches the other out, and then places the latter on his shoulder, and stretches out the other, and continues to do so alternately, it is called the "splitting of a bamboo".

When one of her legs is placed on the head, and the other is stretched out, it is called the "fixing of a nail". This is learnt by practice only.

When both the legs of the woman are contracted, and placed on her stomach, it is called the "crab's position".

When the thighs are raised and placed one upon the other, it is called the "packed position".

When the shanks are placed one upon the other, it is called the "lotus-like position".

When a man, during congress, turns round, and enjoys

the woman without leaving her, while she embraces him round the back all the time, it is called the "turning position" and is learnt only by practice.

Thus says Suvarnanabha, these different ways of lying down, sitting, and standing should be practised in water, because it is easy to do so therein. But Vatsyayana is of opinion that congress in water is improper, because it is prohibited by the religious law.

When a man and a woman support themselves on each other's bodies, or on a wall, or pillar, and thus while standing engage in congress, it is called the "supported congress".

When a man supports himself against a wall, and the woman, sitting on his hands joined together and held underneath her, throws her arms round his neck, and putting her thighs alongside his waist, moves herself by her feet, which are touching the wall against which the man is leaning, it is called the "suspended congress".

When a woman stands on her hands and feet like a quadruped, and her lover mounts her like a bull, it is called the "congress of a cow". At this time everything that is ordinarily done on the bosom should be done on the back. In the same way can be carried on the congress of a dog, the congress of a goat, the congress of a deer, the forcible mounting of an ass, the congress of a cat, the jump of a tiger, the pressing of an elephant, the rubbing of a boar, and the mounting of a horse. And in all these cases the characteristics of these different animals should be manifested by acting like them.

When a man enjoys two women at the same time, both of whom love him equally, it is called the "united congress".

When a man enjoys many women altogether, it is called the "congress of a herd of cows".

The following kinds of congress, viz., sporting in water, or the congress of an elephant with many female elephants which is said to take place only in the water, the congress of a collection of goats, the congress of a collection of deer, take place in imitation of these animals.

In Gramaneri many young men enjoy a woman that may be married to one of them, either one after the other, or at the same time. Thus one of them holds her, another enjoys her, a third uses her mouth, a fourth holds her middle part, and in this way they go on enjoying her several parts alternately.

The same things can be done when several men are sitting in company with one courtesan, or when one courtesan is alone with many men. In the same way this can be done by the women of the King's harem when they accidentally get hold of a man.

The people in the Southern countries have also a congress in the anus, that is called the "lower congress".

Thus ends the various kinds of congress. There are also two verses on the subject as follows.

"An ingenious person should multiply the kinds of congress after the fashion of the different kinds of beasts and of birds. For these different kinds of congress, performed according to the usage of each country, and the liking of each individual, generate love, friendship, and respect in the hearts of women."

CHAPTER VII

Of the Various Modes of Striking, and of the Sounds Appropriate to Them

SEXUAL intercourse can be compared to a quarrel, on account of the contrarieties of love and its tendency to dispute. The place of striking with passion is the body, and on the body the special places are:

> The shoulders.
> The head.
> The space between the breasts.
> The back.
> The jaghana, or middle part of the body.
> The sides.

Striking is of four kinds, viz.:

> Striking with the back of the hand.
> Striking with the fingers a little contracted.

Striking with the fist.

Striking with the open palm of the hand.

On account of its causing pain, striking gives rise to the hissing sound, which is of various kinds, and to the eight kinds of crying, viz.:

The sound Hin.

The thundering sound.

The cooing sound.

The weeping sound.

The sound Phut.

The sound Phât.

The sound Sût.

The sound Plât.

Besides these, there are also words having a meaning, such as "mother", and those that are expressive of prohibition, sufficiency, desire of liberation, pain or praise, and to which may be added sounds like those of the dove, the cuckoo, the green pigeon, the parrot, the bee, the sparrow, the flamingo, the duck, and the quail, which are all occasionally made use of.

Blows with the fist should be given on the back of the woman, while she is sitting on the lap of the man, and she should give blows in return, abusing the man as if she were angry, and making the cooing and the weeping sounds. While the woman is engaged in congress the space between the breasts should be struck with the back of the hand, slowly at first, and then proportionately to the increasing excitement, until the end.

At this time the sounds Hin and others may be made, alternately or optionally, according to habit. When the man, making the sound Phât, strikes the woman on the head, with the fingers of his hand a little contracted, it is called Prasritaka, which means striking with the fingers of the hand a little contracted. In this case the appropriate sounds are the cooing sound, the sound Phât, and the sound Phut in the interior of the mouth, and at the end of congress the sighing and weeping sounds. The sound Phât is an imitation of the sound of a bamboo being split, while the sound Phut is like the sound made by something falling into water. At all times when kissing and such like things are begun, the woman should give a reply with a hissing sound. During the excitement when the woman is not accustomed to striking, she continually utters words expressive of prohibition, sufficiently, or desire of liberation, as well as the words "father", "mother", intermingled with the sighing, weeping and thundering sounds.* Towards the conclusion of the congress, the breasts, the jaghana, and the sides of the woman should be pressed with the open palms of the hand, with some force, until the end of it, and then sounds like those of the quail, or the goose should be made.

There are also two verses on the subject as follows:

"The characteristics of manhood are said to consist of roughness and impetuosity, while weakness, tenderness, sensibility, and an inclination to turn away from unpleasant things are the distinguishing marks of womanhood. The excitement of passion, and peculiarities of habit may sometimes cause contrary results to appear, but these do not last long, and in the end the natural state is resumed."

The wedge on the bosom, the scissors on the head, the piercing instrument on the cheeks, and the pinchers on the breasts and sides, may also be taken into consideration with the other four modes of striking, and thus give eight ways altogether. But these four ways of striking with instruments are peculiar to the people of the southern countries, and the marks caused by them are seen on the breasts of their women. They are local peculiarities, but Vatsyayana is of opinion that the practice of them is painful, barbarous, and base, and quite unworthy of imitation.

In the same way anything that is a local peculiarity should not always be adopted elsewhere, and even in the place where the practice is prevalent, excess of it should always be avoided. Instances of the dangerous use of them may be given as follows. The King of the Panchalas killed the courtesan Madhavasena by means of the wedge during

* Men who are well acquainted with the art of love are well aware how often one woman differs from another in her sighs and sounds during the time of congress. Some women like to be talked to in the most loving way, others in the most lustful way, others in the most abusive way, and so on. Some women enjoy themselves with closed eyes in silence, others make a great noise over it, and some almost faint away. The great art is to ascertain what gives them the greatest pleasure, and what specialities they like best.

congress. King Shatakarni Shatavahana of the Kuntalas deprived his great Queen Malayavati of her life by a pair of scissors, and Naradeva, whose hand was deformed, blinded a dancing girl by directing a piercing instrument in a wrong way.

There are also two verses on the subject as follows:

"About these things there cannot be either enumeration or any definite rule. Congress having once commenced, passion alone gives birth to all the acts of the parties."

Such passionate actions and amorous gesticulations or movements, which arise on the spur of the moment, and during sexual intercourse, cannot be defined, and are as irregular as dreams. A horse having once attained the fifth degree of motion goes on with blind speed, regardless of pits, ditches, and posts in his way; and in the same manner a loving pair become blind with passion in the heat of congress, and go on with great impetuosity, paying not the least regard to excess. For this reason one who is well acquainted with the science of love, and knowing his own strength, as also the tenderness, impetuosity, and strength of the young women, should act accordingly. The various modes of enjoyment are not for all times or for all persons, but they should only be used at the proper time, and in the proper countries and places.

CHAPTER VIII

About Women Acting the Part of a Man; and of the Work of a Man

WHEN a woman sees that her lover is fatigued by constant congress, without having his desire satisfied, she should, with his permission, lay him down upon his back, and give him assistance by acting his part. She may also do this to satisfy the curiosity of her lover, or her own desire of novelty.

There are two ways of doing this, the first is when during congress she turns round, and gets on the top of her lover, in such a manner as to continue the congress, without obstructing the pleasure of it; and the other is when she acts the man's part from the beginning. At such a time, with flowers in her hair hanging loose, and her smiles broken by hard breathings, she should press upon her lover's bosom with her own breasts, and lowering her head frequently, should do in return the same actions which he used to do before, returning his blows and chaffing him, should say, "I was laid down by you, and fatigued with hard congress, I shall now therefore lay you down in return". She should then again manifest her own bashfulness, her fatigue, and her desire of stopping the congress. In this way she should do the work of a man, which we shall presently relate.

Whatever is done by a man for giving pleasure to a woman is called the work of a man, and is as follows:

While the woman is lying on his bed, and is as it were abstracted by his conversation, he should loosen the knot of her under garments, and when she begins to dispute with him, he should overwhelm her with kisses. Then when his lingam is erect he should touch her with his hands in various places, and gently manipulate various parts of the body. If the woman is bashful, and if it is the first time that they have come together, the man should place his hands between her thighs, which she would probably keep close together, and if she is a very young girl, he should first get his hands upon her breasts, which she would probably cover with her own hands, and under her armpits and on her neck. If however she is a seasoned woman, he should do whatever is agreeable either to him or to her, and whatever is fitting for the occasion. After this he should take hold of her hair, and hold her chin in his fingers for the purpose of kissing her. On this, if she is a young girl, she will become bashful and close her eyes. Any how he should gather from the action of the woman what things would be pleasing to her during congress.

Here Suvarnanabha says that while a man is doing to the woman what he likes best during congress, he should always make a point of pressing those parts of her body on which she turns her eyes.

The signs of the enjoyment and satisfaction of the women

are as follows: her body relaxes, she closes her eyes, she puts aside all bashfulness, and shows increased willingness to unite the two organs as closely together as possible. On the other hand, the signs of her want of enjoyment and of failing to be satisfied are as follows: she shakes her hands, she does not let the man get up, feels dejected, bites the man, kicks him, and continues to go on moving after the man has finished. In such cases the man should rub the yoni of the woman with his hand and fingers (as the elephant rubs anything with his trunk) before engaging in congress, until it is softened, and after that is done he should proceed to put his lingam into her.

The acts to be done by the man are:

> Moving forward
> Friction or churning
> Piercing
> Rubbing
> Pressing
> Giving a blow
> The blow of a boar
> The blow of a bull
> The sporting of a sparrow·

(1) When the organs are brought together properly and directly it is called "moving the organ forward".

(2) When the lingam is held with the hand, and turned all round in the yoni, it is called "churning".

(3) When the yoni is lowered, and the upper part of it is struck with the lingam, it is called "piercing".

(4) When the same thing is done on the lower part of the yoni, it is called "rubbing".

(5) When the yoni is pressed by the lingam for a long time, it is called "pressing".

(6) When the lingam is removed to some distance from the yoni, and then forcibly strikes it, it is called "giving a blow".

(7) When only one part of the yoni is rubbed with the lingam, it is called the "blow of a boar".

(8) When both sides of the yoni are rubbed in this way, it is called the "blow of a bull".

(9) When the lingam is in the yoni, and moved up and

down frequently, and without being taken out, it is called the "sporting of a sparrow". This takes place at the end of congress.

When a woman acts the part of a man, she has the following things to do in addition to the nine given above, viz.:

> The pair of tongs
> The top
> The swing

(1) When the woman holds the lingam in her yoni, draws it in, presses it, and keeps it thus in her for a long time, it is called the "pair of tongs".

(2) When, while engaged in congress, she turns round like a wheel, it is called the "top". This is learnt by practice only.

(3) When, on such an occasion, the man lifts up the middle part of his body, and the woman turns round her middle part, it is called the "swing".

When the woman is tired, she should place her forehead on that of her lover, and should thus take rest without disturbing the union of the organs, and when the woman has rested herself the man should turn round and begin the congress again.

There are also some verses on the subject as follows:

"Though a woman is reserved, and keeps her feelings concealed, yet when she gets on the top of a man, she then shows all her love and desire. A man should gather from the actions of the woman of what disposition she is, and in what way she likes to be enjoyed. A woman during her monthly courses, a woman who has been lately confined, and a fat woman should not be made to act the part of a man."

Of the Auparishtaka* or Mouth Congress

THERE are two kinds of eunuchs, those that are disguised as males, and those that are disguised as females. Eunuchs disguised as females imitate their dress, speech, gestures, tenderness, timidity, simplicity, softness and bashfulness. The acts that are done on the jaghana or middle parts of women, are done in the mouths of these eunuchs, and this is called Auparishtaka. These eunuchs derive their imaginable pleasure, and their livelihood from this kind of congress, and they lead the life of courtesans. So much concerning eunuchs disguised as females.

Eunuchs disguised as males keep their desires secret, and when they wish to do anything they lead the life of shampooers. Under the pretence of shampooing, an eunuch of this kind embraces and draws towards himself the thighs of the man whom he is shampooing, and after this he touches the joints of his thighs and his jaghana, or central portions of his body. Then, if he finds the lingam of the man erect, he presses it with his hands, and chaffs him for getting into that state. If after this, and after knowing his intention, the man does not tell the eunuch to proceed, then the latter does it of his own accord and begins the congress. If however he is ordered by the man to do it, then he disputes with him, and only consents at last with difficulty.

* This practice appears to have been prevalent in some parts of India from a very ancient time. The *Shushruta*, a work on medicine some two thousand years old, describes the wounding of the lingam with the teeth as one of the causes of a disease treated upon in that work. Traces of the practice are found as far back as the eighth century, for various kinds of the Auparishtaka are represented in the sculptures of many Shaiva temples at Bhuvaneshwara, near Cuttack, in Orissa, and which were built about that period. From these sculptures being found in such places, it would seem that this practice was popular in that part of the country at that time. It does not seem to be so prevalent now in Hindustan, its place perhaps is filled up by the practice of sodomy, introduced since the Mahomedan period.

The following eight things are then done by the eunuch one after the other, viz.:

> The nominal congress
> Biting the sides
> Pressing outside
> Pressing inside
> Kissing
> Rubbing
> Sucking a mangoe fruit
> Swallowing up

At the end of each of these, the eunuch expresses his wish to stop, but when one of them is finished, the man desires him to do another, and after that is done, then the one that follows it, and so on.

(1) When, holding the man's lingam with his hand, and placing it between his lips, the eunuch moves about his mouth, it is called the "nominal congress".

(2) When, covering the end of the lingam, with his fingers collected together like the bud of a plant or flower, the eunuch presses the sides of it with his lips, using his teeth also, it is called "biting the sides".

(3) When, being desired to proceed, the eunuch presses the end of the lingam with his lips closed together, and kisses it as if he were drawing it out, it is called the "outside pressing".

(4) When, being asked to go on, he puts the lingam further into his mouth, and presses it with his lips and then takes it out, it is called the "inside pressing".

(5) When, holding the lingam in his hand, the eunuch kisses it as if he were kissing the lower lip, it is called "kissing".

(6) When, after kissing it, he touches it with his tongue everywhere, and passes the tongue over the end of it, it is called "rubbing".

(7) When, in the same way, he puts the half of it into his mouth, and forcibly kisses and sucks it, this is called "sucking a mangoe fruit".

(8) And lastly, when, with the consent of the man, the eunuch puts the whole lingam into his mouth, and presses

it to the very end, as if he were going to swallow it up, it is called "swallowing up".

Striking, scratching, and other things may also be done during this kind of congress.

The Auparishtaka is practised also by unchaste and wanton women, female attendants and serving maids, i.e., those who are not married to any body, but who live by shampooing.

The Acharyas (i.e., ancient and venerable authors) are of opinion that this Auparishtaka is the work of a dog and not of a man, because it is a low practice, and opposed to the orders of the Holy Writ, and because the man himself suffers by bringing his lingam into contact with the mouths of eunuchs and women. But Vatsyayana says that the orders of the Holy Writ do not affect those who resort to courtesans, and the law prohibits the practice of the Auparishtaka with married women only. As regards the injury to the male, that can be easily remedied.

The people of Eastern India do not resort to women who practise the Auparishtaka.

The people of Ahichhatra resort to such women, but do nothing with them, so far as the mouth is concerned.

The people of Saketa do with these women every kind of mouth congress, while the people of Nagara do not practise this, but do every other thing.

The people of the Shurasena country, on the southern bank of the Jumna, do everything without any hesitation, for they say that women being naturally unclean, no one can be certain about their character, their purity, their conduct, their practices, their confidences, or their speech. They are not however on this account to be abandoned, because religious law, on the authority of which they are reckoned pure, lays down that the udder of a cow is clean at the time of milking, though the mouth of a cow, and also the mouth of her calf, are considered unclean by the Hindoos. Again a dog is clean when he seizes a deer in hunting, though food touched by a dog is otherwise considered very unclean. A bird is clean when it causes a fruit to fall from a tree by pecking at it, though things eaten by crows and other birds are considered unclean. And the mouth of a woman is clean for kissing and such like things at the time of sexual intercourse. Vatsyayana moreover thinks that in all these things connected with love, everybody should act according to the custom of his country, and his own inclination.

There are also the following verses on the subject.

"The male servants of some men carry on the mouth congress with their masters. It is also practised by some citizens, who know each other well, among themselves. Some women of the harem, when they are amorous, do the acts of the mouth on the yonis of one another, and some men do the same thing with women. The way of doing this (i.e., of kissing the yoni) should be known from kissing the mouth. When a man and woman lie down in an inverted order, i.e., with the head of the one towards the feet of the other and carry on this congress, it is called the "congress of a crow".

For the sake of such things courtesans abandon men possessed of good qualities, liberal and clever, and become attached to low persons, such as slaves and elephant drivers. The Auparishtaka, or mouth congress, should never be done by a learned Brahman, by a minister that carries on the business of a state, or by a man of good reputation, because though the practice is allowed by the Shastras, there is no reason why it should be carried on, and need only be practised in particular cases. As for instance, the taste, and the strength, and the digestive qualities of the flesh of dogs are mentioned in works on medicine, but it does not therefore follow that it should be eaten by the wise. In the same way there are some men, some places and some times, with respect to which these practices can be made use of. A man should therefore pay regard to the place, to the time, and to the practice which is to be carried out, as also as to whether it is agreeable to his nature and to himself, and then he may or may not practise these things according to circumstances. But after all, these things being done secretly, and the mind of the man being fickle, how can it be known what any person will do at any particular time and for any particular purpose.

CHAPTER X

*Of the Way How to Begin and How to End the Congress
Different Kinds of Congress and Love Quarrels*

IN the pleasure-room, decorated with flowers, and fragrant
with perfumes, attended by his friends and servants, the
citizen should receive the woman, who will come bathed and
dressed, and will invite her to take refreshment and to drink
freely. He should then seat her on his left side, and holding
her hair, and touching also the end and knot of her garment,
he should gently embrace her with his right arm. They
should then carry on an amusing conversation on various
subjects, and may also talk suggestively of things which
would be considered as coarse, or not to be mentioned
generally in society. They may then sing, either with or
without gesticulations, and play on musical instruments, talk
about the arts, and persuade each other to drink. At last
when the woman is overcome with love and desire, the
citizen should dismiss the people that may be with him,
giving them flowers, ointments, and betel leaves, and then
when the two are left alone, they should proceed as has been
already described in the previous chapters.

Such is the beginning of sexual union. At the end of the
congress, the lovers with modesty, and not looking at each
other, should go separately to the washing-room. After this,
sitting in their own places, they should eat some betel leaves,
and the citizen should apply with his own hand to the body
of the woman some pure sandal wood ointment, or ointment
of some other kind. He should then embrace her with his
left arm, and with agreeable words should cause her to drink
from a cup held in his own hand, or he may give her water
to drink. They can then eat sweetmeats, or anything else,
according to their likings, and may drink fresh juice,* soup,

* The fresh juice of the cocoa nut tree, the date tree, and other kinds of
palm trees are drunk in India. It will not keep fresh very long, but ferments
rapidly, and is then distilled into liquor.

gruel, extracts of meat, sherbet, the juice of mangoe fruits, the extract of the juice of the citron tree mixed with sugar, or anything that may be liked in different countries, and known to be sweet, soft, and pure. The lovers may also sit on the terrace of the palace or house, and enjoy the moonlight, and carry on an agreeable conversation. At this time, too, while the woman lies in his lap, with her face towards the moon, the citizen should show her the different planets, the morning star, the polar star, and the seven Rishis, or Great Bear.

This is the end of sexual union.

Congress is of the following kinds, viz.:

> Loving congress.
> Congress of subsequent love
> Congress of artificial love
> Congress of transferred love
> Congress like that of eunuchs
> Deceitful congress
> Congress of spontaneous love

(1) When a man and a woman, who have been in love with each other for some time, come together with great difficulty, or when one of the two returns from a journey, or is reconciled after having been separated on account of a quarrel, then congress is called the "loving congress". It is carried on according to the liking of the lovers, and as long as they choose.

(2) When two persons come together, while their love for each other is still in its infancy, their congress is called the "congress of subsequent love".

(3) When a man carries on the congress by exciting himself by means of the sixty-four ways, such as kissing, etc., etc., or when a man and a woman come together, though in reality they are both attached to different persons, their congress is then called "congress of artificial love". At this time all the ways and means mentioned in the Kama Shastra should be used.

(4) When a man, from the beginning to the end of the congress, though having connection with the woman, thinks all

the time that he is enjoying another one whom he loves, it is called the "congress of transferred love".

(5) Congress between a man and a female water carrier, or a female servant of a caste lower than his own, lasting only until the desire is satisfied, is called "congress like that of eunuchs". Here external touches, kisses, and manipulations are not to be employed.

(6) The congress between a courtesan and a rustic, and that between citizens and the women of villages, and bordering countries, is called "deceitful congress".

(7) The congress that takes place between two persons who are attached to one another, and which is done according to their own liking is called "spontaneous congress".

Thus ends the kinds of congress.

We shall now speak of love quarrels.

A woman who is very much in love with a man cannot bear to hear the name of her rival mentioned, or to have any conversation regarding her, or to be addressed by her name through mistake. If such takes place, a great quarrel arises, and the woman cries, becomes angry, tosses her hair about, strikes her lover, falls from her bed or seat, and, casting aside her garlands and ornaments, throws herself down on the ground.

At this time, the lover should attempt to reconcile her with conciliatory words, and should take her up carefully and place her on her bed. But she, not replying to his questions, and with increased anger, should bend down his head by pulling his hair, and having kicked him once, twice, or thrice on his arms, head, bosom or back, should then proceed to the door of the room. Dattaka says that she should then sit angrily near the door and shed tears, but should not go out, because she would be found fault with for going away. After a time, when she thinks that the conciliatory words and actions of her lover have reached their utmost, she should then embrace him, talking to him with harsh and reproachful words, but at the same time showing a loving desire for congress.

When the woman is in her own house, and has quarrelled with her lover, she should go to him and show how angry she is, and leave him. Afterwards the citizen having sent the Vita,* the Vidushaka* or the Pithamurda* to pacify her, she should accompany them back to the house, and spend the night with her lover.

Thus end the love quarrels.

In conclusion.

A man, employing the sixty-four means mentioned by Babhravya, obtains his object, and enjoys the woman of the first quality. Though he may speak well on other subjects, if he does not know the sixty-four divisions, no great respect is paid to him in the assembly of the learned. A man, devoid of other knowledge, but well acquainted with the sixty-four divisions, becomes a leader in any society of men and women. What man will not respect the sixty-four parts,† considering they are respected by the learned, by the cunning, and by the courtezans. As the sixty-four parts are respected, are charming, and add to the talent of women, they are called by the Acharyas dear to women. A man skilled in the sixty-four parts is looked upon with love by his own wife, by the wives of others, and by courtesans.

END OF PART II

* The characteristics of these three individuals have been given in Part I., pages 109-110.

† A definition of the sixty-four parts, or divisions, is given in Chapter II., page 123.

PART III

ABOUT THE ACQUISITION OF A WIFE

CHAPTER I

On Marriage

WHEN a girl of the same caste, and a virgin, is married in accordance with the precepts of Holy Writ, the results of such an union are: the acquisition of Dharma and Artha, offspring, affinity, increase of friends, and untarnished love. For this reason a man should fix his affections upon a girl who is of good family, whose parents are alive, and who is three years or more younger than himself. She should be born of a highly respectable family, possessed of wealth, well connected, and with many relations and friends. She should also be beautiful, of a good disposition, with lucky marks on her body, and with good hair, nails, teeth, ears, eyes, and breasts, neither more nor less than they ought to be, and no one of them entirely wanting, and not troubled with a sickly body. The man should, of course, also possess these qualities himself. But at all events, says Ghotakamukha, a girl who has been already joined with others (i.e., no longer a maiden) should never be loved, for it would be reproachable to do such a thing.

Now in order to bring about a marriage with such a girl as described above, the parents and relations of the man should exert themselves, as also such friends on both sides as may be desired to assist in the matter. These friends should bring to the notice of the girl's parents, the faults, both present and future, of all the other men that may wish to marry her, and should at the same time extol even to exaggeration all the excellencies, ancestral and paternal, of their friend, so as to endear him to them, and particularly to those that may be liked by the girl's mother. One of the friends should also disguise himself as an astrologer, and declare the future good fortune and wealth of his friend by showing the existence of all the lucky omens* and signs,† the good influence of planets, the auspicious entrance of the sun into a sign of the Zodiac, propitious stars and fortunate marks on his body. Others again should rouse the jealousy of the girl's mother by telling her that their friend has a chance of getting from some other quarter even a better girl than hers.

A girl should be taken as a wife, as also given in marriage, when fortune, signs, omens, and the words‡ of others are favourable, for, says Ghotakamukha, a man should not marry at any time he likes. A girl who is asleep, crying, or gone out of the house when sought in marriage, or who is betrothed to another, should not be married. The following also should be avoided:

One who is kept concealed
One who has an ill-sounding name
One who has her nose depressed
One who has her nostril turned up
One who is formed like a male
One who is bent down
One who has crooked thighs
One who has a projecting forehead
One who has a bald head
One who does not like purity
One who has been polluted by another
One who is affected with the Gulma§
One who is disfigured in any way
One who has fully arrived at puberty
One who is a friend
One who is a younger sister

* The flight of a blue jay on a person's left side is considered a lucky omen when one starts on any business; the appearance of a cat before anyone at such a time is looked on as a bad omen. There are many omens of the same kind.

† Such as the throbbing of the right eye of men and the left eye of women, etc.

‡ Before anything is begun it is a custom to go early in the morning to a neighbour's house, and overhear the first words that may be spoken in his family, and according as the words heard are of good or bad import, so draw an inference as to the success or failure of the undertaking.

§ A disease consisting of any glandular enlargement in any part of the body.

One who is a Varshakari*

In the same way a girl who is called by the name of one of the twenty-seven stars, or by the name of a tree, or of a river, is considered worthless, as also a girl whose name ends in "r" or "l". But some authors say that prosperity is gained only by marrying that girl to whom one becomes attached, and that therefore no other girl but the one who is loved should be married by anyone.

When a girl becomes marriageable her parents should dress her smartly, and should place her where she can be easily seen by all. Every afternoon, having dressed her and decorated her in a becoming manner, they should send her with her female companions to sports, sacrifices, and marriage ceremonies, and thus show her to advantage in society, because she is a kind of merchandise. They should also receive with kind words and signs of friendliness those of an auspicious appearance who may come accompanied by their friends and relations for the purpose of marrying their daughter, and under some pretext or other having first dressed her becomingly, should then present her to them. After this they should await the pleasure of fortune, and with this object should appoint a future day on which a determination could be come to with regard to their daughter's marriage. On this occasion when the persons have come, the parents of the girl should ask them to bathe and dine, and should say, "Everything will take place at the proper time", and should not then comply with the request, but should settle the matter later.

When a girl is thus acquired, either according to the custom of the country, or according to his own desire, the man should marry her in accordance with the precepts of the Holy Writ, according to one of the four kinds of marriage.

Thus ends marriage.

There are also some verses on the subject as follows:

"Amusement in society, such as completing verses begun by others, marriages, and auspicious ceremonies should be carried on neither with superiors, nor inferiors, but with our

* A woman, the palms of whose hands and the soles of whose feet are always perspiring.

equals. That should be known as a high connection when a man, after marrying a girl, has to serve her and her relations afterwards like a servant, and such a connection is censured by the good. On the other hand, that reproachable connection, where a man, together with his relations, lords it over his wife, is called a low connection by the wise. But when both the man and the women afford mutual pleasure to each other, and when the relatives on both sides pay respect to one another, such is called a connection in the proper sense of the word. Therefore a man should contract neither a high connection by which he is obliged to bow down afterwards to his kinsmen, nor a low connection, which is universally reprehended by all."

CHAPTER II

Of Creating Confidence in the Girl

FOR the first three days after marriage, the girl and her husband should sleep on the floor, abstain from sexual pleasures, and eat their food without seasoning it either with alkali or salt. For the next seven days they should bathe amidst the sounds of auspicious musical instruments, should decorate themselves, dine together, and pay attention to their relations as well as to those who may have come to witness their marriage. This is applicable to persons of all castes. On the night of the tenth day the man should begin in a lonely place with soft words, and thus create confidence in the girl. Some authors say that for the purpose of winning her over he should not speak to her for three days, but the followers of Babhravya are of opinion that if the man does not speak with her for three days, the girl may be discouraged by seeing him spiritless like a pillar, and, becoming dejected, she may begin to despise him as an eunuch. Vatsyayana says that the man should begin to win her over, and to create confidence in her, but should abstain at first from sexual pleasures. Women being of a tender nature, want tender beginnings, and when they are forcibly approached by men with whom they are but slightly acquainted, they sometimes suddenly become haters of sexual connection, and sometimes even haters of the male sex. The man should therefore approach the girl according to her liking, and should make use of those devices by which he may be able to establish himself more and more into her confidence. These devices are as follows:

He should embrace her first of all in a way she likes most, because it does not last for a long time.

He should embrace her with the upper part of his body because that is easier and simpler. If the girl is grown up, or if the man has known her for some time, he may embrace her by the light of a lamp, but if he is not well acquainted with her, or if she is a young girl, he should then embrace her in darkness.

When the girl accepts the embrace, the man should put a "tambula" or screw of betel nut and betel leaves in her mouth, and if she will not take it, he should induce her to do so by conciliatory words, entreaties, oaths, and kneeling at her feet, for it is an universal rule that however bashful or angry a woman may be, she never disregards a man's kneeling at her feet. At the time of giving this "tambula" he should kiss her mouth softly and gracefully without making any sound. When she is gained over in this respect he should then make her talk, and so that she may be induced to talk he should ask her questions about things of which he knows or pretends to know nothing, and which can be answered in a few words. If she does not speak to him, he should not frighten her, but should ask her the same thing again and again in a conciliatory manner. If she does not then speak he should urge her to give a reply, because as Ghotakamukha says, "All girls hear everything said to them by men, but do not themselves sometimes say a single word". When she is thus importuned, the girl should give replies by shakes of the head, but if she quarrelled with the man she should not even do that. When she is asked by the man whether she wishes for him, and whether she likes him, she should remain silent for a long time, and when at last importuned to reply, should give him a favourable answer by a nod of her head. If the man is previously acquainted with the girl he should converse with her by means of a female friend, who may be favourable to him, and in the confidence of both, and carry on the conversation on both sides. On such an occasion the girl should smile with her head bent down, and if the female friend say more on her part than she was desired to do, she should chide her and dispute with her. The female friend should say in jest even what she is not desired to say by the girl, and add, "She says so", on which the girl should say indistinctly and prettily, "Oh no! I did not say so", and she should then smile and throw an occasional glance towards the man.

If the girl is familiar with the man, she should place near him, without saying anything, the tambula, the ointment, or the garland that he may have asked for, or she may tie them up in his upper garment. While she is engaged in this, the man should touch her young breasts in the sounding way of pressing with the nails, and if she prevents him doing this he should say to her, "I will not do it again if you will embrace me", and should in this way cause her to embrace him. While he is being embraced by her he should pass his hand repeatedly over and about her body. By and bye he should place her in his lap, and try more and more to gain her consent, and if she will not yield to him he should frighten her by saying, "I shall impress marks of my teeth and nails on your lips and breasts, and then make similar marks on my own body, and shall tell my friends that you did them. What will you say then?" In this and other ways, as fear and confidence are created in the minds of children, so should the man gain her over to his wishes.

On the second and third nights, after her confidence has increased still more, he should feel the whole of her body with his hands, and kiss her all over; he should also place his hands upon her thighs and shampoo them, and if he succeed in this he should then shampoo the joints of her thighs. If she tries to prevent him doing this he should say to her, "What harm is there in doing it?" and should persuade her to let him do it. After gaining this point he should touch her private parts, should loosen her girdle and the knot of her dress, and turning up her lower garment should shampoo the joints of her naked thighs. Under various pretences he should do all these things, but he should not at that time begin actual congress. After this he should teach her the sixty-four arts, should tell her how much he loves her, and describe to her the hopes which he formerly entertained regarding her. He should also promise to be faithful to her in future, and should dispel all her fears with respect to rival women, and, at last, after having overcome her bashfulness, he should begin to enjoy her in a way so as not to frighten her. So much about creating confidence in the girl; and there are, moreover, some verses on the subject as follows:

"A man acting according to the inclinations of a girl should try and gain her over so that she may love him and place her confidence in him. A man does not succeed either by implicitly following the inclination of a girl, or by wholly opposing her, and he should therefore adopt a middle course. He who knows how to make himself beloved by women, as well as to increase their honour and create confidence in them, this man becomes an object of their love. But he, who neglects a girl thinking she is too bashful, is despised by her as a beast ignorant of the working of the female mind. Moreover, a girl forcibly enjoyed by one who does not understand the hearts of girls becomes nervous, uneasy and dejected, and suddenly begins to hate the man who has taken advantage of her; and then, when her love is not understood or returned, she sinks into despondency, and becomes either a hater of mankind altogether, or, hating her own man, she has recourse to other men."*

* These last few lines have been exemplified in many ways in many novels of this century.

CHAPTER III

On Courtship, and the Manifestation of the Feelings by Outward Signs and Deeds

A POOR man possessed of good qualities, a man born of a low family possessed of mediocre qualities, a neighbour possessed of wealth, and one under the control of his father, mother or brothers, should not marry without endeavouring to gain over the girl from her childhood to love and esteem them. Thus a boy separated from his parents, and living in the house of his uncle, should try to gain over the daughter of his uncle, or some other girl, even though she be previously betrothed to another. And this way of gaining over a girl, says Ghotakamukha, is unexceptional, because Dharma can be accomplished by means of it, as well as by any other way of marriage.

When a boy has thus begun to woo the girl he loves, he should spend his time with her and amuse her with various games and diversions fitted for their age and acquaintanceship, such as picking and collecting flowers, making garlands of flowers, playing the parts of members of a fictitious family, cooking food, playing with dice, playing with cards, the game of odd and even, the game of finding out the middle finger, the game of six pebbles, and such other games as may be prevalent in the country, and agreeable to the disposition of the girl. In addition to this, he should carry on various amusing games played by several persons together, such as hide and seek, playing with seeds, hiding things in several small heaps of wheat and looking for them, blindman's buff, gymnastic exercises, and other games of the same sort, in company with the girl, her friends and female attendants. The man should also show great kindness to any woman whom the girl thinks fit to be trusted, and should also make new acquaintances, but above all he should attach to himself by kindness and little services the daughter of the girl's nurse, for if she be gained over, even though she comes to know of his design, she does not cause any obstruction, but is sometimes even able to effect an union between him and the girl. And though she knows the true character of the man, she always talks of his many excellent qualities to the parents and relations of the girl, even though she may not be desired to do so by him.

In this way the man should do whatever the girl takes most delight in, and he should get for her whatever she may have a desire to possess. Thus he should procure for her such playthings as may be hardly known to other girls. He may also show her a ball dyed with various colours, and other curiosities of the same sort; and should give her dolls made of cloth, wood, buffalo-horn, ivory, wax, flour, or earth; also utensils for cooking food, and figures in wood, such as a man and woman standing, a pair of rams, or goats, or sheep; also temples made of earth, bamboo, or wood, dedicated to various goddesses; and cages for parrots, cuckoos, starlings, quails, cocks, and partridges; water-vessels of different sorts and of elegant forms, machines for throwing water about, guitars, stands for putting images upon, stools, lac, red arsenic, yellow ointment, vermilion and collyrium, as well as sandal-wood, saffron, betel nut and betel leaves. Such things should be given at different times whenever he gets a good opportunity of meeting her, and some of them should be given in private, and some in public, according to circumstances. In short, he should try in every way to make her look upon him as one who would do for her everything that she wanted to be done.

In the next place he should get her to meet him in some place privately, and should then tell her that the reason of his giving presents to her in secret was the fear that the parents of both of them might be displeased, and then he may add that the things which he had given her had been much desired by other people. When her love begins to show signs of increasing he should relate to her agreeable stories if she expresses a wish to hear such narratives. Or if she takes delight in legerdemain, he should amaze her by performing various tricks of jugglery; or if she feels a great curiosity to see a performance of the various arts, he should show his own skill in them. When she is delighted with singing he should entertain her with music, and on certain days, and at the time of going together to moonlight fairs and festivals, and at the time of her return after being absent from home, he should present her with bouquets of flowers, and with chaplets for the head, and with ear ornaments and rings, for these are the proper occasions on which such things should be presented.

He should also teach the daughter of the girl's nurse all the sixty-four means of pleasure practised by men, and under this pretext should also inform her of his great skill in the art of sexual enjoyment. All this time he should wear a fine dress, and make as good an appearance as possible, for young women love men who live with them, and who are handsome, good looking and well dressed. As for the sayings that though women may fall in love, they still make no effort themselves to gain over the object of their affections, that is only a matter of idle talk.

Now a girl always shows her love by outward signs and actions, such as the following: she never looks the man in the face, and becomes abashed when she is looked at by him; under some pretext or other she shows her limbs to him; she looks secretly at him though he has gone away from her side; hangs down her head when she is asked some question by him, and answers in indistinct words and unfinished sentences, delights to be in his company for a long time, speaks to her attendants in a peculiar tone with the hope of attracting his attention towards her when she is at a distance from him, does not wish to go from the place where he is, under some pretext or other she makes him look at different things, narrates to him tales and stories very slowly so that she may continue conversing with him for a long time, kisses and embraces before him a child sitting in her lap, draws ornamental marks on the foreheads of her female servants, performs sportive and graceful movements when her attendants speak jestingly to her in the presence of her lover, confides in her lover's friends, and respects and obeys them, shows kindness to his servants, converses with them, and engages them to do her work as if she were their mistress, and listens attentively to them when they tell stories about her lover to somebody else, enters his house when induced to do so by the daughter of her nurse, and by her assistance manages to converse and play with him, avoids being seen by her lover when she is not dressed and decorated, gives him by the hand of her female friend her ear ornament, ring, or garland of flowers that he may have asked to see, always wears anything that he may have presented to her, become dejected when any other bridegroom is mentioned by her parents, and does not mix with those who may be of his party, or who may support his claims.

There are also some verses on the subject as follows:

"A man, who has seen and perceived the feelings of the girl towards him, and who has noticed the outward signs and movements by which those feelings are expressed, should do everything in his power to effect an union with her. He should gain over a young girl by childlike sports, a damsel come of age by his skill in the arts, and a girl that loves him by having recourse to persons in whom she confides."

CHAPTER IV

About things to be done only by the Man, and the Acquisition of the Girl thereby. Also what is to be done by a Girl to gain over a Man, and subject him to her

Now when the girl begins to show her love by outward signs and motions, as described in the last chapter, the lover should try to gain her over entirely by various ways and means, such as the following:

When engaged with her in any game or sport he should intentionally hold her hand. He should practise upon her the various kinds of embraces, such as the touching embrace, and others already described in a preceding chapter (Part II, Chapter 2). He should show her a pair of human beings cut out of the leaf of a tree, and such like things, at intervals. When engaged in water sports, he should dive at a distance from her, and come up close to her. He should show an increased liking for the new foliage of trees and such like things. He should describe to her the pangs he suffers on her account. He should relate to her the beautiful dream that he has had with reference to other women. At parties and assemblies of his caste he should sit near her, and touch her under some pretence or other, and having placed his foot upon hers, he should slowly touch each of her toes, and press the ends of the nails; if successful in this, he should get hold of her foot with his hand and repeat the same thing. He should also press a finger of her hand between his toes when she happens to be washing his feet; and whenever he gives anything to her or takes anything from her, he should show her by his manner and look how much he loves her.

He should sprinkle upon her the water brought for rinsing his mouth; and when alone with her in a lonely place, or in darkness, he should make love to her, and tell her the true state of his mind without distressing her in any way.

Whenever he sits with her on the same seat or bed he should say to her, "I have something to tell you in private", and then, when she comes to hear it in a quiet place, he should express his love to her more by manner and signs than by words. When he comes to know the state of her feelings towards him he should pretend to be ill, and should make her come to his house to speak to him. There he should intentionally hold her hand and place it on his eyes and forehead, and under the pretence of preparing some medicine for him he should ask her to do the work for his sake in the following words: "This work must be done by you, and by nobody else". When she wants to go away he should let her go, with an earnest request to come and see him again. This device of illness should be continued for three days and three nights. After this, when she begins coming to see him frequently, he should carry on long conversations with her, for, says Ghotakamukha, "though a man loves a girl ever so much, he never succeeds in winning her without a great deal of talking". At last, when the man finds the girl completely gained over, he may then begin to enjoy her. As for the saying that women grow less timid than usual during the evening, and in darkness, and are desirous of congress at those times, and do not oppose men then, and should only be enjoyed at these hours, it is a matter of talk only.

When it is impossible for the man to carry on his endeavours alone, he should, by means of the daughter of her nurse, or of a female friend in whom she confides, cause the girl to be brought to him without making known to her his design, and he should then proceed with her in the manner above described. Or he should in the beginning send his own female servant to live with the girl as her friend, and should then gain her over by her means.

At last, when he knows the state of her feelings by her outward manner and conduct towards him at religious ceremonies, marriage ceremonies, fairs, festivals, theatres, public assemblies, and such like occasions, he should begin to enjoy her when she is alone, for Vatsyayana lays it down, that women, when resorted to at proper times and in proper places, do not turn away from their lovers.

When a girl, possessed of good qualities and well-bred, though born in a humble family, or destitute of wealth, and not therefore desired by her equals, or an orphan girl, or one deprived of her parents, but observing the rules of her family and caste, should wish to bring about her own marriage when she comes of age, such a girl should endeavour to gain over a strong and good looking young man, or a person whom she thinks would marry her on account of the weakness of his mind, and even without the consent of his parents. She should do this by such means as would endear her to the said person, as well as by frequently seeing and meeting him. Her mother also should constantly cause them to meet by means of her female friends, and the daughter of her nurse. The girl herself should try to get alone with her beloved in some quiet place, and at odd times should give him flowers, betel nut, betel leaves and perfumes. She should also show her skill in the practice of the arts, in shampooing, in scratching and in pressing with the nails. She should also talk to him on the subjects he likes best, and discuss with him the ways and means of gaining over and winning the affections of a girl.

But old authors say that although the girl loves the man ever so much, she should not offer herself, or make the first overtures, for a girl who does this loses her dignity, and is liable to be scorned and rejected. But when the man shows his wish to enjoy her, she should be favourable to him and should show no change in her demeanour when he embraces her, and should receive all the manifestations of his love as if she were ignorant of the state of his mind. But when he tries to kiss her she should oppose him; when he begs to be allowed to have sexual intercourse with her she should let him touch her private parts only and with considerable difficulty; and though importuned by him, she should not yield herself up to him as if of her own accord, but should resist his attempts to have her. It is only, moreover, when she is certain that she is truly loved, and that her lover is indeed devoted to her, and will not change his mind, that she should then give herself up to him, and persuade him to marry her quickly. After losing her virginity she should tell her confidential friends about it.

Here ends the efforts of a girl to gain over a man.

There are also some verses on the subject as follows:

"A girl who is much sought after should marry the man that she likes, and whom she thinks would be obedient to her, and capable of giving her pleasure. But when from the desire of wealth a girl is married by her parents to a rich man without taking into consideration the character or looks of the bridegroom, or when given to a man who has several wives, she never becomes attached to the man, even though he be endowed with good qualities, obedient to her will, active, strong and healthy, and anxious to please her in every way.* A husband who is obedient but yet master of himself, though he be poor and not good looking, is better than one who is common to many women, even though he be handsome and attractive. The wives of rich men, where there are many wives, are not generally attached to their husbands, and are not confidential with them, and even though they possess all the external enjoyments of life, still have recourse to other men. A man who is of a low

---

* There is a good deal of truth in the last few observations. Woman is a monogamous animal, and loves but one, and likes to feel herself alone in the affections of one man, and cannot bear rivals. It may also be taken as a general rule that women either married to, or kept by, rich men love them for their wealth, but not for themselves.

mind, who has fallen from his social position, and who is much given to travelling, does not deserve to be married; neither does one who has many wives and children, or one who is devoted to sport and gambling, and who comes to his wife only when he likes. Of all the lovers of a girl he only is her true husband who possesses the qualities that are liked by her, and such a husband only enjoys real superiority over her, because he is the husband of love."

CHAPTER V

On Certain Forms of Marriage*

WHEN a girl cannot meet her lover frequently in private, she should send the daughter of her nurse to him, it being understood that she has confidence in her, and had previously gained her over to her interests. On seeing the man, the daughter of the nurse should, in the course of conversation, describe to him the noble birth, the good disposition, the beauty, talent, skill, knowledge of human nature and affection of the girl in such a way as not to let him suppose that she had been sent by the girl, and should thus create affection for the girl in the heart of the man. To the girl also she should speak about the excellent qualities of the man, especially of those qualities which she knows are pleasing to the girl. She should, moreover, speak with disparagement of the other lovers of the girl, and talk about the avarice and indiscretion of their parents, and the fickleness of their relations. She should also quote samples of many girls of ancient times, such as Sakuntala and others, who, having united themselves with lovers of their own caste and their own choice, were ever happy afterwards in their society. And she should also tell of other girls who married into great families, and being troubled by

* These forms of marriage differ from the four kinds of marriage mentioned in Chapter I., and are only to be made use of when the girl is gained over in the way mentioned in Chapters III. and IV.

rival wives, became wretched and miserable, and were finally abandoned. She should further speak of the good fortune, the continual happiness, the chastity, obedience, and affection of the man, and if the girl gets amorous about him, she should endeavour to allay her shame* and her fear as well as her suspicions about any disaster that might result from her marriage. In a word, she should act the whole part of a female messenger by telling the girl all about the man's affection for her, the places he frequented, and the endeavours he made to meet her, and by frequently repeating, "It will be all right if the man will take you away forcibly and unexpectedly".

The Forms of Marriage

When the girl is gained over, and acts openly with the man as his wife, he should cause fire to be brought from the house of a Brahman, and having spread the Kusha grass upon the ground, and offered an oblation to the fire, he should marry her according to the precepts of the religious law. After this he should inform his parents of the fact, because it is the opinion of ancient authors that a marriage solemnly contracted in the presence of fire cannot afterwards be set aside.

After the consummation of the marriage, the relations of the man should gradually be made acquainted with the affair, and the relations of the girl should also be apprised of it in such a way that they may consent to the marriage, and overlook the manner in which it was brought about, and when this is done they should afterwards be reconciled by affectionate presents and favourable conduct. In this manner the man should marry the girl according to the Gandharva form of marriage.

When the girl cannot make up her mind, or will not express her readiness to marry, the man should obtain her in any one of the following ways:

* About this, see a story on the fatal effects of love at page 114 of *Early Ideas; a Group of Hindoo Stories,* collected and collated by Anaryan. W. H. Allen and Co., London, 1881.

(1) On a fitting occasion, and under some excuse, he should, by means of a female friend with whom he is well acquainted, and whom he can trust, and who also is well known to the girl's family, get the girl brought unexpectedly to his house, and he should then bring fire from the house of a Brahman, and proceed as before described.

(2) When the marriage of the girl with some other person draws near, the man should disparage the future husband to the utmost in the mind of the mother of the girl, and then having got the girl to come with her mother's consent to a neighbouring house, he should bring fire from the house of a Brahman, and proceed as above.

(3) The man should become a great friend of the brother of the girl, the said brother being of the same age as himself, and addicted to courtesans, and to intrigues with the wives of other people, and should give him assistance in such matters, and also give him occasional presents. He should then tell him about his great love for his sister, as young men will sacrifice even their lives for the sake of those who may be of the same age, habits, and dispositions as themselves. After this the man should get the girl brought by means of her brother to some secure place, and having brought fire from the house of a Brahman should proceed as before.

(4) The man should on the occasion of festivals get the daughter of the nurse to give the girl some intoxicating substance, and then cause her to be brought to some secure place under the pretence of some business, and there having enjoyed her before she recovers from her intoxication, should bring fire from the house of a Brahman, and proceed as before.

(5) The man should, with the connivance of the daughter of the nurse, carry off the girl from her house while she is asleep, and then, having enjoyed her before she recovers from her sleep, should bring fire from the house of a Brahman, and proceed as before.

(6) When the girl goes to a garden, or to some village in the neighbourhood, the man should, with his friends, fall on her guards, and having killed them, or frightened them away, forcibly carry her off, and proceed as before.

There are verses on this subject as follows:

"In all the forms of marriage given in this chapter of this work, the one that precedes is better than the one that follows it, on account of its being more in accordance with the commands of religion, and therefore it is only when it is impossible to carry the former into practice that the latter should be resorted to. As the fruit of all good marriages is love, the Gandharva* form of marriage is respected, even though it is formed under unfavourable circumstances because it fulfils the object sought for. Another cause of the respect accorded to the Gandharva form of marriage is, that it brings forth happiness, causes less trouble in its performance than the other forms of marriage, and is above all the result of previous love."

* About the Gandharvavivaha form of marriage, see note to page 28 of Captain R. F. Burton's *Vickram and the Vampire; or Tales of Hindu Devilry.* Longmans, Green & Co., London, 1870. This form of matrimony was recognised by the ancient Hindus, and is frequent in books. It is a kind of Scotch Wedding—ultra-Caledonian—taking place by mutual consent without any form or ceremony. The Gandharvas are heavenly minstrels of Indra's court, who are supposed to be witnesses.

END OF PART III

PART IV

ABOUT A WIFE

CHAPTER I

On the Manner of Living of a Virtuous Woman, and of Her Behaviour During the Absence of Her Husband

A VIRTUOUS woman, who has affection for her husband, should act in conformity with his wishes as if he were a divine being, and with his consent should take upon herself the whole care of his family. She should keep the whole house well cleaned, and arrange flowers of various kinds in different parts of it, and make the floor smooth and polished so as to give the whole a neat and becoming appearance. She should surround the house with a garden, and place ready in it all the materials required for the morning, noon and evening sacrifices. Moreover she should herself revere the sanctuary of the Household Gods, for says Gonardiya,

"Nothing so much attracts the heart of a householder to his wife as a careful observance of the things mentioned above".

Towards the parents, relations, friends, sisters, and servants of her husband she should behave as they deserve. In the garden she should plant beds of green vegetables, bunches of the sugar cane, and clumps of the fig tree, the mustard plant, the parsley plant, the fennel plant, and the xanthochymus pictorius. Clusters of various flowers such as the trapa bispinosa, the jasmine, the gasminum grandiflorum, the yellow amaranth, the wild jasmine, the tabernamontana coronaria, the nadyaworta, the china rose and others, should likewise be planted, together with the fragrant grass andropogon schœnanthus, and the fragrant root of the plant andropogon miricatus. She should also have seats and arbours made in the garden, in the middle of which a well, tank, or pool should be dug.

The wife should always avoid the company of female beggars, female buddhist mendicants, unchaste and roguish women, female fortune tellers and witches. As regards meals she should always consider what her husband likes and dislikes, and what things are good for him, and what are injurious to him. When she hears the sounds of his footsteps coming home she should at once get up, and be ready to do whatever he may command her, and either order her female servant to wash his feet, or wash them herself. When going anywhere with her husband, she should put on her ornaments, and without his consent she should not either give or accept invitations, or attend marriages and sacrifices, or sit in the company of female friends, or visit the temples of the Gods. And if she wants to engage in any kind of games or sports, she should not do it against his will. In the same way she should always sit down after him, and get up before him, and should never awaken him when he is asleep. The kitchen should be situated in a quiet and retired place, so as not to be accessible to strangers, and should always look clean.

In the event of any misconduct on the part of her husband, she should not blame him excessively, though she be a little displeased. She should not use abusive language towards him, but rebuke him with conciliatory words, whether he be in the company of friends or alone. Moreover, she should not be a scold, for says Gonordiya, "there is no cause of dislike on the part of a husband so great as this characteristic in a wife". Lastly she should avoid bad expressions, sulky looks, speaking aside, standing in the doorway, and looking at passers-by, conversing in the pleasure groves, and remaining in a lonely place for a long time; and finally she should always keep her body, her teeth, her hair and everything belonging to her tidy, sweet, and clean.

When the wife wants to approach her husband in private her dress should consist of many ornaments, various kinds of flowers, and a cloth decorated with different colours, and some sweet-smelling ointments or unguents. But her everyday dress should be composed of a thin, close-textured cloth, a few ornaments and flowers, and a little scent, not too much. She should also observe the fasts and vows of her husband, and when he tries to prevent her doing this, she should persuade him to let her do it.

At appropriate times of the year, and when they happen to be cheap, she should buy earth, bamboos, firewood, skins, and iron pots, as also salt and oil. Fragrant substances, vessels made of the fruit of the plant wrightea anti-dysenterica, or oval leaved wrightea, medicines, and other things which are always wanted, should be obtained when required and kept in a secret place of the house. The seeds of the radish, the potato, the common beet, the Indian wormwood, the mangoe, the cucumber, the egg plant, the kushmanda, the pumpkin gourd, the surana, the bignonia indica, the sandal wood, the premna spinosa, the garlic plant, the onion, and other vegetables, should be bought and sown at the proper seasons.

The wife, moreover, should not tell to strangers, the amount of her wealth, nor the secrets which her husband has confided to her. She should surpass all the women of her own rank in life in her cleverness, her appearance, her knowledge of cookery, her pride, and her manner of serving her husband. The expenditure of the year should be regulated by the profits. The milk that remains after the meals should be turned into ghee or clarified butter. Oil and sugar should be prepared at home; spinning and weaving should also be done there; and a store of ropes and cords, and barks of trees for twisting into ropes should be kept. She should also attend to the pounding and cleaning of rice, using its small grain and chaff in some way or other. She should pay the salaries of the servants, look after the tilling of the fields, and keeping of the flocks and herds, super-intend the making of vehicles, and take care of the rams, cocks, quails, parrots, starlings, cuckoos, peacocks, mon-keys, and deer; and finally adjust the income and expenditure of the day. The worn-out clothes should be given to those servants who have done good work, in order to show them that their services have been appreciated, or they may be applied to some other use. The vessels in which wine is prepared, as well as those in which it is kept, should be carefully looked after, and put away at the proper time. All sales and purchases should also be well attended to. The friends of her husband she should welcome by presenting them with flowers, ointment, incense, betel leaves, and betel nut. Her father-in-law and mother-in-law she should treat as they deserve, always remaining dependent on their will, never contradicting them, speaking to them in few and not harsh words, not laughing loudly in their presence, and acting with their friends and enemies as with her own. In addition to the above she should not be vain, or too much taken up with her enjoyments. She should be liberal towards her servants, and reward them on holidays and festivals; and not give away anything without first making it known to her husband.

Thus ends the manner of living of a virtuous woman.

During the absence of her husband on a journey the virtuous woman should wear only her auspicious ornaments, and observe the fasts in honour of the Gods. While anxious to hear the news of her husband, she should still look after her household affairs. She should sleep near the elder women of the house, and make herself agreeable to them. She should look after and keep in repair the things that are liked by her husband, and continue the works that have been begun by him. To the abode of her relations she should not go except on occasions of joy and sorrow, and then she should go in her usual travelling dress, accompanied by her husband's servants, and not remain there for a long time. The fasts and feasts should be observed with the consent of the elders of the house. The resources should be increased by making purchases and sales according to the practice of the merchants, and by means of honest servants, superintended by herself. The income should be increased, and the expenditure diminished as much as possible. And when her husband returns from his journey, she should receive him at first in her ordinary clothes, so that he may know in what way she has lived during his absence, and should bring to him some presents, as also materials for the worship of the Deity.

Thus ends the part relating to the behaviour of a wife during the absence of her husband on a journey.

There are also some verses on the subject as follows:

"The wife, whether she be a woman of noble family, or a virgin widow* remarried, or a concubine, should lead a chaste life, devoted to her husband, and doing every thing for his welfare. Women acting thus, acquire Dharma, Artha and Kama, obtain a high position, and generally keep their husbands devoted to them."

CHAPTER II

On the Conduct of the Elder Wife towards the Other Wives of Her Husband, and on that of a Younger Wife Towards the Elder Ones. Also on the Conduct of a Virgin Widow Re-married; of a Wife Disliked by Her Husband; of the Women in the King's Harem; and lastly on the Conduct of a Husband Towards Many Wives

THE causes of re-marrying during the lifetime of the wife are as follows:

(1) The folly or ill temper of the wife.
(2) The husband's dislike to her.
(3) The want of offspring.
(4) The continual birth of daughters.
(5) The incontinence of the husband.

From the very beginning a wife should endeavour to attract the heart of her husband, by showing to him continually her devotion, her good temper and her wisdom. If however she bears him no children, she should herself tell her husband to marry another woman. And when the second wife is married, and brought to the house, the first wife should give her a position superior to her own, and look upon her as a sister. In the morning the elder wife

* This probably refers to a girl married in her infancy, or when very young, and whose husband had died before she arrived at the age of puberty. Infant marriages are still the common custom of the Hindoos.

should forcibly make the younger one decorate herself in the presence of their husband, and should not mind all the husband's favour being given to her. If the younger wife does anything to displease her husband the elder one should not neglect her, but should always be ready to give her most careful advice, and should teach her to do various things in the presence of her husband. Her children she should treat as her own, her attendants she should look upon with more regard, even than on her own servants, her friends she should cherish with love and kindness, and her relations with great honour.

When there are many other wives besides herself, the elder wife should associate with the one who is immediately next to her in rank and age, and should instigate the wife who has recently enjoyed her husband's favour to quarrel with the present favourite. After this she should sympathise with the former, and having collected all the other wives together, should get them to denounce the favourite as a scheming and wicked woman, without however committing herself in any way. If the favourite wife happens to quarrel with the husband, then the elder wife should take her part and give her false encouragement, and thus cause the quarrel to be increased. If there be only a little quarrel between the two, the elder wife should do all she can to work it up into a large quarrel. But if after all this she finds the husband still continues to love his favourite wife she should then change her tactics, and endeavour to bring about a conciliation between them, so as to avoid her husband's displeasure.

Thus ends the conduct of the elder wife.

The younger wife should regard the elder wife of her husband as her mother, and should not give anything away, even to her own relations, without her knowledge. She should tell her everything about herself, and not approach her husband without her permission. Whatever is told to her by the elder wife she should not reveal to others, and she should take care of the children of the senior even more than of her own. When alone with her husband she should serve him well, but should not tell him of the pain she suffers from the existence of a rival wife. She may also obtain secretly from her husband some marks of his particular regard for her, and may tell him that she lives only for him, and for the regard that he has for her. She should never reveal her love for her husband, nor her husband's love for her to any person, either in pride or in anger, for a wife that reveals the secrets of her husband is despised by him. As for seeking to obtain the regard of her husband, Gonardiya says, that it should always be done in private, for fear of the elder wife. If the elder wife be disliked by her husband, or be childless, she should sympathise with her, and should ask her husband to do the same, but should surpass her in leading the life of a chaste woman.

Thus ends the conduct of the younger wife towards the elder.

A widow in poor circumstances, or of a weak nature, and who allies herself again to a man, is called a widow remarried.

The followers of Babhravya say that a virgin widow should not marry a person whom she may be obliged to leave on account of his bad character, or of his being destitute of the excellent qualities of a man, she thus being obliged to have recourse to another person. Gonardya is of opinion that as the cause of a widow's marrying again is her desire for happiness, and as happiness is secured by the possession of excellent qualities in her husband, joined to love of enjoyment, it is better therefore to secure a person endowed with such qualities in the first instance. Vatsyayana however thinks that a widow may marry any person that she likes, and that she thinks will suit her.

At the time of her marriage the widow should obtain from her husband the money to pay the cost of drinking parties, and picnics with her relations, and of giving them and her friends kindly gifts and presents; or she may do these things at her own cost if she likes. In the same way she may wear either her husband's ornaments or her own. As to the presents of affection mutually exchanged between the husband and herself there is no fixed rule about them. If she leaves her husband after marriage of her own accord, she should restore to him whatever he may have given her, with the exception of the mutual presents. If however she is driven out of the house by her husband she should not return anything to him.

After her marriage she should live in the house of her husband like one of the chief members of the family, but should treat the other ladies of the family with kindness, the servants with generosity, and all the friends of the house with familiarity and good temper. She should show that she is better acquainted with the sixty-four arts than the other ladies of the house, and in any quarrels with her husband she should not rebuke him severely, but in private do everything that he wishes, and make use of the sixty-four ways of enjoyment. She should be obliging to the other wives of her husband, and to their children she should give presents, behave as their mistress, and make ornaments and playthings for their use. In the friends and servants of her husband she should confide more than in his other wives, and finally she should have a liking for drinking parties, going to picnics, attending fairs and festivals, and for carrying out all kinds of games and amusements.

Thus ends the conduct of a virgin widow re-married.

A woman who is disliked by her husband, and annoyed and distressed by his other wives, should associate with the wife who is liked most by her husband, and who serves him more than the others, and should teach her all the arts with which she is acquainted. She should act as the nurse of her husband's children, and having gained over his friends to her side, should through them make him acquainted of her devotion to him. In religious ceremonies she should be a leader, as also in vows and fasts, and should not hold too good an opinion of herself. When her husband is lying on his bed she should only go near him when it is agreeable to him, and should never rebuke him, or show obstinacy in any way. If her husband happens to quarrel with any of his other wives, she should reconcile them to each other, and if he desires to see any woman secretly, she should manage to bring about the meeting between them. She should moreover make herself acquainted with the weak points of her husband's character, but always keep them secret, and on the whole behave herself in such a way as may lead him to look upon her as a good and devoted wife.

Here ends the conduct of a wife disliked by her husband.

The above sections will show how all the women of the King's seraglio are to behave, and therefore we shall now speak separately only about the king.

The female attendants in the harem (called severally Kanchukiyas,* Mahallarikas,† and Mahallikas‡) should bring flowers, ointments and clothes from the King's wives to the King, and he having received these things should give them as presents to the servants, along with the things worn by him the previous day. In the afternoon the King, having dressed and put on his ornaments, should interview the women of the harem, who should also be dressed and decorated with jewels. Then having given to each of them such a place and such respect as may suit the occasion as they may deserve, he should carry on with them a cheerful conversation. After that he should see such of his wives as may be virgin widows re-married, and after them the concubines and dancing girls. All of these should be visited in their own private rooms.

When the King rises from his noonday sleep, the woman whose duty it is to inform the King regarding the wife who is to spend the night with him should come to him accompanied by the female attendants of that wife whose turn may have arrived in the regular course, and of her who may have been accidentally passed over as her turn arrived, and of her who may have been unwell at the time of her turn. These attendants should place before the King the ointments and unguents sent by each of these wives, marked with the seal of her ring, and their names and their reasons for sending the ointments should be told to the King. After this the King accepts the ointment of one of

* A name given to the maid servants of the zenana of the Kings in ancient times, on account of their always keeping their breasts covered with a cloth called Kanchuki. It was customary in the olden time for the maid servants to cover their breasts with a cloth, while the Queens kept their breasts uncovered. This custom is distinctly to be seen in the Ajunta cave paintings.

† The meaning of this word is a superior woman, so it would seem that a Mahallarika must be a person in authority over the maid servants of the house.

‡ This was also appertaining to the rank of women employed in the harem. In latter times this place was given to eunuchs.

them, who then is informed that her ointment has been accepted, and that her day has been settled.*

At festivals, singing parties and exhibitions, all the wives of the King should be treated with respect and served with drinks.

But the women of the harem should not be allowed to go out alone, neither should any women outside the harem be allowed to enter it except those whose character is well known. And lastly the work which the King's wives have to do should not be too fatiguing.

Thus ends the conduct of the King towards the women of the harem, and of their own conduct.

A man marrying many wives should act fairly towards them all. He should neither disregard nor pass over their faults, and should not reveal to one wife the love, passion, bodily blemishes, and confidential reproaches of the other. No opportunity should be given to any one of them of speaking to him about their rivals, and if one of them should begin to speak ill of another, he should chide her and tell her that she has exactly the same blemishes in her character. One of them he should please by secret confidence, another by secret respect, and another by secret flattery, and he should please them all by going to gardens, by amusements, by presents, by honouring their relations, by telling them secrets, and lastly by loving unions. A young woman who is of a good temper, and who conducts herself according to the precepts of the Holy Writ, wins her husband's attachment, and obtains a superiority over her rivals.

Thus ends the conduct of a husband towards many wives.

END OF PART IV

* As Kings generally had many wives, it was usual for them to enjoy their wives by turns. But as it happened sometimes that some of them lost their turns owing to the King's absence, or to their being unwell, then in such cases the women whose turns had been passed over, and those whose turns had come, used to have a sort of lottery, and the ointment of all the claimants were sent to the King, who accepted the ointment of one of them, and thus settled the question.

PART V

ABOUT THE WIVES OF OTHER MEN

Of the Characteristics of Men and Women—the Reasons why Women Reject the Addresses of Men—about Men who have Success with Women, and about Women who are Easily Gained Over

THE wives of other people may be resorted to on the occasions already described in Part I, Chapter 5, of this work, but the possibility of their acquisition, their fitness for cohabitation, the danger to oneself in uniting with them, and the future effect of these unions, should first of all be examined. A man may resort to the wife of another, for the purpose of saving his own life, when he perceives that his love for her proceeds from one degree of intensity to another. These degrees are ten in number, and are distinguished by the following marks:

1. Love of the eye.
2. Attachment of the mind.
3. Constant reflection.
4. Destruction of sleep.
5. Emaciation of the body.
6. Turning away from objects of enjoyment.
7. Removal of shame.
8. Madness.
9. Fainting.
10. Death.

Ancient authors say that a man should know the disposition, truthfulness, purity, and will of a young woman, as also the intensity, or weakness of her passions, from the form of her body, and from her characteristic marks and signs. But Vatsyayana is of opinion that the forms of bodies, and the characteristic marks or signs are but erring tests of character, and that women should be judged by their conduct, by the outward expression of their thoughts, and by the movements of their bodies.

Now as a general rule Gonikaputra says that a woman falls in love with every handsome man she sees, and so does every man at the sight of a beautiful woman, but frequently they do not take any further steps, owing to various considerations. In love the following circumstances are peculiar to the woman. She loves without regard to right or wrong,* and does not try to gain over a man simply for the attainment of some particular purpose. Moreover, when a man first makes up to her she naturally shrinks from him, even though she may be willing to unite herself with him. But when the attempts to gain her are repeated and renewed, she at last consents. But with a man, even though he may have begun to love, he conquers his feelings from a regard for morality and wisdom, and although his thoughts are often on the woman, he does not yield, even though an attempt be made to gain him over. He sometimes makes an attempt or effort to win the object of his affections, and having failed, he leaves her alone for the future. In the same way, when a woman is once gained, he often becomes in-different about her. As for the saying that a man does not care for what is easily gained, and only desires a thing which can-not be obtained without difficulty, it is only a matter of talk.

The causes of a woman rejecting the addresses of a man are as follows:

1. Affection for her husband.

2. Desire of lawful progeny.

3. Want of opportunity.

4. Anger at being addressed by the man too familiarly.

5. Difference in rank of life.

6. Want of certainty on account of the man being devoted to travelling.

7. Thinking that the man may be attached to some other person.

* On peut tout attendre et tout supposer d'une femme amoureuse.— Balzac.

184

8. Fear of the man's not keeping his intentions secret.

9. Thinking that the man is too devoted to his friends, and has too great a regard for them.

10. The apprehension that he is not in earnest.

11. Bashfulness on account of his being an illustrious man.

12. Fear on account of his being powerful, or possessed of too impetuous passion, in the case of the deer woman.

13. Bashfulness on account of his being too clever.

14. The thought of having once lived with him on friendly terms only.

15. Contempt of his want of knowledge of the world.

16. Distrust of his low character.

17. Disgust at his want of perception of her love for him.

18. In the case of an elephant woman, the thought that he is a hare man, or a man of weak passion.

19. Compassion lest any thing should befall him on account of his passion.

20. Despair at her own imperfections.

21. Fear of discovery.

22. Disillusion at seeing his grey hair or shabby appearance.

23. Fear that he may be employed by her husband to test her chastity.

24. The thought that he has too much regard for morality.

Whichever of the above causes a man may detect, he should endeavour to remove it from the very beginning. Thus, the bashfulness that may arise from his greatness or his ability, he should remove by showing his great love and affection for her. The difficulty of the want of opportunity, or of his inaccessibility, he should remove by showing her some easy way of access. The excessive respect entertained by the woman for him should be removed by making himself very familiar. The difficulties that arise from his being thought a low character he should remove by showing his valour and his wisdom; those that come from neglect by extra attention; and those that arise from fear by giving her proper encouragement.

The following are the men who generally obtain success with women.

1. Men well versed in the science of love.

2. Men skilled in telling stories.

3. Men acquainted with women from their childhood.

4. Men who have secured their confidence.

5. Men who send presents to them.

6. Men who talk well.

7. Men who do things that they like.

8. Men who have not loved other women previously.

9. Men who act as messengers.

10. Men who know their weak points.

11. Men who are desired by good women.

12. Men who are united with their female friends.

13. Men who are good looking.

14. Men who have been brought up with them.

15. Men who are their neighbours.

16. Men who are devoted to sexual pleasures, even though these be their own servants.

17. The lovers of the daughters of their nurse.

18. Men who have been lately married.

19. Men who like picnics and pleasure parties.

20. Men who are liberal.

21. Men who are celebrated for being very strong (Bull men).

22. Enterprising and brave men.

23. Men who surpass their husbands in learning and good looks, in good qualities, and in liberality.

24. Men whose dress and manner of living are magnificent.

The following are the women who are easily gained over.

1. Women who stand at the doors of their houses.

2. Women who are always looking out on the street.

3. Women who sit conversing in their neighbour's house.

4. A woman who is always staring at you.

5. A female messenger.

6. A woman who looks sideways at you.

7. A woman whose husband has taken another wife without any just cause.

8. A woman who hates her husband, or who is hated by him.

9. A woman who has nobody to look after her, or keep her in check.

10. A woman who has not had any children.

11. A woman whose family or caste is not well known.

12. A woman whose children are dead.

13. A woman who is very fond of society.

14. A woman who is apparently very affectionate with her husband.

15. The wife of an actor.

16. A widow.

17. A poor woman.

18. A woman fond of enjoyments.

19. The wife of a man with many younger brothers.

20. A vain woman.

21. A woman whose husband is inferior to her in rank or abilities.

22. A woman who is proud of her skill in the arts.

23. A woman disturbed in mind by the folly of her husband.

24. A woman who has been married in her infancy to a rich man, and not liking him when she grows up, desires a man possessing a disposition, talents, and wisdom suitable to her own tastes.

25. A woman who is slighted by her husband without any cause.

26. A woman who is not respected by other women of the same rank or beauty as herself.

27. A woman whose husband is devoted to travelling.

28. The wife of a jeweller.

29. A jealous woman.

30. A covetous woman.

31. An immoral woman.

32. A barren woman.

33. A lazy woman.

34. A cowardly woman.

35. A humpbacked woman.

36. A dwarfish woman.

37. A deformed woman.

38. A vulgar woman.

39. An ill-smelling woman.

40. A sick woman.

41. An old woman.

There are also two verses on the subject as follows:

"Desire, which springs from nature, and which is increased by art, and from which all danger is taken away by wisdom, becomes firm and secure. A clever man, depending on his own ability, and observing carefully the ideas and thoughts of women, and removing the causes of their turning away from men, is generally successful with them."

CHAPTER II

About Making Acquaintance with the Woman, and of the Effort to Gain Her Over

ANCIENT authors are of opinion that girls are not so easily seduced by employing female messengers as by the efforts of the man himself, but that the wives of others are more easily got at by the aid of female messengers than by the personal efforts of the man. But Vatsyayana lays it down that whenever it is possible a man should always act himself in these matters, and it is only when such is impracticable, or impossible, that female messengers should be employed. As for the saying that women who act and talk boldly and freely are to be won by the personal efforts of the man, and women who do not possess those qualities are to be got at by female messengers, it is only a matter of talk.

Now when a man acts himself in the matter he should first of all make the acquaintance of the woman he loves in the following manner.

1st. He should arrange to be seen by the woman either on a natural or special opportunity. A natural opportunity is when one of them goes to the house of the other, and a special opportunity is when they meet either at the house of a friend, or a caste-fellow, or a minister, or a physician, as also on the occasion of marriage ceremonies, sacrifices, festivals, funerals, and garden parties.

2nd. When they do meet, the man should be careful to look at her in such a way as to cause the state of his mind to be made known to her; he should pull about his moustache, make a sound with his nails, cause his own ornaments to tinkle, bite his lower lip, and make various other signs of that description. When she is looking at him he should speak to his friends about her and other women, and should show to her his liberality and his appreciation of enjoyments. When sitting by the side of a female friend he should yawn and twist his body, contract his eyebrows, speak very slowly as if he was weary, and listen to her indifferently. A conversation having two meanings should also be carried on with a child or some other person, apparently having regard to a third person, but really having reference to the woman he loves, and in this way his love should be made manifest under the pretext of referring to others rather than to herself. He should make marks that have reference to her, on the earth with his nails, or with a stick, and should embrace and kiss a child in her presence, and give it the mixture of betel nut and betel leaves with his tongue, and press its chin with his fingers in a caressing way. All these things should be done at the proper time and in proper places.

3rd. The man should fondle a child that may be sitting on her lap, and give it something to play with, and also take the same back again. Conversation with respect to the child may also be held with her, and in this manner he should gradually become well acquainted with her, and he should also make himself agreeable to her relations. Afterwards, this acquaintance should be made a pretext for visiting her house frequently, and on such occasions he should converse on the subject of love in her absence, but within her hearing. As his intimacy with her increases he should place in her charge some kind of deposit or trust, and take away from it a small portion at a time; or he may give her some fragrant substances, or betel nuts to be kept for him by her. After this he should endeavour to make her well acquainted with his own wife, and get them to carry on confidential conversations, and to sit together in lonely places. In order to see her frequently he should arrange so that the same goldsmith, the same jeweller, the same basket maker, the same dyer, and the same washerman should be employed by the two families. And he should also pay her long visits openly under the pretence of being engaged with her on business, and one business should lead to another, so as to keep up the intercourse between them. Whenever she wants anything, or is in need of money, or wishes to acquire skill in one of the arts, he should cause her to understand that he is willing and able to do anything that she wants, to give her money, or teach her one of the arts, all these things being quite within his ability and power. In the same way he should hold discussions with her in company with other people, and they should talk of the doings and sayings of other persons, and examine different things, like jewellery, precious stones, etc. On such occasions he should show her certain things with the values of which she may be unacquainted, and if she begins to dispute with him about the things or their value, he should not contradict her, but point out that he agrees with her in every way.

Thus ends the ways of making the acquaintance of the woman desired.

Now after a girl has become acquainted with the man as above described, and has manifested her love to him by the various outward signs; and by the motions of her body, the man should make every effort to gain her over. But as girls are not acquainted with sexual union, they should be treated with the greatest delicacy, and the man should proceed with considerable caution, though in the case of other women, accustomed to sexual intercourse, this is not necessary. When the intentions of the girl are known, and her bashfulness put aside, the man should begin to make use of her money, and an interchange of clothes, rings and flowers should be made. In this the man should take particular care that the things given by him are handsome and valuable. He should moreover receive from her a mixture of betel nut and betel leaves, and when he is going to a party he should ask for the flower in her hair, or for the flower in her hand.

If he himself gives her a flower it should be a sweet smelling one, and marked with marks made by his nails or teeth. With increasing assiduity he should dispel her fears, and by degrees get her to go with him to some lonely place, and there he should embrace and kiss her. And finally at the time of giving her some betel nut, or of receiving the same from her, or at the time of making an exchange of flowers, he should touch and press her private parts, thus bringing his efforts to a satisfactory conclusion.

When a man is endeavouring to seduce one woman, he should not attempt to seduce any other at the same time. But after he has succeeded with the first, and enjoyed her for a considerable time, he can keep her affections by giving her presents that she likes, and then commence making up to another woman. When a man sees the husband of a woman going to some place near his house, he should not enjoy the woman then, even though she may be easily gained over at that time. A wise man having a regard for his reputation should not think of seducing a woman who is apprehensive, timid, not to be trusted, well guarded, or possessed of a father-in-law, or mother-in-law.

CHAPTER III

Examination of the State of a Woman's Mind

WHEN a man is trying to gain over a woman he should examine the state of her mind, and act as follows.

If she listens to him, but does not manifest to him in any way her own intentions, he should then try to gain her over by means of a go-between.

If she meets him once, and again comes to meet him better dressed than before, or comes to him in some lonely place, he should be certain that she is capable of being enjoyed by the use of a little force. A woman who lets a man make up to her, but does not give herself up, even after a long time, should be considered as a trifler in love, but owing to the fickleness of the human mind, even such a woman can be conquered by always keeping up a close acquaintance with her.

When a woman avoids the attentions of a man, and on account of respect for him, and pride in herself, will not meet him or approach him, she can be gained over with difficulty, either by endeavouring to keep on familiar terms with her, or else by an exceedingly clever go-between.

When a man makes up to a woman, and she reproaches him with harsh words, she should be abandoned at once.

When a woman reproaches a man, but at the same time acts affectionately towards him, she should be made love to in every way.

A woman, who meets a man in lonely places, and puts up with the touch of his foot, but pretends, on account of the indecision of her mind, not to be aware of it, should be conquered by patience, and by continued efforts as follows:

If she happens to go to sleep in his vicinity he should put his left arm round her, and see when she awakes whether she repulses him in reality, or only repulses him in such a way as if she was desirous of the same thing being done to her again. And what is done by the arm can also be done by the foot. If the man succeeds in this point he should embrace her more closely, and if she will not stand the embrace and gets up, but behaves with him as usual the next day, he should consider then that she is not unwilling to be enjoyed by him. If however she does not appear again, the man should try to get over her by means of a go-between; and if, after having disappeared for some time she again appears, and behaves with him as usual, the man should then consider that she would not object to be united with him.

When a woman gives a man an opportunity, and makes her own love manifest to him, he should proceed to enjoy her. And the signs of a woman manifesting her love are these:

1. She calls out to a man without being addressed by him in the first instance.

2. She shows herself to him in secret places.

3. She speaks to him tremblingly and inarticulately.

4. She has the fingers of her hand, and the toes of her feet

moistened with perspiration, and her face blooming with delight.

5. She occupies herself with shampooing his body and pressing his head.

6. When shampooing him she works with one hand only, and with the other she touches and embraces parts of his body.

7. She remains with both hands placed on his body motionless as if she had been surprised by something, or was overcome by fatigue.

8. She sometimes bends down her face upon his thighs, and when asked to shampoo them does not manifest any unwillingness to do so.

9. She places one of her hands quite motionless on his body, and even though the man should press it between two members of his body, she does not remove it for a long time.

10. Lastly, when she has resisted all the efforts of the man to gain her over, she returns to him next day to shampoo his body as before.

When a woman neither gives encouragement to a man, nor avoids him, but hides herself and remains in some lonely place, she must be got at by means of the female servant who may be near her. If when called by the man she acts in the same way, then she should be gained over by means of a skilful go-between. But if she will have nothing to say to the man, he should consider well about her before he begins any further attempts to gain her over.

Thus ends the examination of the state of a woman's mind.

A man should first get himself introduced to a woman, and then carry on a conversation with her. He should give her hints of his love for her, and if he finds from her replies that she receives these hints favourably, he should then set to work to gain her over without any fear. A woman who shows her love by outward signs to the man at his first interview should be gained over very easily. In the same way a lascivious woman, who when addressed in loving words replies openly in words expressive of her love, should be considered to have been gained over at that very moment.

With regard to all women, whether they be wise, simple, or confiding, this rule is laid down that those who make an open manifestation of their love are easily gained over.

CHAPTER IV

About the Business of a Go-between

IF a woman has manifested her love or desire, either by signs or by motions of the body, and is afterwards rarely or never seen any where, or if a woman is met for the first time, the man should get a go-between to approach her.

Now the go-between, having wheedled herself into the confidence of the woman by acting according to her disposition, should try to make her hate or despise her husband by holding artful conversations with her, by telling her about medicines for getting children, by talking to her about other people, by tales of various kinds, by stories about the wives of other men, and by praising her beauty, wisdom, generosity and good nature, and then saying to her: "It is indeed a pity that you, who are so excellent a woman in every way, should be possessed of a husband of this kind. Beautiful lady, he is not fit even to serve you." The go-between should further talk to the woman about the weakness of the passion of her husband, his jealousy, his roguery, his ingratitude, his aversion to enjoyments, his dullness, his meanness, and all the other faults that he may have, and with which she may be acquainted. She should particularly harp upon that fault or that failing by which the wife may appear to be the most affected. If the wife be a deer woman, and the husband a hare man, then there would be no fault in that direction, but in the event of his being a hare man, and she a mare woman or elephant woman, then this fault should be pointed out to her.

Gonikaputra is of opinion that when it is the first affair of the woman, or when her love has only been very secretly shown, the man should then secure and send to her a go-between, with whom she may be already acquainted, and in whom she confides.

But to return to our subject. The go-between should tell the woman about the obedience and love of the man, and as her confidence and affection increase, she should then explain to her the thing to be accomplished in the following way. "Hear this, Oh beautiful lady, that this man, born of a good family, having seen you, has gone mad on your account. The poor young man, who is tender by nature, has never been distressed in such a way before, and it is highly probable that he will succumb under his present affliction, and experience the pains of death." If the woman listens with a favourable ear, then on the following day the go-between, having observed marks of good spirits in her face, in her eyes, and in her manner of conversation, should again converse with her on the subject of the man, and should tell her the stories of Ahalya* and Indra, of Sakoontala† and Dushyanti, and such others as may be fitted for the occasion. She should also describe to her the strength of the man, his talents, his skill in the sixty-four sorts of enjoyments mentioned by Babhravya, his good looks, and his liaison with some praiseworthy woman, no matter whether this last ever took place or not.

In addition to this, the go-between should carefully note the behaviour of the woman, which if favourable would be as follows: she would address her with a smiling look, would seat herself close beside her, and ask her, "Where have you been? What have you been doing? Where did you dine? Where did you sleep? Where have you been sitting?" Moreover the woman would meet the go-between in lonely places and tell her stories there, would yawn contemplatively, draw long sighs, give her presents, remember her on occasions of festivals, dismiss her with a wish to see her

* The wife of the sage Gautama, she was seduced by Indra the king of the Gods.

† The heroine of one of the best, if not the best, of Hindoo plays, and the best known in Sanscrit dramatic literature. It was first brought to notice by Sir William Jones, and has been well and poetically translated by Dr. Monier Williams under the title of *Sakoontala, or the Lost Ring,* an Indian drama, translated into English prose and verse from the Sanscrit of Kalidasa.

again, and say to her jestingly, "Oh, well-speaking woman, why do you speak these bad words to me?" would discourse on the sin of her union with the man, would not tell her about any previous visits or conversations that she may have had with him, but wish to be asked about these, and lastly would laugh at the man's desire, but would not reproach him in any way.

Thus ends the behaviour of the woman with the go-between.

When the woman manifests her love in the manner above described, the go-between should increase it by bringing to her love tokens from the man. But if the woman be not acquainted with the man personally, the go-between should win her over by extolling and praising his good qualities, and by telling stories about his love for her. Here Auddalaka says that when a man or woman are not personally acquainted with each other, and have not shown each other any signs of affection, the employment of a go-between is useless.

The followers of Babhravya on the other hand affirm that even though they be personally unacquainted, but have shown each other signs of affection there is an occasion for the employment of a go-between. Gonikaputra asserts that a go-between should be employed, provided they are acquainted with each other, even though no signs of affection may have passed between them. Vatsyayana however lays it down that even though they may not be personally acquainted with each other, and may not have shown each other any signs of affection, still they are both capable of placing confidence in a go-between.

Now the go-between should show the woman the presents, such as the betel nut and the betel leaves, the perfumes, the flowers, and the rings which the man may have given to her for the sake of the woman, and on these presents should be impressed the marks of the man's teeth, and nails, and other signs. On the cloth that he may send he should draw with saffron both his hands joined together as if in earnest entreaty.

The go-between should also show to the woman ornamental figures of various kinds cut in leaves, together with ear ornaments, and chaplets made of flowers containing love letters expressive of the desire of the man,* and she should cause her to send affectionate presents to the man in return. After they have mutually accepted each other's presents, then a meeting should be arranged between them on the faith of the go-between.

The followers of Babhravya say that this meeting should take place at the time of going to the temple of a Deity, or on occasions of fairs, garden parties, theatrical performances, marriages, sacrifices, festivals and funerals, as also at the time of going to the river to bathe, or at times of natural calamities,† fear of robbers or hostile invasions of the country.

Gonikaputra is of opinion however that these meetings had better be brought about in the abodes of female friends, mendicants, astrologers and ascetics. But Vatsyayana decides that that place is only well suited for the purpose which has proper means of ingress and egress, and where arrangements have been made to prevent any accidental occurrence, and when a man who has once entered the house, can also leave it at the proper time without any disagreeable encounter.

Now go-betweens or female messengers are of the following different kinds, viz.:

(1) A go-between who takes upon herself the whole burden of the business.

(2) A go-between who does only a limited part of the business.

(3) A go-between who is the bearer of a letter only.

* It is presumed that something like the following French verses are intended.

> Quand on a jurè le plus profound hommage,
> Voulez vous qu'infidele on change de language,
> Vous seul captive mon esprit et mon coeur
> Que je puisse dans vos bras seuls gouter le bonheur;
> Je voudrais, mais en vain, que mon coeur en delire
> Couche ou ce papier n'oserait vous dire.
> Avec soin, de ces vers lisez leur premiers mots,
> Vous verrez quel remede il faut a tous mes maux.

Or these:

> Quand on vous voit, on vous aime;
> Quand on vous aime, ou vous voit on.

† It is supposed that storms, earthquakes, famines and pestilent diseases are here alluded to.

(4) A go-between acting on her own account.

(5) The go-between of an innocent young woman.

(6) A wife serving as a go-between.

(7) A mute go-between.

(8) A go-between who acts the part of the wind.

(1) A woman who, having observed the mutual passion of a man and woman, brings them together and arranges it by the power of her own intellect, such an one is called a go-between who takes upon herself the whole burden of the business. This kind of go-between is chiefly employed when the man and the woman are already acquainted with each other, and have conversed together, and in such cases she is sent not only by the man (as is always done in all other cases) but by the woman also. The above name is also given to a go-between who, perceiving that the man and the woman are suited to each other, tries to bring about a union between them, even though they be not acquainted with each other.

(2) A go-between who, perceiving that some part of the affair is already done, or that the advances on the part of the man are already made, completes the rest of the business, is called a go-between who performs only a limited part of the business.

(3) A go-between, who simply carries messages between a man and a woman, who love each other, but who cannot frequently meet, is called the bearer of a letter or message.

This name is also given to one who is sent by either of the lovers to acquaint either the one or the other with the time and place of their meeting.

(4) A woman who goes herself to a man, and tells him of her having enjoyed sexual union with him in a dream, and expresses her anger at his wife having rebuked him for calling her by the name of her rival instead of by her own name and gives him something bearing the marks of her teeth and nails, and informs him that she knew she was formerly desired by him, and asks him privately whether she or his wife is the best looking, such a person is called a woman who is a go-between for herself. Now such a woman should be met and interviewed by the man in private and secretly.

The above name is also given to a woman who having made agreement with some other woman to act as her go-between, gains over the man to herself, by the means of making him personally acquainted with herself, and thus causes the other woman to fail. The same applies to a man who, acting as a go-between for another, and having no previous connection with the woman, gains her over for himself, and thus causes the failure of the other man.

(5) A woman, who has gained the confidence of the innocent young wife of any man, and who has learned her secrets without exercising any pressure on her mind, and found out from her how her husband behaves to her, if this woman then teaches her the art of securing his favour, and decorates her so as to show her love, and instructs her how and when to be angry, or to pretend to be so, and then, having herself made marks of the nails and teeth on the body of the wife, gets the latter to send for her husband to show these marks to him, and thus excite him for enjoyment, such is called the go-between of an innocent young woman. In such cases the man should send replies to his wife through the same woman.

(6) When a man gets his wife to gain the confidence of a woman whom he wants to enjoy, and to call on her and talk to her about the wisdom and ability of her husband, that wife is called a wife serving as a go-between. In this case the feelings of the woman with regard to the man should also be made known through the wife.

(7) When any man sends a girl or a female servant to any woman under some pretext or other, and places a letter in her bouquet of flowers, or in her ear ornaments, or marks something about her with his teeth or nails, that girl or female servant is called a mute go-between. In this case the man should expect an answer from the woman through the same person.

(8) A person, who carries a message to a woman, which has a double meaning, or which relates to some past transactions, or which is unintelligible to other people, is called a go-between who acts the part of the wind. In this case the reply should be asked for through the same woman.

Thus ends the different kinds of go-betweens.

A female astrologer, a female servant, a female beggar, or a female artist are well acquainted with the business of a go-between, and very soon gain the confidence of other women. Any one of them can raise enmity between any two persons if she wishes to do so, or extol the loveliness of any woman that she wishes to praise, or describe the arts practised by other women in sexual union. They can also speak highly of the love of a man, of his skill in sexual enjoyment, and of the desire of other women, more beautiful even than the woman they are addressing, for him, and explain the restraint under which he may be at home.

Lastly a go-between can, by the artfulness of her conversation unite a woman with a man, even though he may not have been thought of by her, or may have been considered beyond his aspirations. She can also bring back a man to a woman, who, owing to some cause or other, has separated himself from her.

CHAPTER V

About the Love of Persons in Authority for the Wives of Other Men

KINGS and their ministers have no access to the abodes of others, and moreover their mode of living is constantly watched and observed and imitated by the people at large, just as the animal world, seeing the sun rise, get up after him, and when he sits in the evening, lie down again in the same way. Persons in authority should not therefore do any improper act in public, as such are impossible from their position, and would be deserving of censure. But if they find that such an act is necessary to be done, they should make use of the proper means as described in the following paragraphs.

The head man of the village, the King's officer employed there, and the man* whose business it is to glean corn, can

* This is a phrase used for a man who does the work of everybody, and who is fed by the whole village.

gain over female villagers simply by asking them. It is on this account that this class of woman are called unchaste women by voluptuaries.

The union of the above mentioned men with this class of woman takes place on the occasions of unpaid labour, of filling the granaries in their houses, of taking things in and out of the house, of cleaning the houses, of working in the fields, and of purchasing cotton, wool, flax, hemp and thread, and at the season of the purchase, sale and exchange of various other articles, as well as at the time of doing various other works. In the same way the superintendents of cow pens enjoy the women in the cow pens; and the officers, who have the superintendence of widows, of the women who are without supporters, and of women who have left their husbands, have sexual intercourse with these women. The intelligent accomplish their object by wandering at night in the village, and while villagers also unite with the wives of their sons, being much alone with them. Lastly the superintendents of markets have a great deal to do with the female villagers at the time of their making purchases in the market.

During the festival of the eighth moon, i.e., during the bright half of the month of Nargashirsha, as also during the moon-light festival of the month of Kartika, and the spring festival of Chaitra, the women of cities and towns generally visit the women of the King's harem in the royal palace. These visitors go to the several apartments of the women of the harem, as they are acquainted with them, and pass the night in conversation, and in proper sports, and amusement, and go away in the morning. On such occasions a female attendant of the King (previously acquainted with the woman whom the King desires), should loiter about, and accost this woman when she sets out to go home, and induce her to come and see the amusing things in the palace. Previous to these festivals even, she should have caused it to be intimated to this woman that on the occasion of this festival she would show her all the interesting things in the royal palace. Accordingly she should show her the bower of the coral creeper, the garden house with its floor inlaid with precious stones, the bower of grapes, the building on the water, the secret passages in the walls of the palace, the pictures, the sporting animals, the machines, the birds, and the cages of the lions and the tigers. After this, when alone with her, she should tell her about the love of the King for her, and should describe to her the good fortune which would attend upon her union with the King, giving her at the time a strict promise of secrecy. If the woman does not accept the offer, she should conciliate and please her with handsome presents befitting the position of the King, and having accompanied her for some distance should dismiss her with great affection.

(2) Or, having made the acquaintance of the husband of the woman whom the King desires, the wives of the King should get the wife to pay them a visit in the harem, and on this occasion a female attendant of the King, having been sent thither, should act as above described.

(3) Or, one of the King's wives should get acquainted with the woman that the King desires, by sending one of the female attendants to her, who should, on their becoming more intimate, induce her to come and see the royal abode. Afterwards when she has visited the harem, and acquired confidence, a female confidante of the King, sent thither, should act as before described.

(4) Or, the King's wife should invite the woman, whom the King desires, to come to the royal palace, so that she might see the practice of the art in which the King's wife may be skilled, and after she has come to the harem, a female attendant of the King, sent thither, should act as before described.

(5) Or, a female beggar, in league with the King's wife, should say to the woman desired by the King, and whose husband may have lost his wealth, or may have some cause of fear from the King: "This wife of the King has influence over him, and she is, moreover, naturally kind-hearted, we must therefore go to her in this matter. I shall arrange for your entrance into the harem, and she will do away with all cause of danger and fear from the King." If the woman accepts this offer, the female beggar should take her two or three times to the harem, and the King's wife there should give her a promise of protection. After this, when the

woman, delighted with her reception and promise of protection, again goes to the harem, then a female attendant of the King, sent thither, should act as directed.

(6) What has been said above regarding the wife of one who has some cause of fear from the King applies also to the wives of those who seek service under the King, or who are oppressed by the King's ministers, or who are poor, or who are not satisfied with their position, or who are desirous of gaining the King's favour, or who wish to become famous among the people, or who are oppressed by the members of their own caste, or who want to injure their caste fellows, or who are spies of the King, or who have any other object to attain.

(7) Lastly, if the woman desired by the King be living with some person who is not her husband, then the King should cause her to be arrested, and having made her a slave, on account of her crime, should place her in the harem. Or the King should cause his ambassador to quarrel with the husband of the woman desired by him, and should then imprison her as the wife of an enemy of the King, and by this means should place her in the harem.

Thus ends the means of gaining over the wives of others secretly.

The above mentioned ways of gaining over the wives of other men are chiefly practised in the palaces of Kings. But a King should never enter the abode of another person, for Abhira,* the King of the Kottas was killed by a washerman while in the house of another, and in the same way Jayasana the King of the Kashis was slain by the commandment of his cavalry.

But according to the customs of some countries there are facilities for Kings to make love to the wives of other men. Thus in the country of the Andras† the newly married daughters of the people thereof enter the King's harem with some presents on the tenth day of their marriage, and having been enjoyed by the King are then dismissed. In the country of the Vatsagulmas‡ the wives of the chief ministers

---

* The exact date of the reign of these kings is now known. It is supposed to have been about the beginning of the Christian era.

† The modern country of Tailangam which is to the South of Rajamundry.

‡ Supposed to be a tract of the country to the south of Malwa.

approach the King at night to serve him. In the country of the Vaidarbhas* the beautiful wives of the inhabitants pass a month in the King's harem under the pretence of affection for the King. In the country of the Aparatakas† the people give their beautiful wives as presents to the ministers and the Kings. And lastly in the country of the Saurashtras‡ the women of the city and the country enter the royal harem for the King's pleasure either together or separately.

There are also two verses on the subject as follows:

"The above and other ways are the means employed in different countries by Kings with regard to the wives of other persons. But a King, who has the welfare of his people at heart, should not on any account put them into practice."

"A King, who has conquered the six§ enemies of mankind, becomes the master of the whole earth."

CHAPTER VI

About the Women of the Royal Harem; and of the Keeping of One's Own Wife

THE women of the royal harem cannot see or meet any men on account of their being strictly guarded, neither do they have their desires satisfied, because their only husband is common to many wives. For this reason among themselves they give pleasure to each other in various ways as now described.

Having dressed the daughters of their nurses, or their female friends, or their female attendants, like men, they accomplish their object by means of bulbs, roots, and fruits having the form of the lingam, or they lie down upon the

---

* Now known by the name of Berar. Its capital was Kundinpura, which has been identified with the modern Oomravati.

† Also called Aparantakas, being the northern and southern Concan.

‡ The modern provinces of Katteeawar. Its capital was called Girinaguda, or the modern Junagurh.

§ These are Lust, Anger, Avarice, Spiritual Ignorance, Pride and Envy.

statue of a male figure, in which the lingam is visible and erect.

Some Kings, who are compassionate, take or apply certain medicines to enable them to enjoy many wives in one night, simply for the purpose of satisfying the desire of their women, though they perhaps have no desire of their own. Others enjoy with great affection only those wives that they particularly like, while others only take them, according as the turn of each wife arrives in due course. Such are the ways of enjoyment prevalent in Eastern countries, and what is said about the means of enjoyment of the female is also applicable to the male.

By means of their female attendants the ladies of the royal harem generally get men into their apartments in the disguise or dress of women. Their female attendants, and the daughters of their nurses, who are acquainted with their secrets, should exert themselves to get men to come to the harem in this way by telling them of the good fortune attending it, and by describing the facilities of entering and leaving the palace, the large size of the premises, the carelessness of the sentinels, and the irregularities of the attendants about the persons of the royal wives. But these women should never induce a man to enter the harem by telling him falsehoods, for that would probably lead to his destruction.

As for the man himself he had better not enter a royal harem, even though it may be easily accessible, on account of the numerous disasters to which he may be exposed there. If however he wants to enter it, he should first ascertain whether there is an easy way to get out, whether it is closely surrounded by the pleasure garden, whether it has separate enclosures belonging to it, whether the sentinels are careless, whether the King has gone abroad, and then, when he is called by the women of the harem, he should carefully observe the localities, and enter by the way pointed out by them. If he is able to manage it, he should hang about the harem every day, and, under some pretext or other, make friends with the sentinels, and show himself attached to the female attendants of the harem, who may have become acquainted with his design, and to whom he should express his regret at not being able to obtain the object of his desire. Lastly he should cause the whole business of a go-between to be done by the woman who may have access to the harem, and he should be careful to be able to recognise the emissaries of the King.

When a go-between has no access to the harem, then the man should stand in some place where the lady, whom he loves, and whom he is anxious to enjoy, can be seen.

If that place is occupied by the King's sentinels, he should then disguise himself as a female attendant of the lady who comes to the place, or passes by it. When she looks at him he should let her know his feelings by outward signs and gestures, and should show her pictures, things with double meaning, chaplets of flowers, and rings. He should carefully mark the answer she gives, whether by word or by sign, or by gesture, and should then try and get into the harem. If he is certain of her coming to some particular place he should conceal himself there, and at the appointed time should enter along with her as one of the guards. He may also go in and out, concealed in a folded bed, or bed covering, or with his body made invisible,* by means of external applications, a receipt for one of which is as follows:

The heart of an ichneumon, the fruit of the long gourd (Tumbi), and the eyes of a serpent should all be burnt without letting out the smoke, the ashes should then be ground and mixed in equal quantities with water. By putting this mixture upon the eyes a man can go about unseen.

Other means of invisibility are prescribed by Duyana Brahmans and Jogashiras.

Again the man may enter the harem during the festival of the eighth moon in the month of Nargashirsha, and during the moonlight festivals when the female attendants of the harem are all busily occupied, or in confusion.

The following principles are laid down on this subject.

The entrance of young men into harems, and their exit from them, generally take place when things are being

* The way to make oneself invisible; the knowledge of the art of transmigration, or changing ourselves or others into any shape or form by the use of charms and spells; the power of being in two places at once, and other occult sciences are frequently referred to in all Oriental literature.

brought into the palace, or when things are being taken out of it, or when drinking festivals are going on, or when the female attendants are in a hurry, or when the residence of some of the royal ladies is being changed, or when the King's wives go to gardens, or to fairs, or when they enter the palace on their return from them, or lastly, when the King is absent on a long pilgrimage. The women of the royal harem know each other's secrets, and having but one object to attain, they give assistance to each other. A young man, who enjoys all of them, and who is common to them all, can continue enjoying his union with them so long as it is kept quiet, and is not known abroad.

Now in the country of the Aparatakas the royal ladies are not well protected, and consequently many young men are passed into the harem by the women who have access to the royal palace. The wives of the King of the Ahira country accomplish their objects with those sentinels in the harem who bear the name of Kashtriyas. The royal ladies in the country of the Vatsagulmas cause such men as are suitable to enter into the harem along with their female messengers. In the country of the Vaidarbhas the sons of the royal ladies enter the royal harem when they please, and enjoy the women, with the exception of their own mothers. In the Stri-rajya the wives of the King are enjoyed by his caste fellows and relations. In the Ganda country the royal wives are enjoyed by Brahmans, friends, servants and slaves. In the Samdhava country, servants, foster children, and other persons like them enjoy the women of the harem. In the country of the Haimavatas adventurous citizens bribe the sentinels and enter the harem. In the country of the Vanyas and the Kalmyas, Brahmans, with the knowledge of the King, enter the harem under the pretence of giving flowers to the ladies, and speak with them from behind a curtain, and from such conversation union afterwards takes place. Lastly the women in the harem of the King of the Prachyas conceal one young man in the harem for every batch of nine or ten of the women.

Thus act the wives of others.

For these reasons a man should guard his own wife. Old authors say that a King should select for sentinels in his harem such men as have their freedom from carnal desires well tested. But such men, though free themselves from carnal desire, by reason of their fear of avarice, may cause other persons to enter the harem, and therefore Gonikaputra says, that Kings should place such men in the harem as may have had their freedom from carnal desires, their fears, and their avarice well tested. Lastly Vatsyayana says that under the influence of Dharma* people might be admitted, and therefore men should be selected who are free from carnal desires, fear, avarice, and Dharma.†

The followers of Babhravya say that a man should cause his wife to associate with a young woman who would tell him the secrets of other people, and thus find out from her about his wife's chastity. But Vatsyayana says, that as wicked persons are always successful with women, a man should not cause his innocent wife to be corrupted by bringing her into the company of a deceitful woman.

The following are the causes of the destruction of a woman's chastity.

Always going into society, and sitting in company.

Absence of restraint.

The loose habits of her husband.

Want of caution in her relations with other men.

Continued and long absence of her husband.

Living in a foreign country.

Destruction of her love and feelings by her husband.

The company of loose women.

The jealousy of her husband.

There are also the following verses on the subject:

"A clever man, learning from the Shastras the ways of winning over the wives of other people, is never deceived in the case of his own wives. No one, however, should make use of these ways for seducing the wives of others, because they do not always succeed, and, moreover, often cause disasters, and the destruction of Dharma and Artha. This book,

* This may be considered as meaning religious influence, and alludes to persons who may be gained over by that means.

† It will be noted from the above remarks that eunuchs do not appear to have been employed in the King's harem in those days, though they seem to have been employed for other purposes. See Part II., page 122.

which is intended for the good of the people, and to teach them the ways of guarding their own wives, should not be made use of merely for gaining over the wives of others."

END OF PART V

PART VI

ABOUT COURTESANS

Introductory Remarks

THIS Part VI, about courtesans, was prepared by Vatsyayana, from a treatise on the subject, that was written by Dattaka, for the women of Pataliputra (the modern Patna), some two thousand years ago. Dattaka's work does not appear to be extant now, but this abridgement of it is very clever, and quite equal to any of the productions of Emile Zola, and other writers of the realistic school of today.

Although a great deal has been written on the subject of the courtesan, nowhere will be found a better description of her, of her belongings, of her ideas, and of the working of her mind, than is contained in the following pages.

The details of the domestic and social life of the early Hindoos would not be complete without mention of the courtesan, and Part VI is entirely devoted to this subject. The Hindoos have ever had the good sense to recognise courtesans as a part and portion of human society, and so long as they behaved themselves with decency and propriety, they were regarded with a certain respect. Anyhow, they have never been treated in the East with that brutality and contempt so common in the West, while their education has always been of a superior kind to that bestowed upon the rest of womankind in Oriental countries.

In the earlier days the well-educated Hindoo dancing girl and courtesan doubtless resembled the Hetera of the Greeks, and being educated and amusing, were far more acceptable as companions than the generality of the married or unmarried women of that period. At all times and in all countries, there has ever been a little rivalry between the chaste and the unchaste. But while some women are born courtesans, and follow the instincts of their nature in every class of society, it has been truly said by some authors that every woman has got an inkling of the profession in her nature, and does her best, as a general rule, to make herself agreeable to the male sex.

The subtlety of women, their wonderful perceptive powers, their knowledge and their intuitive appreciation of men and things, are all shown in the following pages, which may be looked upon as a concentrated essence that has been since worked up into detail by many writers in every quarter of the globe.

CHAPTER I

Of the Causes of a Courtesan Resorting to Men; of the Means of Attaching to Herself the Man Desired; and of the Kind of Man that it is Desirable to be Acquainted With

By having intercourse with men courtesans obtain sexual pleasure, as well as their own maintainance. Now when a courtesan takes up with a man from love, the action is natural; but when she resorts to him for the purpose of getting money, her action is artificial or forced. Even in the latter case, however, she should conduct herself as if her love were indeed natural, because men repose their confidence on those women who apparently love them. In making known her love to the man, she should show an entire freedom from avarice, and for the sake of her future credit she should abstain from acquiring money from him by unlawful means.

A courtesan, well dressed and wearing her ornaments, should sit or stand at the door of her house, and without exposing herself too much, should look on the public road so as to be seen by the passers by, she being like an object on view for sale.* She should form friendships with such

* In England the lower classes of courtesans walk the streets; in India and other places in the East, they sit at the windows, or at the doors of their houses.

persons as would enable her to separate men from other women, and attach them to herself, to repair her own misfortunes, to acquire wealth, and to protect her from being bullied, or set upon by persons with whom she may have dealings of some kind or another.

These persons are:

The guards of the town, or the police.

The officers of the courts of justice.

Astrologers.

Powerful men, or men with interest.

Learned men.

Teachers of the sixty-four arts.

Pithamardas or confidants.

Vitas or parasites.

Vidushakas or jesters.

Flower sellers.

Perfumers.

Vendors of spirits.

Washermen.

Barbers.

Beggars.

And such other persons as may be found necessary for the particular object to be acquired.

The following kinds of men may be taken up with, simply for the purpose of getting their money.

Men of independent income.

Young men.

Men who are free from any ties.

Men who hold places of authority under the King.

Men who have secured their means of livelihood without difficulty.

Men possessed of unfailing sources of income.

Men who consider themselves handsome.

Men who are always praising themselves.

One who is an eunuch, but wishes to be thought a man.

One who hates his equals.

One who is naturally liberal.

One who has influence with the King or his ministers.

One who is always fortunate.

One who is proud of his wealth.

One who disobeys the orders of his elders.

One upon whom the members of his caste keep an eye.

An only son whose father is wealthy.

An ascetic who is internally troubled with desire.

A brave man.

A physician of the King.

Previous acquaintances.

On the other hand, those who are possessed of excellent qualities are to be resorted to for the sake of love, and fame. Such men are as follows:

Men of high birth, learned, with a good knowledge of the world, and doing the proper things at the proper times, poets, good story tellers, eloquent men, energetic men, skilled in various arts, far-seeing into the future, possessed of great minds, full of perseverance, of a firm devotion, free from anger, liberal, affectionate to their parents, and with a liking for all social gatherings, skilled in completing verses begun by others and in various other sports, free from all disease, possessed of a perfect body, strong, and not addicted to drinking, powerful in sexual enjoyment, sociable, showing love towards women and attracting their hearts to himself, but not entirely devoted to them, possessed of independent means of livelihood, free from envy, and last of all, free from suspicion.

Such as the good qualities of a man.

The woman also should have the following characteristics, viz.:

She should be possessed of beauty, and amiability, with auspicious body marks. She should have a liking for good qualities in other people, as also a liking for wealth. She should take delight in sexual unions resulting from love, and should be of a firm mind, and of the same class as the man with regard to sexual enjoyment.

She should always be anxious to acquire and obtain experience and knowledge, be free from avarice, and always have a liking for social gatherings, and for the arts.

The following are the ordinary qualities of all women, viz.:

To be possessed of intelligence, good disposition, and good manners; to be straighforward in behaviour, and to be grateful; to consider well the future before doing anything; to possess activity, to be of consistent behaviour, and to have a knowledge of the proper times and places for doing things; to speak always without meanness, loud laughter, malignity, anger, avarice, dullness, or stupidity, to have a knowledge of the Kama Sutra, and to be skilled in all the arts connected with it.

The faults of the women are to be known by the absence of any of the above mentioned good qualities.

The following kinds of men are not fit to be resorted to by courtesans, viz.:

One who is consumptive; one who is sickly; one whose mouth contains worms; one whose breath smells like human excrement; one whose wife is dear to him; one who speaks harshly; one who is always suspicious; one who is avaricious; one who is pitiless; one who is a thief; one who is self-conceited; one who has a liking for sorcery; one who does not care for respect or disrespect; one who can be gained over even by his enemies by means of money; and lastly, one who is extremely bashful.

Ancient authors are of opinion that the causes of a courtesan resorting to men are love, fear, money, pleasure, returning some act of enmity, curiosity, sorrow, constant intercourse, Dharma, celebrity, compassion, the desire of having a friend, shame, the likeness of the man to some beloved person, the search after good fortune, the getting rid of the love of somebody else, the being of the same class as the man with respect to sexual union, living in the same place, constancy, and poverty. But Vatsyayana decides that desire of wealth, freedom from misfortune, and love, are the only causes that affect the union of courtesans with men.

Now a courtesan should not sacrifice money to her love, because money is the chief thing to be attended to. But in cases of fear, etc., she should pay regard to strength and other qualities. Moreover, even though she be invited by any man to join him, she should not at once consent to a union, because men are apt to despise things which are easily acquired. On such occasions she should first send the shampooers, and the singers, and the jesters, who may be in her service, or, in their absence the Pithamardas, or confidants, and others, to find out the state of his feelings, and the condition of his mind. By means of these persons she should ascertain whether the man is pure or impure, affected, or the reverse, capable of attachment, or indifferent, liberal or niggardly; and if she finds him to her liking, she should then employ the Vita and others to attach his mind to her.

Accordingly, the Pithamarda should bring the man to her house, under the pretence of seeing the fights of quails, cocks, and rams, of hearing the maina (a kind of starling) talk, or of seeing some other spectacle, or the practice of some art; or he may take the woman to the abode of the man. After this, when the man comes to her house the woman should give him something capable of producing curiosity, and love in his heart, such as an affectionate present telling him that it was specially designed for his use. She should also amuse him for a long time by telling him such stories, and doing such things as he may take most delight in. When he goes away she should frequently send to him a female attendant, skilled in carrying on a jesting conversation, and also a small present at the same time. She should also sometimes go to him herself under the pretence of some business, and accompanied by the Pithamarda.

Thus end the means of attaching to herself the man desired.

There are also some verses on the subject as follows:

"When a lover comes to her abode, a courtesan should give him a mixture of betel leaves and betel nut, garlands of flowers, and perfumed ointments, and, showing her skill in arts, should entertain him with a long conversation. She should also give him some loving presents, and make an exchange of her own things with his, and at the same time should show him her skill in sexual enjoyment. When a courtesan is thus united with her lover she should always delight him by affectionate gifts, by conversation, and by the application of tender means of enjoyment."

CHAPTER II

Of Living Like a Wife

WHEN a courtesan is living as a wife with her lover, she should behave like a chaste woman, and do everything to his satisfaction. Her duty in this respect, in short, is, that she should give him pleasure, but should not become attached to him, though behaving as if she were really attached.

Now the following is the manner in which she is to conduct herself, so as to accomplish the above mentioned purpose. She should have a mother dependent on her, one who should be represented as very harsh, and who looked upon money as her chief object in life. In the event of there being no mother, then an old and confidential nurse should play the same role. The mother or nurse, on their part, should appear to be displeased with the lover, and forcibly take her away from him. The woman herself should always show pretended anger, dejection, fear, and shame on this account, but should not disobey the mother or nurse at any time.

She should make out to the mother or nurse that the man is suffering from bad health, and making this a pretext for going to see him, she should go on that account. She is, moreover, to do the following things for the purpose of gaining the man's favour, viz.:

Sending her female attendant to bring the flowers used by him on the previous day, in order that she may use them herself as a mark of affection, also asking for the mixture of betel nut and leaves that have remained uneaten by him; expressing wonder at his knowledge of sexual intercourse, and the several means of enjoyment used by him; learning from him the sixty-four kinds of pleasure mentioned by Babhravya; continually practising the ways of enjoyment as taught by him, and according to his liking; keeping his secrets; telling him her own desires and secrets; concealing her anger; never neglecting him on the bed when he turns his face towards her; touching any parts of his body according to his wish; kissing and embracing him when he is asleep; looking at him with apparent anxiety when he is wrapt in thought, or thinking of some other subject than herself; showing neither complete shamelessness, nor excessive bashfulness when he meets her, or sees her standing on the terrace of her house from the public road; hating his enemies; loving those who are dear to him; showing a liking for that which he likes; being in high or low spirits according to the state that he is in himself; expressing a curiosity to see his wives; not continuing her anger for a long time; suspecting even the marks and wounds made by herself with her nails and teeth on his body to have been made by some other woman; keeping her love for him unexpressed by words, but showing it by deeds, and signs, and hints; remaining silent when he is asleep, intoxicated, or sick; being very attentive when he describes his good actions, and reciting them afterwards to his praise and benefit; giving witty replies to him if he be sufficiently attached to her; listening to all his stories, except those that relate to her rivals; expressing feelings of dejection and sorrow if he sighs, yawns, or falls down; pronouncing the words "live long" when he sneezes; pretending to be ill, or to have the desire of pregnancy, when she feels dejected; abstaining from praising the good qualities of anybody else, and from censuring those who possess the same faults as her own man; wearing anything that may have been given to her by him; abstaining from putting on her ornaments, and from taking food when he is in pain, sick, low-spirited, or suffering from misfortune, and condoling and lamenting with him over the same; wishing to accompany him if he happens to leave the country himself or if he be banished from it by the King; expressing a desire not to live after him; telling him that the whole object and desire of her life was to be united with him; offering previously promised sacrifices to the Deity when he acquires wealth, or has some desire fulfilled, or when he has recovered from some illness or disease; putting on ornaments every day; not acting too freely with him; reciting his name and the name of his family in her songs; placing his hand on her loins, bosom and fore-

218

head, and falling asleep after feeling the pleasure of his touch; sitting on his lap and falling asleep there; wishing to have a child by him; desiring not to live longer than he does; abstaining from revealing his secrets to others; dissuading him from vows and fasts by saying "let the sin fall upon me"; keeping vows and fasts along with him when it is impossible to change his mind on the subject; telling him that vows and fasts are difficult to be observed, even by herself, when she has any dispute with him about them; looking on her own wealth and his without any distinction; abstaining from going to public assemblies without him, and accompanying him when he desires her to do so; taking delight in using things previously used by him, and in eating food that he has left uneaten; venerating his family, his disposition, his skill in the arts, his learning, his caste, his complexion, his native country, his friends, his good qualities, his age, and his sweet temper; asking him to sing, and to do other such like things, if able to do them; going to him without paying any regard to fear, to cold, to heat, or to rain; saying with regard to the next world that he should be her lover even there; adapting her tastes, disposition and actions to his liking; abstaining from sorcery; disputing continually with her mother on the subject of going to him, and, when forcibly taken by her mother to some other place, expressing her desire to die by taking poison, by starving herself to death, by stabbing herself with some weapon, or by hanging herself; and lastly assuring the man of her constancy and love by means of her agents, and receiving money herself, but abstaining from any dispute with her mother with regard to pecuniary matters.

When the man sets out on a journey, she should make him swear that he will return quickly, and in his absence should put aside her vows of worshipping the Deity, and should wear no ornaments except those that are lucky. If the time fixed for his return has passed, she should endeavour to ascertain the real time of his return from omens, from the reports of the people, and from the positions of the planets, the moon and the stars. On occasions of amusement, and of auspicious dreams, she should say "Let me be soon united to him". If, moreover, she feels melancholy, or sees any

219

inauspicious omen, she should perform some rite to appease the Deity.

When the man does return home she should worship the God Kama (i.e., the Indian Cupid), and offer oblations to other Deities, and having caused a pot filled with water to be brought by her friends, she should perform the worship in honour of the crow who eats the offerings which we make to the manes of deceased relations. After the first visit is over she should ask her lover also to perform certain rites, and this he will do if he is sufficiently attached to her.

Now a man is said to be sufficiently attached to a woman when his love is disinterested; when he has the same object in view as his beloved one; when he is quite free from any suspicions on her account; and when he is indifferent to money with regard to her.

Such is the manner of a courtesan living with a man like a wife, and set forth here for the sake of guidance from the rules of Dattaka. What is not laid down here should be practised according to the custom of the people, and the nature of each individual man.

There are also two verses on the subject as follows:

"The extent of the love of women is not known, even to those who are the objects of their affection, on account of its subtlety, and on account of the avarice, and natural intelligence of womankind."

"Women are hardly ever known in their true light, though they may love men, or become indifferent towards them; may give them delight, or abandon them; or may extract from them all the wealth that they may possess."

CHAPTER III

*Of the Means of Getting Money. Of the Signs of the Change of a
Lover's Feelings, and of the Way to Get Rid of Him*

MONEY is got out of a lover in two ways, viz.:

By natural or lawful means, and by artifices. Old authors
are of opinion that when a courtesan can get as much money
as she wants from her lover, she should not make use of
artifice. But Vatsyayana lays down that though she may get
some money from him by natural means, yet when she
makes use of artifice he gives her doubly more, and therefore
artifice should be resorted to for the purpose of extorting
money from him at all events.

Now the artifices to be used for getting money from her
lover are as follows:

1st. Taking money from him on different occasions, for
the purpose of purchasing various articles, such as ornaments, food, drink, flowers, perfumes and cloths, and either
not buying them, or getting from him more than their cost.

2nd. Praising his intelligence to his face.

3rd. Pretending to be obliged to make gifts on occasion
of festivals connected with vows, trees, gardens, temples, or
tanks.*

4th. Pretending that at the time of going to his house, her
jewels have been stolen either by the King's guards, or by
robbers.

5th. Alleging that her property has been destroyed by
fire, by the falling of her house, or by the carelessness of her
servants.

6th. Pretending to have lost the ornaments of her lover
along with her own.

* On the completion of a vow a festival takes place. Some trees such as the
Peepul and Banyan trees, are invested with sacred threads like the Brahman's,
and on the occasion of this ceremony a festival is given. In the same way
when gardens are made, and tanks or temples built, then also festivals are
observed.

7th. Causing him to hear through other people of the expenses incurred by her in coming to see him.

8th. Contracting debts for the sake of her lover.

9th. Disputing with her mother on account of some expense incurred by her for her lover, and which was not approved of by her mother.

10th. Not going to parties and festivities in the houses of her friends for the want of presents to make to them, she having previously informed her lover of the valuable presents given to her by these very friends.

11th. Not performing certain festive rites under the pretence that she has no money to perform them with.

12th. Engaging artists to do something for her lover.

13th. Entertaining physicians and ministers for the purpose of attaining some object.

14th. Assisting friends and benefactors both on festive occasions, and in misfortune.

15th. Performing household rites.

16th. Having to pay the expenses of the ceremony of marriage of the son of a female friend.

17th. Having to satisfy curious wishes during her state of pregnancy.

18th. Pretending to be ill, and charging her cost of treatment.

19th. Having to remove the troubles of a friend.

20th. Selling some of her ornaments, so as to give her lover a present.

21st. Pretending to sell some of her ornaments, furniture, or cooking utensils to a trader, who has been already tutored how to behave in the matter.

22nd. Having to buy cooking utensils of greater value than those of other people, so that they might be more easily distinguished, and not changed for others of an inferior description.

23rd. Remembering the former favours of her lover, and causing them always to be spoken of by her friends and followers.

24th. Informing her lover of the great gains of other courtesans.

25th. Describing before them, and in the presence of her

lover, her own great gains, and making them out to be greater even than theirs, though such may not have been really the case.

26th. Openly opposing her mother when she endeavours to persuade her to take up with men with whom she has been formerly acquainted, on account of the great gains to be got from them.

27th. Lastly, pointing out to her lover the liberality of his rivals.

Thus ends the ways and means of getting money.

A woman should always know the state of the mind, of the feelings, and of the disposition of her lover towards her, from the changes of his temper, his manner, and the colour of his face.

The behaviour of a waning lover is as follows:

1st. He gives the woman either less than is wanted, or something else than that which is asked for.

2nd. He keeps her in hopes by promises.

3rd. He pretends to do one thing, and does something else.

4th. He does not fulfil her desires.

5th. He forgets his promises, or does something else than that which he has promised.

6th. He speaks with his own servants in a mysterious way.

7th. He sleeps in some other house under the pretence of having to do something for a friend.

8th. Lastly, he speaks in private with the attendants of a woman with whom he was formerly acquainted.

Now when a courtesan finds that her lover's disposition towards her is changing, she should get possession of all his best things before he becomes aware of her intentions, and allow a supposed creditor to take them away forcibly from her in satisfaction of some pretended debt. After this, if the lover is rich, and has always behaved well towards her, she should ever treat him with respect; but if he is poor and destitute, she should get rid of him as if she had never been acquainted with him in any way before.

The means of getting rid of a lover are as follows:

1st. Describing the habits and vices of the lover as disagreeable and censurable, with the sneer of the lip, and the stamp of the foot.

2nd. Speaking on a subject with which he is not acquainted.

3rd. Showing no admiration for his learning, and passing a censure upon it.

4th. Putting down his pride.

5th. Seeking the company of men who are superior to him in learning and wisdom.

6th. Showing a disregard for him on all occasions.

7th. Censuring men possessed of the same faults as her lover.

8th. Expressing dissatisfaction at the ways and means of enjoyment used by him.

9th. Not giving him her mouth to kiss.

10th. Refusing access to her Jaghana, i.e., the part of the body between the navel and the thighs.

11th. Showing a dislike for the wounds made by his nails and teeth.

12th. Not pressing close up against him at the time when he embraces her.

13th. Keeping her limbs without movement at the time of congress.

14th. Desiring him to enjoy her when he is fatigued.

15th. Laughing at his attachment to her.

16th. Not responding to his embraces.

17th. Turning away from him when he begins to embrace her.

18th. Pretending to be sleepy.

19th. Going out visiting, or into company, when she perceives his desire to enjoy her during the day time.

20th. Mis-constructing his words.

21st. Laughing without any joke, or at the time of any joke made by him laughing under some pretence.

22nd. Looking with side glances at her own attendants, and clapping her hands when he says anything.

23rd. Interrupting him in the middle of his stories, and beginning to tell other stories herself.

24th. Reciting his faults and his vices, and declaring them to be incurable.

25th. Saying words to her female attendants calculated to cut the heart of her lover to the quick.

26th. Taking care not to look at him when he comes to her.

27th. Asking him what cannot be granted.

28th. And, after all, finally dismissing him.

There are also two verses on this subject as follows:

"The duty of a courtesan consists in forming connections with suitable men after due and full consideration, and attaching the person with whom she is united to herself; in obtaining wealth from the person who is attached to her, and then dismissing him after she has taken away all his possessions."

"A courtesan leading in this manner the life of a wife is not troubled with too many lovers, and yet obtains abundance of wealth."

CHAPTER IV

About Reunion with a Former Lover

WHEN a courtesan abandons her present lover after all his wealth is exhausted, she may then consider about her reunion with a former lover. But she should return to him only if he has acquired fresh wealth, or is still wealthy, and if he is still attached to her. And if this man be living at the time with some other woman she should consider well before she acts.

Now such a man can only be in one of the six following conditions, viz.:

1st. He may have left the first woman of his own accord, and may even have left another woman since then.

2nd. He may have been driven away from both women.

3rd. He may have left the one woman of her own accord, and been driven away by the other.

4th. He may have left the one woman of his own accord, and be living with another woman.

5th. He may have been driven away from the one woman, and left the other of his own accord.

6th. He may have been driven away by the one woman, and may be living with another.

(1) Now if the man has left both women of his own accord, he should not be resorted to, on account of the fickleness of his mind, and his indifference to the excellences of both of them.

(2) As regards the man who may have been driven away from both women, if he has been driven away from the last one because the woman could get more money from some other man, then he should be resorted to, for if attached to the first woman he would give her more money, through vanity and emulation to spite the other woman. But if he has been driven away by the woman on account of his poverty, or stinginess, he should not then be resorted to.

(3) In the case of the man who may have left the one woman of his own accord, and been driven away by the other, if he agrees to return to the former and give her plenty of money beforehand, then he should be resorted to.

(4) In the case of the man who may have left the one woman of his own accord, and be living with another woman, the former (wishing to take up with him again), should first ascertain if he left her in the first instance in the hope of finding some particular excellence in the other woman, and that not having found any such excellence, he was willing to come back to her, and to give her much money on account of his conduct, and on account of his affection still existing for her.

Or, whether, having discovered many faults in the other woman, he would now see even more excellences in herself than actually exist, and would be prepared to give her much money for these qualities.

Or, lastly, to consider whether he was a weak man, or a man fond of enjoying many women, or one who liked a poor woman, or one who never did anything for the woman that he was with. After maturely considering all these things, she should resort to him or not, according to circumstances.

(5) As regards the man who may have been driven away from the one woman, and left the other of his own accord, the former woman (wishing to reunite with him), should first ascertain whether he still has any affection for her, and would consequently spend much money upon her; or whether, being attached to her excellent qualities, he did not take delight in any other women; or whether, being driven away from her formerly before completely satisfying his sexual desires, he wished to get back to her, so as to be revenged for the injury done to him; or whether he wished to create confidence in her mind, and then take back from her the wealth which she formerly took from him, and finally destroy her; or, lastly, whether he wished first to separate her from her present lover, and then to break away from her himself. If, after considering all these things, she is of opinion that his intentions are really pure and honest, she can reunite herself with him. But if his mind be at all tainted with evil intentions, he should be avoided.

(6) In the case of the man who may have been driven away by one woman, and be living with another, if the man makes overtures to return to the first one, the courtesan should consider well before she acts, and while the other woman is engaged in attracting him to herself, she should try in her turn (though keeping herself behind the scenes) to gain him over, on the grounds of any of the following considerations, viz.:

1st. That he was driven away unjustly and for no proper reason, and now that he has gone to another woman, every effort must be used to bring him back to myself.

2nd. That if he were once to converse with me again, he would break away from the other woman.

3rd. That the pride of my present lover would be put down by means of the former one.

4th. That he has become wealthy, has secured a higher position, and holds a place of authority under the King.

5th. That he is separate from his wife.

6th. That he is now independent.

7th. That he lives apart from his father, or brother.

8th. That by making peace with him, I shall be able to get hold of a very rich man, who is now prevented from coming to be by my present lover.

9th. That as he is not respected by his wife, I shall now be able to separate him from her.

10th. That the friend of this man loves my rival, who hates me cordially, I shall therefore by this means separate the friend from his mistress.

11th. And lastly, I shall bring discredit upon him by bringing him back to me, thus showing the fickleness of his mind.

When a courtesan is resolved to take up again with a former lover, her Pithamurda and other servants should tell him that his former expulsion from the woman's house was caused by the wickedness of her mother; that the woman loved him just as much as ever at that time, but could not help the occurrence on account of her deference to her mother's will; that she hated the union of her present lover, and disliked him excessively. In addition to this, they should create confidence in his mind by speaking to him of her former love for him, and should allude to the mark of that love that she has ever remembered. This mark of her love should be connected with some kind of pleasure that may have been practised by him, such as his way of kissing her, or manner of having connection with her.

Thus end the ways of bringing about a reunion with a former lover.

When a woman has to choose between two lovers, one of whom was formerly united with her, while the other is a stranger, the Acharyas (sages) are of opinion that the first one is preferable, because his disposition and character being already known by previous careful observation, he can be easily pleased and satisfied; but Vatsyayana thinks that a former lover, having already spent a great deal of his wealth, is not able or willing to give much money again, and is not therefore to be relied upon so much as a stranger. Particular cases may however arise differing from this general rule on account of the different natures of men.

There are also verses on the subject as follows:

"Reunion with a former lover may be desirable so as to separate some particular woman from some particular man, or some particular man from some particular woman, or to have a certain effect upon the present lover."

"When a man is excessively attached to a woman, he is afraid of her coming into contact with other men: he does not then regard or notice her faults; and he gives her much wealth through fear of her leaving him."

"A courtesan should be agreeable to the man who is attached to her, and despise the man who does not care for her. If while she is living with one man, a messenger comes to her from some other man, she may either refuse to listen to any negotiations on his part, or appoint a fixed time for him to visit her, but she should not leave the man who may be living with her and who may be attached to her."

"A wise woman should only renew her connection with a former lover if she is satisfied that good fortune, gain, love, and friendship, are likely to be the result of such a reunion."

CHAPTER V

Of Different Kinds of Gain

WHEN a courtesan is able to realise much money every day, by reason of many customers, she should not confine herself to a single lover; under such circumstances, she should fix her rate for one night, after considering the place, the season, and the condition of the people, and having regard to her own good qualities and good looks, and after comparing her rates with those of other courtesans. She can inform her lovers, and friends, and acquaintances about these charges. If, however, she can obtain a great gain from a single lover, she may resort to him alone, and live with him like a wife.

Now, the Sages are of opinion, that, when a courtesan has the chance of an equal gain from two lovers at the same time, a preference should be given to the one who would give her the kind of thing which she wants. But Vatsyayana says that the preference should be given to the one who gives her gold, because it cannot be taken back like some other things, it can be easily received, and is also the means of procuring anything that may be wished for. Of such things as gold, silver, copper, bell metal, iron, pots, furniture, beds, upper garments, under vestments, fragrant substances, vessels made of gourds, ghee, oil, corn, cattle, and other things of a like nature, the first, viz., gold, is superior to all the others.

When the same labour is required to gain any two lovers, or when the same kind of thing is to be got from each of them, the choice should be made by the advice of a friend, or it may be made from their personal qualities, or from the signs of good or bad fortune that may be connected with them.

When there are two lovers, one of whom is attached to the courtesan, and the other is simply very generous, the Sages say that the preference should be given to the generous lover, but Vatsyayana is of opinion that the one who is really attached to the courtesan should be preferred, because he can be made to be generous, even as a miser gives money if he becomes fond of a woman, but a man who is simply generous cannot be made to love with real attachment. But amongst those who are attached to her, if there is one who is poor, and one who is rich, the preference is of course to be given to the latter.

When there are two lovers, one of whom is generous, and the other ready to do any service for the courtesan, some Sages say that the one who is ready to do the service should be preferred, but Vatsyayana is of opinion that a man who does a service thinks that he has gained his object when he has done something once, but a generous man does not care for what he has given before. Even here the choice should be guided by the likelihood of the future good to be derived from her union with either of them.

When one of the two lovers is grateful, and the other liberal, some Sages say that the liberal one should be preferred, but Vatsyayana is of opinion that the former should be chosen, because liberal men are generally haughty, plain spoken, and wanting in consideration towards others. Even though these liberal men have been on friendly terms for a long time, yet if they see any fault in the courtesan, or are told lies about her by some other woman, they do not care for past services, but leave abruptly. On the other hand the grateful man does not at once break off from her, on account of a regard for the pains she may have taken to please him. In this case also the choice is to be guided with respect to what may happen in future.

When an occasion for complying with the request of a friend, and a chance of getting money come together, the Sages say that the chance of getting money should be preferred. But Vatsyayana thinks that the money can be obtained tomorrow as well as today, but if the request of a friend be not at once complied with, he may become disaffected. Even here, in making the choice, regard must be paid to future good fortune.

On such an occasion, however, the courtesan might pacify her friend by pretending to have some work to do, and telling him that his request will be complied with next day, and in this way secure the chance of getting the money that has been offered her.

When the chance of getting money, and the chance of avoiding some disaster come at the same time, the Sages are of opinion that the chance of getting money should be preferred, but Vatsyayana says that money has only a limited importance, while a disaster that is once averted may never occur again. Here, however, the choice should be guided by the greatness or smallness of the disaster.

The gains of the wealthiest and best kind of courtesans are to be spent as follows:

Building temples, tanks, and gardens; giving a thousand cows to different Brahmans; carrying on the worship of the Gods, and celebrating festivals in their honour; and, lastly, performing such vows as may be within their means.

The gains of other courtesans are to be spent as follows:

Having a white dress to wear every day; getting sufficient food and drink to satisfy hunger and thirst; eating daily a perfumed Tambula, i.e., a mixture of betel nut and betel leaves; and wearing ornaments gilt with gold. The Sages

231

say that these represent the gains of all the middle and lower classes of courtesans, but Vatsyayana is of opinion that their gains cannot be calculated, or fixed in any way, as these depend on the influence of the place, the customs of the people, their own appearance, and many other things.

When a courtesan wants to keep some particular man from some other woman; or wishes to get him away from some woman to whom he may be attached; or to deprive some woman of the gains realised by her from him; or if she thinks that she would raise her position; or enjoy some great good fortune; or become desirable to all men by uniting herself with this man; or if she wishes to get his assistance in averting some misfortune; or is really attached to him and loves him; or wishes to injure some body through his means; or has regard to some former favour conferred upon her by him; or wishes to be united with him merely from desire; for any of the above reasons, she should agree to take from him only a small sum of money in a friendly way.

When a courtesan intends to abandon a particular lover, and take up with another one; or when she has reason to believe that her lover will shortly leave her, and return to his wives; or that having squandered all his money, and become penniless, his guardian, or master, or father would come and take him away; or that her lover is about to lose his position, or lastly, that he is of a very fickle mind, she should, under any of these circumstances, endeavour to get as much money as she can from him as soon as possible.

On the other hand, when the courtesan thinks that her lover is about to receive valuable presents; or get a place of authority from the King; or be near the time of inheriting a fortune; or that his ship would soon arrive laden with merchandise; or that he has large stocks of corn and other commodities; or that if anything was done for him it would not be done in vain; or that he is always true to his word; then should she have regard to her future welfare, and live with the man like a wife.

There are also verses on the subject as follows:

"In considering her present gains, and her future welfare, a courtesan should avoid such persons as have gained their means of subsistence with very great difficulty, as also those who have become selfish and hard-hearted by becoming the favourites of Kings."

"She should make every endeavour to unite herself with prosperous and well-to-do people, and with those whom it is dangerous to avoid, or to slight in any way. Even at some cost to herself she should become acquainted with energetic and liberal-minded men, who when pleased would give her a large sum of money, even for very little service, or for some small thing."

Of Gains and Losses; Attendant Gains and Losses; and Doubts; as also of the Different Kinds of Courtesans

IT sometimes happens that while gains are being sought for, or expected to be realised, that losses only are the result of our efforts, the causes of these losses are:

Weakness of intellect.
Excessive love.
Excessive pride.
Excessive self-conceit.
Excessive simplicity.
Excessive confidence.
Excessive anger.
Carelessness.
Recklessness.
Influence of evil genius.
Accidental circumstances.

The results of these losses are:

Expense incurred without any result.
Destruction of future good fortune.
Stoppage of gains about to be realised.
Loss of what is already obtained.
Acquisition of a sour temper.
Becoming unaimiable to everybody.
Injury to health.

Loss of hair and other accidents.

Now gain is of three kinds, viz.: gain of wealth, gain of religious merit, and gain of pleasure; and similarly, loss is of three kinds, viz.: loss of wealth, loss of religious merit, and loss of pleasure. At the time when gains are sought for, if other gains come along with them, these are called attendant gains. When gain is uncertain, the doubt of its being a gain is called a simple doubt. When there is a doubt whether either of two things will happen or not, it is called a mixed doubt. If while one thing is being done two results take place, it is called a combination of two results, and if several results follow from the same action, it is called a combination of results on every side.

We shall now give examples of the above.

As already stated, gain is of three kinds, and loss, which is opposed to gain, is also of three kinds.

(a) When by living with a great man a courtesan acquires present wealth, and in addition to this becomes acquainted with other people, and thus obtains a chance of future fortune and an accession of wealth, and becomes desirable to all, this is called a gain of wealth attended by other gain.

(b) When by living with a man a courtesan simply gets money, this is called a gain of wealth not attended by any other gain.

(c) When a courtesan receives money from other people besides her lover, the results are: the chance of the loss of future good from her present lover; the chance of disaffection of a man securely attached to her; the hatred of all; and the chance of a union with some low person, tending to destroy her future good. This gain is called a gain of wealth attended by losses.

(d) When a courtesan, at her own expense, and without any results in the shape of gain, has connection with a great man, or an avaricious minister, for the sake of diverting some misfortune, or removing some cause that may be threatening the destruction of a great gain, this loss is said to be a loss of wealth attended by gains of the future good which it may bring about.

(e) When a courtesan is kind, even at her own expense, to a man who is very stingy, or to a man proud of his looks, or to an ungrateful man skilled in gaining the heart of others, without any good resulting from these connections to her in the end, this loss is called a loss of wealth not attended by any gain.

(*f*) When a courtesan is kind to any such man as described above, but who in addition are favourites of the King, and moreover cruel and powerful, without any good result in the end, and with a chance of her being turned away at any moment, this loss is called a loss of wealth attended by other losses.

In this way gains and losses, and attendant gains and losses in religious merit and pleasures may become known to the reader, and combinations of all of them may also be made.

Thus end the remarks on gains and losses, and attendant gains and losses.

In the next place we come to doubts, which are again of three kinds, viz.: doubts about wealth, doubts about religious merit, and doubts about pleasures.

The following are examples:

(*a*) When a courtesan is not certain how much a man may give her, or spend upon her, this is called a doubt about wealth.

(*b*) When a courtesan feels doubtful whether she is right in entirely abandoning a lover from whom she is unable to get money, she having taken all his wealth from him in the first instance, this doubt is called a doubt about religious merit.

(*c*) When a courtesan is unable to get hold of a lover to her liking, and is uncertain whether she will derive any pleasure from a person surrounded by his family, or from a low person, this is called a doubt about pleasure.

(*d*) When a courtesan is uncertain whether some powerful but low principled fellow would cause loss to her on account of her not being civil to him, this is called a doubt about the loss of wealth.

(*e*) When a courtesan feels doubtful whether she would lose religious merit by abandoning a man who is attached to her without giving him the slightest favour, and thereby causing him unhappiness in this world and the next,* this doubt is called a doubt about the loss of a religious merit.

(f) When a courtesan is uncertain as to whether she might create disaffection by speaking out, and revealing her love and thus not get her desire satisfied, this is called a doubt about the loss of pleasure.

Thus end the remarks on doubts.

Mixed Doubts

(a) The intercourse or connection with a stranger, whose disposition is unknown, and who may have been introduced by a lover, or by one who possessed authority, may be productive either of gain or loss, and therefore this is called a mixed doubt about the gain and loss of wealth.

(b) When a courtesan is requested by a friend, or is impelled by pity to have intercourse with a learned Brahman, a religious student, a sacrificer, a devotee, or an ascetic who may have all fallen in love with her, and who may be consequently at the point of death, by doing this she might either gain or lose religious merit, and therefore this is called a mixed doubt about the gain and loss of religious merit.

(c) If a courtesan relies solely upon the report of other people (i.e., hearsay) about a man, and goes to him without ascertaining herself whether he possesses good qualities or not, she may either gain or lose pleasure in proportion as he may be good or bad, and therefore this is called a mixed doubt about the gain and loss of pleasure.

Uddalika has described the gains and losses on both sides as follows.

(a) If, when living with a lover, a courtesan gets both wealth and pleasure from him, it is called a gain on both sides.

(b) When a courtesan lives with a lover at her own expense without getting any profit out of it, and the lover even takes back from her what he may have formerly given her, it is called a loss on both sides.

* The souls of men who die with their desires unfulfilled are said to go to the world of the Manes, and not direct to the Supreme Spirit.

(*c*) When a courtesan is uncertain whether a new acquaintance would become attached to her, and, moreover, if he became attached to her, whether he would give her any thing, it is then called a doubt on both sides about gains.

(*d*) When a courtesan is uncertain whether a former enemy, if made up by her at her own expense, would do her some injury on account of his grudge against her; or, if becoming attached to her, would take away angrily from her any thing that he may have given to her, this is called a doubt on both sides about loss.

Babhravya has described the gains and losses on both sides as follows.

(*a*) When a courtesan can get money from a man whom she may go to see, and also money from a man whom she may not go to see, this is called a gain on both sides.

(*b*) When a courtesan has to incur further expense if she goes to see a man, and yet runs the risk of incurring an irremediable loss if she does not go to see him, this is called a loss on both sides.

(*c*) When a courtesan is uncertain, whether a particular man would give her anything on her going to see him, without incurring expense on her part, or whether on her neglecting him another man would give her something, this is called a doubt on both sides about gain.

(*d*) When a courtesan is uncertain whether, on going at her own expense to see an old enemy, he would take back from her what he may have given her, or whether by her not going to see him he would cause some disaster to fall upon her, this is called a doubt on both sides about loss.

By combining the above, the following six kinds of mixed results are produced, viz.:

(*a*) Gain on one side, and loss on the other.

(*b*) Gain on one side, and doubt of gain on the other.

(*c*) Gain on one side, and doubt of loss on the other.

(*d*) Loss on one side, and doubt of gain on the other.

(*e*) Doubt of gain on one side, and doubt of loss on the other.

(*f*) Doubt of loss on one side, and loss on the other.

A courtesan, having considered all the above things, and taken counsel with her friends, should act so as to acquire gain, the chances of great gain, and the warding off of any great disaster. Religious merit and pleasure should also be formed into separate combinations like those of wealth, and then all should be combined with each other, so as to form new combinations.

When a courtesan consorts with men she should cause each of them to give her money as well as pleasure. At particular times, such as the Spring Festivals, etc., she should make her mother announce to the various men, that on a certain day her daughter would remain with the man who would gratify such and such a desire of hers.

When young men approach her with delight, she should think of what she may accomplish through them.

The combination of gains and losses on all sides are: gain on one side, and loss on all others; loss on one side and gain on all others; gain on all sides, loss on all sides.

A courtesan should also consider doubts about gain and doubts about loss with reference both to wealth, religious merit and pleasure.

Thus ends the consideration of gain, loss, attendant gains, attendant losses and doubts.

The different kinds of courtesans are:

A bawd.

A female attendant.

An unchaste woman.

A dancing girl.

A female artisan.

A woman who has left her family.

A woman living on her beauty.

And, finally, a regular courtesan.

All the above kinds of courtesans are acquainted with various kinds of men, and should consider the ways of getting money from them, of pleasing them, of separating themselves from them, and of reuniting with them. They should also take into consideration particular gains and losses, attendant gains and losses, and doubts in accordance with their several conditions.

Thus end the considerations of courtesans.

There are also two verses on the subject as follows:

"Men want pleasure, while women want money, and

therefore this Part, which treats of the means of gaining wealth, should be studied."

"There are some women who seek for love, and there are others who seek for money; for the former the ways of love are told in previous portions of this work, while the ways of getting money, as practised by courtesans, are described in this Part."

END OF PART VI

PART VII

ABOUT THE MEANS OF ATTRACTING OTHERS TO YOURSELF

CHAPTER I

On Personal Adornment; on Subjugating the Hearts of Others; and on Tonic Medicines

WHEN a person fails to obtain the object of his desires by any of the ways previously related, he should then have recourse to other ways of attracting others to himself.

Now, good looks, good qualities, youth, and liberality are the chief and most natural means of making a person agreeable in the eyes of others. But in the absence of these a man or a woman must have resort to artificial means, or to art, and the following are some recipes that may be found useful.

(*a*) An ointment made of the tabernamontana coronaria, the costus speciosus or arabicus, and the flacourtia cataphracta, can be used as an unguent of adornment.

(*b*) If a fine powder is made of the above plants, and applied to the wick of a lamp, which is made to burn with the oil of blue vitrol, the black pigment or lamp black produced therefrom, when applied to the eye-lashes, has the effect of making a person look lovely.

(*c*) The oil of the hogweed, the echites putescens, the sarina plant, the yellow amaranth, and the leaf of the nymphae, if applied to the body, has the same effect.

(*d*) A black pigment from the same plants produces a similar effect.

(*e*) By eating the powder of the nelumbrium speciosum, the blue lotus, and the mesna roxburghii, with ghee and honey, a man becomes lovely in the eyes of others.

(*f*) The above things, together with the tabernamontana coronaria, and the xanthochymus pictorius, if used as an ointment, produce the same results.

(*g*) If the bone of a peacock or of an hyena be covered with gold, and tied on the right hand, it makes a man lovely in the eyes of other people.

(*h*) In the same way, if a bead, made of the seed of the jujube, or of the conch shell, be enchanted by the incantations mentioned in the Atharvana Veda, or by the incantations of those well skilled in the science of magic, and tied on the hand, it produces the same result as described above.

(*i*) When a female attendant arrives at the age of puberty, her master should keep her secluded, and when men ardently desire her on account of her seclusion, and on account of the difficulty of approaching her, he should then bestow her hand on such a person as may endow her with wealth and happiness.

This is a means of increasing the loveliness of a person in the eyes of others.

In the same way, when the daughter of a courtesan arrives at the age of puberty, the mother should get together a lot of young men of the same age, disposition, and knowledge as her daughter, and tell them that she would give her in marriage to the person who would give her presents of a particular kind.

After this the daughter should be kept in seclusion as far as possible, and the mother should give her in marriage to the man who may be ready to give her the presents agreed upon. If the mother is unable to get so much out of the man, she should show some of her own things as having been given to the daughter by the bridegroom.

Or, the mother may allow her daughter to be married to the man privately, as if she was ignorant of the whole affair, and then pretending that it has come to her knowledge, she may give her consent to the union.

The daughter, too, should make herself attractive to the sons of wealthy citizens, unknown to her mother, and make them attached to her, and for this purpose should meet them at the time of learning to sing, and in places where music is played, and at the houses of other people, and then request her mother, through a female friend, or servant, to be allowed to unite herself to the man who is most agreeable to her.*

When the daughter of a courtesan is thus given to a man, the ties of marriage should be observed for one year, and after that she may do what she likes. But even after the end of the year, when otherwise engaged, if she should be now and then invited by her first husband to come and see him, she should put aside her present gain, and go to him for the night.

Such is the mode of temporary marriage among courtesans, and of increasing their loveliness, and their value in the eyes of others. What has been said about them should also be understood to apply to the daughters of dancing women, whose mothers should give them only to such persons as are likely to become useful to them in various ways.

Thus end the ways of making oneself lovely in the eyes of others.

(*a*) If a man, after anointing his lingam with a mixture of the powders of the white thorn apple, the long pepper, and the black pepper, and honey, engages in sexual union with a woman, he makes her subject to his will.

(*b*) The application of a mixture of the leaf of the plant vatodbhranta, of the flowers thrown on a human corpse when carried out to be burnt, and the powder of the bones of the peacock, and of the jiwanjiva bird produces the same effect.

(*c*) The remains of a kite who has died a natural death, ground into powder, and mixed with cowach and honey, has also the same effect.

(*d*) Anointing oneself with an ointment made of the plant emblica myrabolans has the power of subjecting women to one's will.

(*e*) If a man cuts into small pieces the sprouts of the

* It is a custom of the courtesans of Oriental countries to give their daughters temporarily in marriage when they come of age, and after they have received an education in the Kama Sutra and other arts. Full details are given of this at page 76 of *Early Ideas,* a group of Hindoo stories, collected and collated by Anaryan. W. H. Allen & Co., London, 1881.

243

vajnasunhi plant, and dips them into a mixture of red arsenic and sulphur, and then dries them seven times, and applies this powder mixed with honey to his lingam, he can subjugate a woman to his will directly that he has had sexual union with her, or, if, by burning these very sprouts at night and looking at the smoke, he sees a golden moon behind, he will then be successful with any woman; or if he throws some of the powder of these same sprouts mixed with the excrement of a monkey upon a maiden, she will not be given in marriage to anybody else.

(f) If pieces of the arris root are dressed with the oil of the mango, and placed for six months in a hole made in the trunk of the sisu tree, and are then taken out and made up into an ointment, and applied to the lingam, this is said to serve as the means of subjugating women.

(g) If the bone of a camel is dipped into the juice of the plant eclipta prostata, and then burnt, and the black pigment produced from its ashes is placed in a box also made of the bone of a camel, and applied together with antimony to the eye lashes with a pencil also made of the bone of a camel, then that pigment is said to be very pure, and wholesome for the eyes, and serves as a means of subjugating others to the person who uses it. The same effect can be produced by black pigment made of the bones of hawks, vultures and peacocks.

Thus end the ways of subjugating others to one's own will.

Now the means of increasing sexual vigour are as follows:

(*a*) A man obtains sexual vigour by drinking milk mixed with sugar, the root of the uchchata plant, the piper chaba, and liquorice.

(*b*) Drinking milk mixed with sugar, and having the testicle of a ram or a goat boiled in it, is also productive of vigour.

(*c*) The drinking of the juice of the hedysarum gangeticum, the kuili, and the kshirika plant mixed with milk, produces the same effect.

(*d*) The seed of the long pepper along with the seeds of the sanseviera roxburghiana, and the hedysarum gangeticum plant, all pounded together, and mixed with milk, is productive of a similar result.

(*e*) According to ancient authors, if a man pounds the seeds or roots of the trapa bispinosa, the kasurika, the tuscan jasmine and liquorice, together with the kshirakapoli (a kind of onion), and puts the powder into milk mixed with sugar and ghee, and having boiled the whole mixture on a moderate fire, drinks the paste so formed, he will be able to enjoy innumerable women.

(*f*) In the same way, if a man mixes rice with the eggs of the sparrow, and having boiled this in milk, adds to it ghee and honey, and drinks as much of it as necessary, this will produce the same effect.

(*g*) If a man takes the outer covering of sesamum seeds, and soaks them with the eggs of sparrows, and then, having boiled them in milk, mixed with sugar and ghee, along with the fruits of the trapa bispinosa and the kasurika plant, and adding to it the flour of wheat and beans, and then drinks this composition, he is said to be able to enjoy many women.

(*h*) If ghee, honey, sugar and liquorice in equal quantities, the juice of the fennel plant, and milk are mixed together, this nectar-like composition is said to be holy, and provocative of sexual vigour, a preservative of life, and sweet to the taste.

(*i*) The drinking of a paste composed of the asparagus racemosus, the shvadaushtra plant, the guduchi plant, the long pepper and liquorice, boiled in milk, honey and ghee, in the spring, is said to have the same effect as the above.

(*j*) Boiling the asparagus racemosus, and the shvadaushtra plant, along with the pounded fruits of the premna spinosa in water, and drinking the same, is said to act in the same way.

(*k*) Drinking boiled ghee, or clarified butter, in the morning during the spring season, is said to be beneficial to health and strength and agreeable to the taste.

(*l*) If the powder of the seed of the shvadaushtra plant and the flower of barley are mixed together in equal parts, and a portion of it, i.e., two palas in weight, is eaten every morning on getting up, it has the same effect as the preceding recipe.

There are also verses on the subject as follows:

"The means* of producing love and sexual vigour should be learnt from the science of medicine, from the Vedas, from those who are learned in the arts of magic, and from confidential relatives. No means should be tried which are doubtful in their effects, which are likely to cause injury to the body, which involve the death of animals, and which bring us in contact with impure things. Such means should only be used as are holy, acknowledged to be good, and approved of by Brahmans, and friends."

CHAPTER II

Of the Ways of Exciting Desire, and Miscellaneous Experiments and Recipes

IF a man is unable to satisfy a Hastini, or elephant woman, he should have recourse to various means to excite her passion. At the commencement he should rub her yoni with his hand or fingers, and not begin to have intercourse with her until she becomes excited, or experiences pleasure. This is one way of exciting a woman.

Or, he may make use of certain Apadravyas, or things which are put on or around the lingam to supplement its length or its thickness, so as to fit it to the yoni. In the opinion of Babhravya, these Apadravyas should be made of gold, silver, copper, iron, ivory, buffalo's horn, various kinds of wood, tin or lead, and should be soft, cool, provocative of sexual vigour, and well fitted to serve the

* From the earliest times Oriental authors have occupied themselves about aphrodisiacs. The following note on the subject is taken from page 29 of a translation of the Hindoo Art of Love, otherwise the Anunga Runga, alluded to in the preface of this work, Part I., pages 81 and 83;—"Most Eastern treatises divide aphrodisiacs into two different kinds; 1., the mechanical or natural, such as scarification, flagellation, etc.; and 2., the medicinal or artificial. To the former belong the application of insects, as is practised by some savage races; and all orientalists will remember the tale of the old Brahman, whose young wife insisted upon his being again stung by a wasp."

intended purpose. Vatsyayana, however, says that they may be made according to the natural liking of each individual.

The following are the different kinds of Apadravyas.

(1) "The armlet" (Valaya) should be of the same size as the lingam, and should have its outer surface made rough with globules.

(2) "The couple" (Sanghati) is formed of two armlets.

(3) "The bracelet" (Chudaka) is made by joining three or more armlets, until they come up to the required length of the lingam.

(4) "The single bracelet" is formed by wrapping a single wire around the lingam, according to its dimensions.

(5) The Kantuka or Jalaka is a tube open at both ends, with a hole through it, outwardly rough and studded with soft globules, and made to fit the side of the yoni, and tied to the waist.

When such a thing cannot be obtained, then a tube made of the wood apple, or tubular stalk of the bottle gourd, or a reed made soft with oil and extracts of plants and tied to the waist with strings, may be made use of, as also a row of soft pieces of wood tied together.

The above are the things that can be used in connection with or in the place of the lingam.

The people of the southern countries think that true sexual pleasure cannot be obtained without perforating the lingam, and they therefore cause it to be pierced like the lobes of the ears of an infant pierced for earrings.

Now, when a young man perforates his lingam he should pierce it with a sharp instrument, and then stand in water so long as the blood continues to flow. At night he should engage in sexual intercourse, even with vigour, so as to clean the hole. After this he should continue to wash the hole with decoctions, and increase the size by putting into it small pieces of cane, and the wrightia antidysenterica, and thus gradually enlarging the orifice. It may also be washed with liquorice mixed with honey, and the size of the hole increased by the fruit stalks of the sima-patra plant. The hole should also be anointed with a small quantity of oil.

In the hole made in the lingam a man may put Apadravyas of various forms, such as the "round", the "round on one side", the "wooden mortar", the "flower", the "arm-let", the "bone of the heron", the "goad of the elephant", the "collection of eight balls", the "lock of hair", the "place where four roads meet", and other things named according to their forms and means of using them. All these Apad-ravyas should be rough on the outside according to their requirements.

The ways of enlarging the lingam must be now related.

When a man wishes to enlarge his lingam, he should rub it with the bristles of certain insects that live in trees, and then, after rubbing it for ten nights with oils, he should again rub it with the bristles as before. By continuing to do this a swelling will be gradually produced in the lingam, and he should then lie on a cot, and cause his lingam to hang down through a hole in the cot. After this he should take away all the pain from the swelling by using cool con-coctions. The swelling, which is called "Suka", and is often brought about among the people of the Dravida country, lasts for life.

If the lingam is rubbed with the following things, viz.: the plant physalis flexuosa, the shavara-kandaka plant, the jalasuka plant, the fruit of the egg plant, the butter of a she buffalo, the hastri-charma plant and the juice of the vajra-rasa plant, a swelling lasting for one month will be produced.

By rubbing it with oil boiled in the concoctions of the above things, the same effect will be produced, but lasting for six months.

The enlargement of the lingam is also effected by rubbing it or moistening it with oil boiled on a moderate fire along with the seeds of the pomegranate, and the cucumber, the juices of the valuka plant, the hasti-charma plant, and the egg-plant.

In addition to the above, other means may be learnt from experienced and confidential persons.

The miscellaneous experiments and recipes are as follows:

(a) If a man mixes the powder of the milk hedge plant, and the kantaka plant with the excrement of a monkey and the powdered root of the lanjalika plant, and throws this mixture on a woman, she will not love anybody else after-wards.

(*b*) If a man thickens the juice of the fruits of the cassia fistula, and the eugenia jambolana by mixing them with the powder of the soma plant, the vernonia anthelmintica, the eclipta prostata, and the lohopa-jihirka and applies this composition to the yoni of a woman and then has sexual intercourse with her, his love for her will be destroyed.

(*c*) The same effect is produced if a man has connection with a woman who has bathed in the butter-milk of a she-buffalo mixed with the powders of the gopalika plant, the banu-padika plant, and the yellow amaranth.

(*d*) An ointment made of the flowers of the nauclea cadamba, the hog plum, and the eugenia jambolana, and used by a woman, causes her to be disliked by her husband.

(*e*) Garlands made of the above flowers, when worn by the woman, produce the same effect.

(*f*) An ointment made of the fruit of the asteracantha longifolia (kokilaksha) will contract the yoni of a Hastini or elephant woman, and this contraction lasts for one night.

(*g*) An ointment made by pounding the roots of the nelumbrium speciosum and of the blue lotus and the powder of the plant physalis flexuosa mixed with ghee and honey, will enlarge the yoni of the Mrigi or deer woman.

(*h*) An ointment made of the fruit of the emblica myrabolans soaked in the milky juice of the milk hedge plant, of the soma plant, the calotropis gigantea and the juice of the fruit of the vernonia anthelmintica, will make the hair white.

(*i*) The juice of the roots of the madayantaka plant, the yellow amaranth, the anjanika plant, the clitoria ternateea and the shlakshnaparni plant, used as a lotion, will make the hair grow.

(*j*) An ointment made by boiling the above roots in oil, and rubbed in, will make the hair black and will also gradually restore hair that has fallen off.

(*k*) If lac is saturated seven times in the sweat of the testicle of a white horse, and applied to a red lip, the lip will become white.

(*l*) The colour of the lips can be regained by means of the madayantika and other plants mentioned above under (*i*).

(*m*) A woman who hears a man playing on a reed pipe which has been dressed with the juices of the bahupadika plant, the tabernamontana coronaria, the costus speciosus or arabicus, the pinus deodora, the euphorbia antiquorùm, the vajra and the kantaka plant, becomes his slave.

(n) If food be mixed with the fruit of the thorn apple (Dathura) it causes intoxication.

(o) If water be mixed with oil and the ashes of any kind of grass except the kusha grass, it becomes the colour of milk.

(p) If yellow myrabolans, the hog plum, the shrawana plant and the priyangu plant be all pounded together and applied to iron pots, these pots become red.

(q) If a lamp, trimmed with oil extracted from the shrawana and priyangn plants, its wick being made of cloth and the slough of the skins of snakes, is lighted, and long pieces of wood placed near it, those pieces of wood will resemble so many snakes.

(r) Drinking the milk of a white cow who has a white calf at her foot is auspicious, produces fame, and preserves life.

(s) The blessings of venerable Brahmans, well propitiated, have the same effect.

There are also some verses in conclusion:

"Thus have I written in a few words the 'Science of love', after reading the texts of ancient authors, and following the ways of enjoyment mentioned in them."

"He who is acquainted with the true principles of this science pays regard to Dharma, Artha, Kama and to his own experiences, as well as to the teachings of others, and does not act simply on the dictates of his own desire. As for the errors in the science of love which I have mentioned in this work, on my own authority as an author, I have, immediately after mentioning them, carefully censured and prohibited them."

"An act is never looked upon with indulgence for the simple reason that it is authorised by the science, because it ought to be remembered that it is the intention of the science that the rules which it contains should only be acted upon in particular cases. After reading and considering the works of Babhravya and other ancient authors, and thinking over the meaning of the rules given by them, the Kama Sutra was composed, according to the precepts of Holy

Writ, for the benefit of the world, by Vatsyayana, while leading the life of a religious student, and wholly engaged in the contemplation of the Deity."

"This work is not intended to be used merely as an intrument for satisfying our desires. A person, acquainted with the true principles of this science, and who preserves his Dharma, Artha and Kama, and has regard for the practices of the people, is sure to obtain the mastery over his senses."

"In short, an intelligent and prudent person, attending to Dharma and Artha, and attending to Kama also, without becoming the slave of his passions, obtains success in everything that he may undertake."

END OF PART VII

CONCLUDING REMARKS
TO THE ORIGINAL EDITION

Thus ends, in seven parts, the Kama Sutra of Vatsyayana, which might otherwise be called a treatise on men and women, their mutual relationship and connection with each other.

It is a work that should be studied by all, both old and young; the former will find in it real truths, gathered by experience, and already tested by themselves, while the latter will derive the great advantage of learning things, which some perhaps may otherwise never learn at all, or which they may only learn when it is too late ("too late" those immortal words of Mirabeau) to profit by the learning.

It can also be fairly commended to the student of social science and of humanity, and above all to the student of those early ideas, which have gradually filtered down through the sands of time, and which seem to prove that the human nature of today is much the same as the human nature of the long ago.

It has been said of Balzac (the great, if not the greatest of French novelists) that he seemed to have inherited a natural and intuitive perception of the feelings of men and women, and has described them with an analysis worthy of a man of science. The author of the present work must also have had a considerable knowledge of the humanities. Many of his remarks are so full of simplicity and truth, that they have stood the test of time, and stand out still as clear and true as when they were first written, some eighteen hundred years ago.

As a collection of facts, told in plain and simple language, it must be remembered that in those early days there was apparently no idea of embellishing the work, either with a literary style, a flow of language, or a quantity of superfluous padding. The author tells the world what he knows in very concise language, without any attempt to produce an interesting story. From his facts how many novels could be written! Indeed much of the matter contained in parts III, IV, V and VI has formed the basis of many of the stories and the tales of past centuries.

There will be found in Part VII some curious recipes. Many of them appear to be as primitive as the book itself, but in later works of the same nature these recipes and prescriptions appear to have increased, both as regards quality and quantity. In the *Anunga Runga* or "The Stage of Love", mentioned at page 81 of the Preface in Part I, there are found no less than thirty-three different subjects for which one hundred and thirty recipes and prescriptions are given.

As the details may be interesting, these subjects are described as follows:

1. For hastening the paroxysm of the woman.
2. For delaying the orgasm of the man.
3. Aphrodisiacs.
4. For thickening and enlarging the lingam, rendering it sound and strong, hard and lusty.
5. For narrowing and contracting the yoni.
6. For perfuming the yoni.
7. For removing and destroying the hair of the body.
8. For removing the sudden stopping of the monthly ailment.
9. For abating the immoderate appearance of the monthly ailment.
10. For purifying the womb.
11. For causing pregnancy.
12. For preventing miscarriage and other accidents.
13. For ensuring easy labour and ready deliverence.
14. For limiting the number of children.
15. For thickening and beautifying the hair.
16. For obtaining a good black colour to it.
17. For whitening and bleaching it.
18. For renewing it.
19. For clearing the skin of the face from eruptions that break out and leave black spots upon it.
20. For removing the black colour of the epidermis.

21. For enlarging the breasts of women.

22 For raising and hardening pendulous breasts.

23. For giving a fragrance to the skin.

23. For removing the evil savour of perspiration.

25. For anointing the body after bathing.

26. For causing a pleasant smell to the breath.

27. Drugs and charms for the purposes of fascinating, overcoming and subduing either men or women.

28. Recipes for enabling a woman to attract and preserve her husband's love.

29. Magical collyriums for winning love and friendship.

30. Prescriptions for reducing other persons to submission.

31. Philter pills, and other charms.

32. Fascinating incense, or fumigation.

33. Magical verses which have the power of fascination.

Of the one hundred and thirty recipes given, many of them are absurd, but not more perhaps than many of the recipes and prescriptions in use in Europe not so very long ago. Love-philters, charms and herbal remedies have been, in early days, as freely used in Europe as in Asia, and doubtless some people believe in them still in many places.

And now, one word about the author of the work, the good old sage Vatsyayana. It is much to be regretted that nothing can be discovered about his life, his belongings, and his surroundings. At the end of Part VII he states that he wrote the work while leading the life of a religious student (probably at Benares) and while wholly engaged in the contemplation of the Deity. He must have arrived at a certain age at that time, for throughout he gives us the benefit of his experience, and of his opinions, and these bear the stamp of age rather than of youth; indeed the work could hardly have been written by a young man.

In a beautiful verse of the Vedas of the Christians it has been said of the peaceful dead, that they rest from their labours, and that their works do follow them. Yes, indeed, the works of men of genius do follow them, and remain as a lasting treasure. And though there may be disputes and discussions about the immortality of the body or the soul, nobody can deny the immortality of genius, which ever remains as a bright and guiding star to the struggling humanities of succeeding ages. This work, then, which has stood the test of centuries, has placed Vatsyayana among the immortals, and on This, and on Him no better elegy or eulogy can be written than the following lines:

"So long as lips shall kiss, and eyes shall see,
So long lives This, and This gives life to Thee."

FINIS